AF473700

OTTO
FRIED

OTTO FRIED

Heaven can wait
Heaven can't wait

HERAUSGEGEBEN VON / EDITED BY
Beate Reifenscheid

SilvanaEditoriale

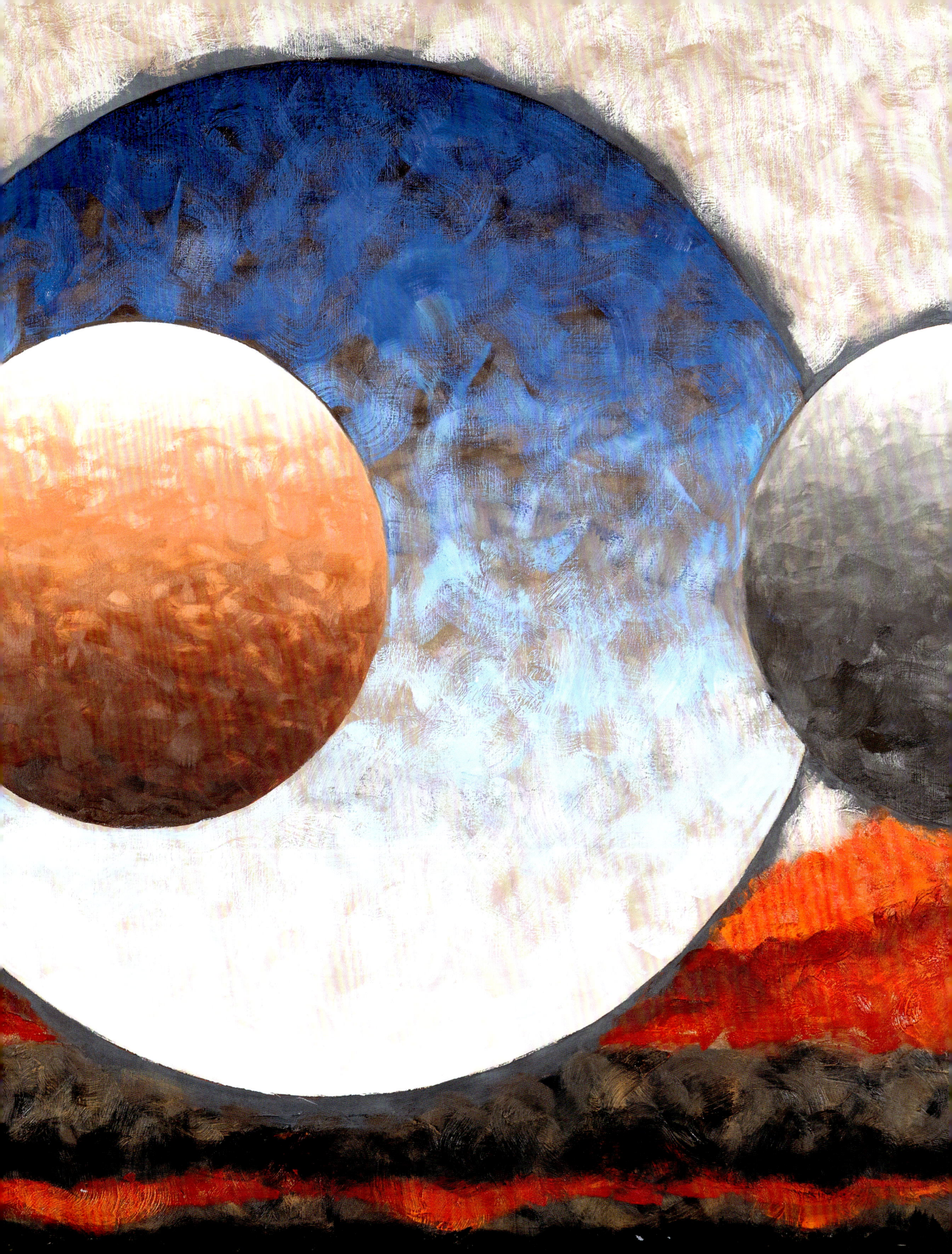

Inhalt Contents

Foreword

BEATE REIFENSCHEID
Director

It is one of those biographies no longer being in the spotlight of world public, but conveying nevertheless something of German history at the time of National Socialism, a time which should not be forgotten. Otto Fried was born as an offspring of the Fried-Salomon family in Horchheim, near Koblenz, in 1923 and sent to America in 1936. It was a protective measure to escape anti-Semitic Germany. The Fried-Salomons were however lucky, because their father was soon released from Buchenwald concentration camp where he had been interned, due to the fact that the Nazis didn´t want to liquidate potential owners in advance, before they expropriate their properties. The parents also managed to escape to Portland, where Otto Fried had already settled. After WWII, he finally studied art and then travelled to Paris, where he worked in the studio of Fernand Léger from 1949 to 1951. It is one of those sustainable examples of arts promotion and international exchange-oriented funding programme, which should open up for new opportunities and horizons across borders. Otto Fried took advantage of these opportunities and found early connections to various exhibitions in Paris, Portland, New York and finally also in Germany. In 1958, he was to be allowed to exhibit his first works in the Deutschherrenhaus, now Ludwig Museum, in his hometown of Koblenz. In a way, a circle is closing since works from his Paris studio will be shown here this year.

This exhibition aims to pay tribute to the work of Otto Fried and at the same time focus on his special biography. Without Otto Fried's gentle cooperation, but above all accompanied by the intensive support of his close kinswoman, Professor Barbara Wolbert, the wider family circle and his gallerist Silvie Brame (Brame & Laurenceau, Paris), as well as Otto Fried's lawyer in Paris, Laurent Lahmani, the exhibition would not have been possible in its complexity. Special thanks have to be said also to all lenders who supported the exhibition with their artworks. Furthermore, the Koblenz City Archives, whose former director, Hans-Josef Schmidt, has been friends with Otto Fried, willingly helped us. The Mittelrhein-Museum in Koblenz supported the exhibition with two important loans, and also the congregation of the church of St. Maximin in Horchheim, to which Otto Fried had donated a work in 2002, deserves to be thanked. In particular, a large painting by Otto Fried from 1998 required some restoration work, carefully taken over by the restoration studio Holly.

Our special thanks go to the Peter and Irene Ludwig Foundation, which has significantly supported this exhibition. In particular, I would like to thank Dr. Brigitte Franzen, Executive Director and the Board of Trustees for their sustained support in this project. Our thanks are as well addressed to Michele Pizzi and his team at Silvana Editoriale, Milan, who once again demonstrated their great devotion to perfect this publication, and in addition to the authors Lisa Forrell and Barbara Wolbert for their sensitive and personal contributions on Otto Fried, as well as Achim Moeller for the kind permission to reprint the Interview of Kenneth Snelson and Otto Fried. We would also like to thank the photographers Marc Waymel and Eric Bardeau (Paris) as well as Susanne Schmidt-Dominé (Düsseldorf) for the photographs they provided from their archives, and Jost Gabriel (Koblenz) for photographing the artworks. Last but not least, I would like to thank the entire team of the Ludwig Museum, who took intensive care of the preparation and realisation of the exhibition, which has been a real challenge, especially due to the restrictions during the Coronavirus crisis. To Larissa Wesp, scientific volunteer at the Ludwig Museum, goes in particular the merit of the very good result of the accompanying preparation of the exhibition and the editing of this catalogue. The exhibition will once again sustainably increase the perception of Otto Fried's artistic work, and this catalogue will help to make this possible even outside the Ludwig Museum as a physical place for the contemplation of his artworks. Both see themselves as a contribution to the enlivenment of an individual and at the same time universal artistic credo, whose origins were shaped by the dark times of National Socialism, overcome by art.

Vorwort

BEATE REIFENSCHEID
Direktorin

Es ist eine dieser Biografien, die nicht im Rampenlicht der Weltöffentlichkeit stehen, die aber gleichwohl etwas von deutscher Geschichte während der Zeit des Nationalsozialismus vermitteln, die nicht in Vergessenheit geraten sollten. Otto Fried wurde als Sprössling der Fleischerfamilie Fried-Salomon in Horchheim, bei Koblenz, 1923 geboren und bereits 1936 nach Amerika geschickt. Es war eine Schutzmaßnahme, um dem antisemitischen Deutschland zu entkommen. Die Fried-Salomons hatten noch Glück, denn trotz Internierung des Vaters im KZ Buchenwald, wurde dieser bald wieder entlassen, da die Nazis zwecks Enteignung von Besitz die Eigentümer nicht vorab liquidierten. Auf Umwegen gelang auch den Eltern die Flucht nach Portland, wo Otto Fried sich bereits eingelebt hatte. Er fand nach dem Krieg schließlich zur Kunst und reiste nach Paris, wo er von 1949 bis 1951 im Atelier von Fernand Léger arbeitete. Es ist eines dieser nachhaltigen Beispiele von Kunstförderung und auf internationalen Austausch ausgerichteter Förderprogramme, das über Grenzen hinweg neue Möglichkeiten und Horizonte öffnen sollte. Otto Fried nutzte diese Chancen und fand früh Anschluss an diverse Ausstellungen in Paris, Portland, New York und schließlich auch in Deutschland. Ausgerechnet im Deutschherrenhaus, dem heutigen Ludwig Museum, in seiner Heimatstadt Koblenz sollte er dann 1958 seine ersten Werke ausstellen dürfen. In gewisser Weise schließt sich nun ein Zirkel, wenn in diesem Jahr Arbeiten aus seinem Pariser Atelier hier gezeigt werden können.
Diese Ausstellung möchte das Werk von Otto Fried würdigen und sich zugleich seiner besonderen Biografie widmen. Ohne Otto Frieds sanfte Mitarbeit, vor allem aber begleitet durch die intensive Unterstützung seiner ihm nahestehenden Verwandten, Professor Barbara Wolbert, des weiteren Familienkreises und seiner Galeristin Silvie Brame (Brame & Laurenceau, Paris), sowie Otto Frieds Anwalt in Paris, Laurent Lahmani, wäre die Ausstellung in ihrer Komplexität nicht möglich gewesen. Gedankt sei auch allen Leihgebern, welche die Ausstellung mit Ihren Werken unterstützen. Aufschlussreiche Dokumente und Informationen stellte das Stadtarchiv Koblenz bereit, dessen ehemaliger Leiter, Hans-Josef Schmidt, ein Bekannter Otto Frieds, uns bereitwillig half. Ebenso unterstützten das Mittelrhein-Museum in Koblenz, das zwei wichtige Leihgaben auslieh, und schließlich die Gemeinde der Kirche Sankt Maximin in Horchheim, der Otto Fried 2002 ein Werk geschenkt hatte. Insbesondere ein großes Gemälde von Otto Fried aus dem Jahr 1998 bedurfte einiger restauratorischer Bearbeitung, was das Restaurierungsatelier Holly umsichtig übernahm.
Unser besonderer Dank richtet sich an die Peter und Irene Ludwig Stiftung, die diese Ausstellung maßgeblich gefördert hat. Namentlich gedankt sei Dr. Brigitte Franzen, Vorständin, sowie dem Kuratorium für die nachhaltige Unterstützung bei diesem Vorhaben. Der Dank richtet sich auch an Michele Pizzi und sein Team bei Silvana Editoriale, Mailand, die sich erneut mit großer Hingabe um die Publikation dieses bedeutenden Œuvres verdient gemacht haben. Darüber hinaus an die Autorinnen Lisa Forrell und Barbara Wolbert, für ihre sensiblen und persönlichen Beiträge, sowie an Achim Moeller für die Bereitstellung des im Katalog enthaltenen Interviews. Auch den Fotografen Marc Waymel und Eric Bardeau (Paris) sowie Susanne Schmidt-Dominé (Düsseldorf) sei gedankt für die Fotografien, die sie aus Ihren Archiven zur Verfügung stellten, sowie Jost Gabriel (Koblenz) für das Fotografieren der Kunstwerke. Nicht zuletzt sei dem gesamten Team des Ludwig Museums nachhaltig gedankt, das sich intensiv um die Vorbereitung und Durchführung der Ausstellung gekümmert hat, was insbesondere durch die Restriktionen während der Corona-Virus-Krise eine echte Herausforderung war. Hier ist es ganz besonders Larissa Wesp, wissenschaftliche Volontärin im Ludwig Museum, zu verdanken, dass die Vorbereitung der Ausstellung und die Redaktion des Katalogs mühelos gelangen. Die Ausstellung wird einmal mehr die Wahrnehmung von Otto Frieds künstlerischem Werk nachhaltig steigern und dieser Katalog dazu beitragen, dass auch außerhalb des Ludwig Museums als physischem Ort von Werkbetrachtung dies möglich wird. Beide verstehen sich als Beitrag zur Verlebendigung eines individuellen und zugleich allgemeingültigen künstlerischen Credos, dessen Ursprung von den dunklen Zeiten des Nationalsozialismus geprägt war und diesen durch die Kunst überwand.

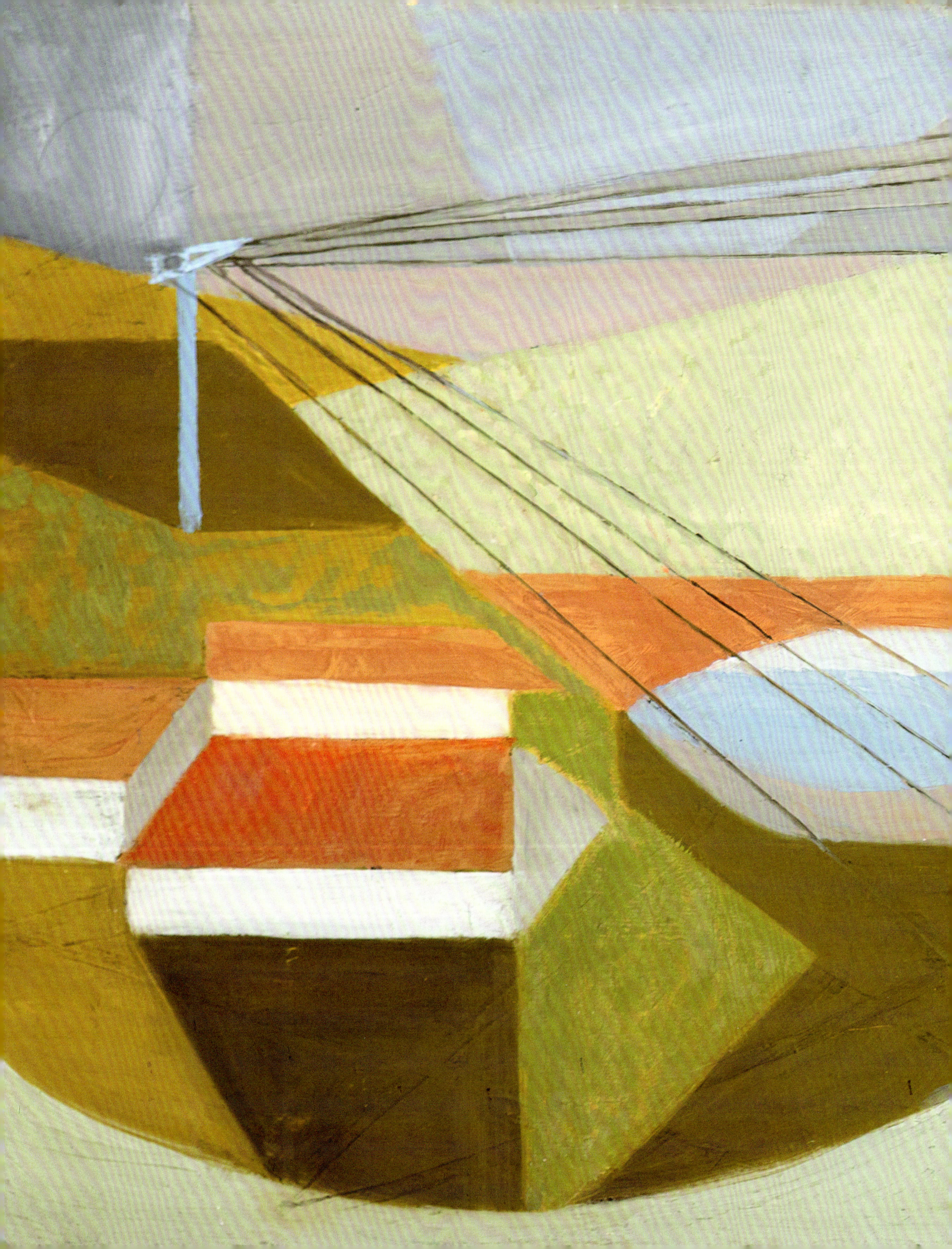

BEATE REIFENSCHEID

Frühe Jahre:
Vom Expressionismus zur Abstraktion

Will man so seine Tage im hohen Alter verbringen? Mitten in der Corona-Pandemie sitzt Otto Fried, mittlerweile 97-jährig, in seiner eleganten Pariser Wohnung, im obersten Stock eines wundervollen Stadthauses im schönen Faubourg St. Honoré. Das historische Gebäude befindet sich einen Steinwurf entfernt von den Tuilerien und unweit des Louvre – im Herzen von Paris, ganz in der Nähe des Elysée-Palasts. Ein Fahrstuhl steigt leise ruckelnd in die obere Etage, aber lieber wählt man die alte Stiege, deren dunkle Eichenbohlen bei jedem einzelnen Schritt sanft knarzen. Hier sitzt er also, isoliert von dem Rest der Welt, die derzeit nun nur noch aus seinen Betreuerinnen besteht, die sich rührend um ihn kümmern. Besuch findet nicht mehr statt, schon allein um ihn vor Infektionsgefahren zu schützen. Shutdown – auch für altehrwürdige Künstler. Traurige Zeiten, die derzeit die Welt fest im Griff halten.

BEATE REIFENSCHEID

Early Years:
From Expressionism to Abstraction

Do you want to spend your days in old age in this manner? Just in the middle of the corona pandemic, Otto Fried, now 97 years old, is sitting in his elegant Paris apartment, on the top floor of a wonderful town house in the beautiful Faubourg St. Honoré. The historic building is a stone's throw from the Tuileries and not far from the Louvre – in the heart of Paris, very close to the Elysée Palace. An elevator jerks up to the upper floor, but it's better to choose the old staircase, whose dark oak planks creak gently at every step. So here he sits, isolated from the rest of the world, which currently consists only of his care-takers. Visits no longer take place, if only to protect him from the risk of infection. Shutdown – also for time-honored artists. Sad times that currently hold the world under control. There may be some tragedy in the fact that his life was so full of hurdles and obstacles. His early youth was marked by exclusion and isolation, because when the National Socialists came to power in Germany, Jewish fellow citizens

Landscape with Bridge
Detail
1951
Öl auf Leinwand / Oil on canvas
50,17 x 99,7 cm
Sammlung des Künstlers/
Collection of the Artist

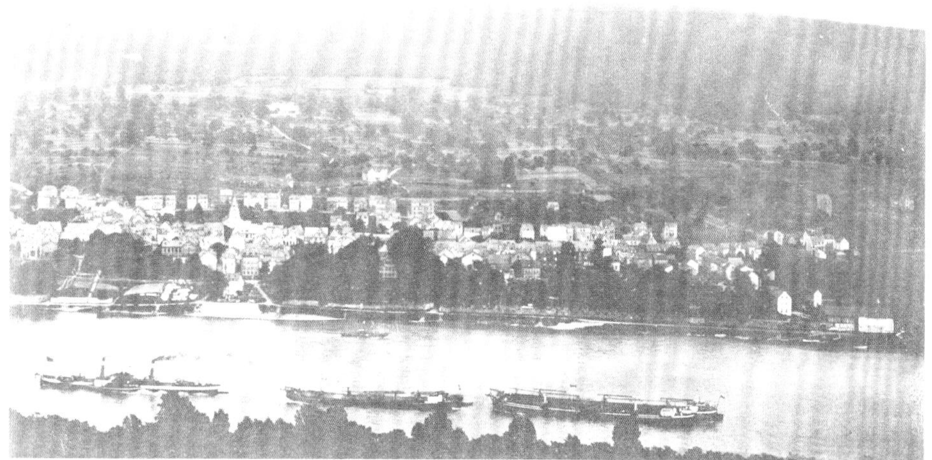

Koblenz-Horchheim um 1914 /
Koblenz-Horchheim around 1914

were increasingly subject to reprisals and, a little later, to persecution. The Nazis raged with their unspeakable politics, with their defamation of fellow Jews, whom they hunted freely from 1933 and finally deported and exterminated to an unimaginable scale in concentration camps. The anti-Semitic climate had intensified in Germany ever since Hitler came to power, and Otto Fried's parents were rightly very concerned about the well-being of their family. The Fried-Salomon family lived in Horchheim, a small district on the opposite side of the Rhine from the historic city center of Koblenz, where the father ran his own butchery and slaughterhouse. Otto had a short, happy childhood with his older brother, but as early as 1936, at the age of only 13, his parents sent him to distant relatives in Portland, Oregon – into the "new world", as it was said even then. The parents had the right fear that the survival of their family was at stake.

Thus Otto Fried was luckily able to seize the opportunity to leave, but he had to go alone on his own from Hamburg to San Francisco by ship, and from there by train to Portland, where a host family welcomed him. Even though he obviously finds only positive words for his time in Oregon, it must have been painful to leave the tranquility of his hometown and the security of his family behind him and find his new way as a teenager in a completely foreign world with a new language. The outbreak of World War II in September 1939 could only have intensified these feelings.

Is it the naivety of the young Otto Fried, who will have experienced a certain tranquility with his host family far from the actual war, or is it rather the deliberate fading out of a reality that would otherwise be perceived as unbearable to lead him towards nature? He likes to describe how he was fascinated by the lush landscape around Portland, the green of the meadows, the imposing rock formations, the two streams that showed a certain synchronicity with the rivers in his hometown Koblenz and the blue of the sky, with its very unique luminosity and energy. In his landscapes, again and again he comes back to exactly these first sensations, captivated above all by the vastness that suggests infinity. He is fascinated by the wild formations of the clouds and the atmospheric changes in the sky. His short excursion into biology, which he began to study after the mili-

Es mag eine gewisse Tragik darin liegen, dass sein Leben so voller Hürden und Hindernissen war. Bereits seine frühe Jugend war von Ausgrenzung und Isolation geprägt, denn als die Nationalsozialisten in Deutschland die Macht übernahmen, waren jüdische Mitbürger zunehmend Repressalien und wenig später auch der Verfolgung ausgesetzt. Die Nazis wüteten mit ihrer unsäglichen Politik, mit ihrer Diffamierung jüdischer Mitbürger, auf die sie ab 1933 ungehindert Jagd machten und schließlich in unvorstellbarem Maßstab in Konzentrationslager deportierten und auslöschten. Das antisemitische Klima verschärfte sich in Deutschland zusehends seit der Machtübernahme Hitlers und zu Recht machten sich Otto Frieds Eltern schon bald große Sorgen um das Wohl ihrer Familie. Die Familie Fried-Salomon lebte in Horchheim, einem kleinen Stadtteil auf der gegenüberliegenden Rheinseite des historischen Stadtkerns von Koblenz am Rhein, wo der Vater eine eigene Metzgerei mit Schlachthaus unterhielt. Mit seinem älteren Bruder verlebte Otto eine kurze, wohl glückliche Kindheit, aber schon 1936, mit nur 13 Jahren, schickten seine Eltern ihn zu entfernten Verwandten nach Portland, Oregon – in die „neue Welt", wie man selbst damals noch sagte. Die Eltern hatten sehr genau ein Gespür dafür, dass das Überleben der Familie auf dem Spiel stand.

Es ist einem glücklichen Umstand zu verdanken, dass Otto Fried die Chance zur Ausreise ergreifen konnte, aber er musste allein, ganz auf sich gestellt, von Hamburg aus mit dem Schiff nach San Francisco und von dort mit dem Zug nach Portland, wo eine Gastfamilie ihn aufnahm. Auch wenn er selbst offensichtlich immer nur positive Worte für seine Zeit in Oregon findet, so muss es doch auch schmerzlich gewesen sein, die Beschaulichkeit seiner Heimatstadt und die Geborgenheit seiner Familie hinter sich zu lassen und als Jugendlicher sich in einer gänzlich fremden Welt und neuen Sprache zurecht zu finden. Der Ausbruch des Zweiten Weltkriegs im September 1939 kann diese Gefühle letztlich nur verstärkt haben.

Ist es der Naivität des Jugendlichen Otto Fried geschuldet, der fernab des eigentlichen Kriegsgeschehens eine gewisse Beschaulichkeit bei seiner Gastfamilie erlebt haben wird, oder ist es eher das bewusste Ausblenden der Realität, die ansonsten als unerträglich wahrgenommen würde, das ihn zur Natur führte? Gerne beschreibt er selbst, wie ihn die üppige Landschaft um Portland faszinierte, das Grün der Wiesen, die imposanten Felsformationen, die beiden Ströme, die eine gewisse Synchronizität mit den Flüssen in seiner Heimatstadt Koblenz aufwiesen und das Blau des Himmels, das allem eine ganz eigene Leuchtkraft und Energie zu verleihen schien. Immer wieder kommt er in seinen Landschaftsbildern auf genau diese ersten Empfindungen zurück und es ist vor allem die Weite, die Unendlichkeit suggeriert, die ihn in ihren Bann schlägt. Es faszinieren ihn die wilden Formationen der Wolken und die atmosphärischen Veränderungen am Himmel. Sein kurzer Ausflug in die Biologie, die zu studieren er sich nach dem Kriegsdienst anschickt, fesselt ihn dann doch nicht nachhaltig, und so entschließt er sich 1947, seinen eigenen Neigungen nachzugeben und sich dem Kunststudium zu widmen. Er beginnt an der University of Oregon, im Department of Art and Architecture, mit dem Studium der Malerei.

Es ist das Amerika der Mittvierziger – ein Land, das selbst in den Zweiten Weltkrieg involviert war und dessen Bevölkerung bis zum Angriff auf Pearl Harbor, Hawaii, noch relativ wenig hautnah leiden musste, weil es nicht selbst militärisch attackiert wurde. Portland, mit seiner Lage im Norden der USA und nahe der Pa-

tary service, did not captivate him permanently, and so in 1947 he decided to give in to his own inclinations and devote himself to studying art. He began to study painting at the University of Oregon, in the Department of Art and Architecture. It is America in the mid-forties - a country that, while being anyway involved in the Second World War, didn't suffer from it directly until the attack on Pearl Harbor, Hawaii, when it was militarily attacked. Portland, with its location in the north of the USA and near the Pacific coast, may have felt even further away from the war and from its own mobilization and armament than the east coast states. The art that prevailed in the 1930s and 1940s was characterized on the one hand by a new realism that had only just developed an independent American form and on the other by increasing influences, especially those of the exiled artists, who had mainly immigrated from Europe to America. They often succeeded in deepening and transforming their own artistic traditions from European avant-garde movements into the new context. From this tension between forms of American realism and the new impulses of the avant-garde scene, new things quickly developed, especially from the late 1940s, when the so-called New York School with its Abstract Expressionism was formed. Far from European perception and its influence, realism prevailed in various, highly individual forms, as it was primarily shaped by artists such as Edward Hopper, Marsden Hartley and Grant Wood. They were all influenced by the major social changes that had been triggered in particular by the Great Depression of 1929. They deliberately turned away from the superiority of the European avant-garde, which they had met not only at the Armory Show of 1913, but above all through the exhibitions that the up-and-coming photographer Alfred Stieglitz regularly organized in his New York Gallery 291.[1] Before the First World War, artists such as Marcel Duchamp, Man Ray and Pablo Picasso, Georges Braques and Auguste Rodin presented their latest works here and thus gained access to American museums and collectors very quickly. Their dominance was not always unproblematic for American artists. For its part, the new style was not created without European impulses and concrete connections. In the case of Grant Wood in particular, a closeness to the New Objectivity, as represented in Germany by Christian Schad or Alexander Kanoldt, is formally undeniable, whereas Marsden Hartley, in particular due to his time in Germany (1913–1915), was largely inspired by Wassily Kandinsky and Franz Marc. The America of the 1940s is inconceivable without these profound ties to the European avant-garde before and after World War I and till World War II, and it was only just beginning to develop its own standards that were to prove revolutionary after 1945.

Nevertheless, it is likely that there were hardly any influences from these American artists that Otto Fried noticed as a young student in Portland. Beyond the presumed classical academic standards in artistic education, Otto Fried met the very dedicated teacher Jack Wilkinson,[2] who had just returned from France. With enthusiasm he revealed his students the latest developments in the European avant-garde, which in a way helped to forge an international perspective. He may also have drawn the attention on those artists who had recently come to America, such as the already famous Hans Hofmann, whose influence was decisive for numerous protagonists of the New York School, but also that of the following generation – such as Nell Blaine, Larry Rivers and Helene Fran-

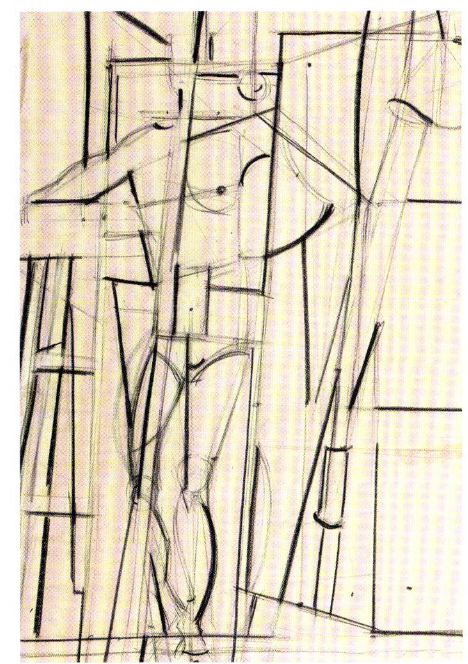

Ohne Titel / Untitled
Circa 1948–1950
Grafit auf Papier /
Graphite on paper
56 x 36,5 cm
Sammlung des Künstlers /
Collection of the Artist

zifikküste, mag da gefühlt noch weiter vom Kriegsgeschehen und von der eigenen Mobilmachung sowie Aufrüstung entfernt gewesen sein, als die Ostküstenstaaten. Die Kunst, die in den 1930er und 1940er Jahren vorherrschte, war zum einen geprägt von einem neuen Realismus, der gerade erst eine eigenständige amerikanische Form entwickelt hatte und zum anderen von zunehmenden Einflüssen, insbesondere die der Exilkünstler, die vornehmlich aus Europa eingewandert waren. Ihnen gelang es oftmals, ihre eigenen künstlerischen Traditionen aus der europäischen Avantgardebewegung in dem neuen Kontext weiter zu vertiefen und zu transformieren. Aus diesem Spannungsgefüge zwischen Formen des amerikanischen Realismus und neuen Impulsen aus der Avantgardeszene entwickelte sich rasch Neues, insbesondere ab Ende der 1940er Jahre als sich die sog. New York School mit ihrem Abstrakten Expressionismus formierte. Fernab der europäischen Wahrnehmung und deren Einfluss setzte sich der Realismus in unterschiedlichen, höchst individuellen Ausformungen durch, wie er vornehmlich von Künstlern wie Edward Hopper, Marsden Hartley und Grant Wood geprägt wurde. Sie alle waren von den großen sozialen Veränderungen beeinflusst, die insbesondere durch die Weltwirtschaftskrise von 1929 ausgelöst worden waren. Sie wandten sich bewusst ab von der Übermacht der europäischen Avantgarde, die sie nicht nur auf der Armory Show von 1913 kennengelernt hatten, sondern vor allem durch jene Ausstellungen, die der aufstrebende Fotograf Alfred Stieglitz in seine New Yorker Gallery 291 regelmäßig ausrichtete.[1] Hier hatten bereits vor dem Ersten Weltkrieg Künstler wie Marcel Duchamp, Man Ray und Pablo Picasso, Georges Braques, Auguste Rodin etc. ihre neuesten Arbeiten präsentiert und so sehr rasch Zugang zu amerikanischen Museen und Sammlern gewonnen. Ihre Dominanz war für die amerikanischen Künstler nicht immer unproblematisch. Die neue Stilrichtung war ihrerseits nicht ohne europäische Impulse und konkrete Verbindungen entstanden. Gerade bei Grant Wood ist eine Nähe zur Neuen Sachlichkeit, wie sie in Deutschland durch Christian Schad oder Alexander Kanoldt vertreten wurde, formal nicht zu leugnen, wohingegen Marsden Hartley insbesondere durch seine Zeit in Deutschland (1913–1915) maßgeblich von Wassily Kandinsky und Franz Marc inspiriert worden war. Das Amerika der 1940er Jahre ist ohne diese intensiven Verflechtungen zur europäischen Avantgarde vor und nach dem Ersten bis hin zum Zweiten Weltkrieg nicht denkbar und es begann gerade erst, eigene Maßstäbe zu entwickeln, die sich nach 1945 als revolutionär erweisen sollten.

Dennoch, es werden vermutlich kaum Einflüsse dieser amerikanischen Künstler gewesen sein, die Otto Fried als junger Student in Portland wahrgenommen hat. Jenseits der zu vermutenden klassisch-akademischen Standards in der künstlerischen Ausbildung traf Otto Fried hier jedoch auf den ausgesprochen engagierten Lehrmeister Jack Wilkinson,[2] der seinerseits gerade aus Frankreich zurückgekehrt war. Er vermittelte seinen Studenten mit Verve die neuesten Entwicklungen der europäischen Avantgarde, was in gewisser Weise mit dazu beitrug, dass sich hier eine Perspektive auf den internationalen Diskurs eröffnete. Er mag auch den Blick gelenkt haben auf jene Künstler, die schon kurz zuvor nach Amerika gekommen waren, wie z.B. der bereits berühmte Hans Hofmann, dessen Einfluss maßgeblich war für zahlreiche Protagonisten der New York School, aber auch jene der nachfolgenden Generation – wie Nell Blaine, Larry Rivers und Helene Frankenthaler.[3] Er nahm vieles vorweg, was wenig später im Abstrakten Expressionismus auf teils überdimensionalen

kenthaler.[3] He anticipated a lot of things that a little later would be expressed in Abstract Expressionism in a purely gestural way on partly oversized canvases. The war years experienced the coming up of the surrealists Max Ernst, André Masson, André Breton as well as of individual personalities such as Marc Chagall, Otto Freundlich, or like Walter Gropius, Mies van der Rohe or Josef Albers, respectively founder and teachers of Bauhaus. More constructive styles came with them onto the American art scene and influenced it as a counterpoint to gestures, later represented by Barnett Newman and the hard-edge painters such as Ad Reinhard. Piet Mondrian, who had fled to the United States in 1940, also established the concepts of his De Stijl movement and the expansion of the famous circle of artists "Abstraction / Création", which in turn was the first cosmopolitan association for abstract art in Paris until 1937. All of this brought about new impulses and orientations in the "new world",[4] especially in New York. Never were art, literature, theater, film etc. more progressive in America than in those years of the Second World War and the period immediately after. In any case, Jack Wilkinson (1913–1974) had returned from Paris in 1941, where he had met Fernand Léger, among others. At the University of Oregon, he developed the first courses for design in the States and taught the students to "look behind" the underlying principles and to trust imagination in their own works. He soon became a legendary teacher and facilitator of contemporary art. His pupil Otto Fried vividly described his teaching, which was felt to be excessive: "Since he was a man interested in all subjects, we had discussions in the fields of philosophy, psychology, mathematics, design, and of course, aesthetics. One class started at 9:00 am and continued until 8:00 at night, ten students started out, locations changed, and Jack was still talking and illuminating. The group narrowed to three and then two, with Jack still talking."[5] It is also thanks to Wilkinson that he invited the architect, philosopher and thought leader Richard Buckminster Fuller[6] to the University of Oregon. He would later express his appreciation of Otto Fried's art.[7] The US government's funding program, the so-called GI Bill, enabled Fried to finance his studies and also his stay in Europe. It was thanks to the initiative and recommendation of his teacher that Otto Fried went to Fernand Léger.

It was definitely the most important thing that Otto Fried could get after his studies, and he took the opportunity to get back to Europe for two years to further widen his artistic studies there and gain new experiences in the then most fashionable metropolis of Paris.[8] Paris had once again become an important "hotspot" of artistic avant-garde, as it was here – after the end of World War II – that all those young talents who wanted to join forces to rebuild Europe and radically reinvent and design art met. It was initially a tentative link to the time before 1910, when Paris had once been the center of the European avant-garde, before it was replaced by Munich for a short period because the "Blaue Reiter" established there to a cosmopolitan size. Thanks to the intensive network that Kandinsky, Marc and Macke had built up, the latter was able to win over artists from many neighboring countries towards their abstraction ideas, work with them and exhibit them: Robert Delauney, Sonja Delauney-Terk, Arnold Schönberg, Edvard Munch, Malewitch and others. These encounters, which in the end were inspired by Kandinsky's revolutionary approach described in his writing *About the Spiritual in Art* (1911), created a new openness towards artistic discussion and exchange that had never before been so intense in

Leinwänden rein gestisch zum Ausdruck gebracht wurde. In den Kriegsjahren kamen zudem die Surrealisten Max Ernst, André Masson, André Breton hinzu, aber auch Einzelpersönlichkeiten wie Marc Chagall, Otto Freundlich und einige andere, die, wie Walter Gropius, Mies van der Rohe oder Josef Albers, Gründer bzw. Lehrende am Bauhaus gewesen waren. Mit ihnen gelangten verstärkt konstruktive Stilrichtungen in die amerikanische Kunstszene und beeinflussten diese als Gegenpol zum Gestischen, u.a. später vertreten durch Barnett Newman und die Hardedge-Maler wie Ad Reinhard. Aber auch Piet Mondrian, der 1940 in die USA geflohen war, etablierte hier die Konzepte seiner De-Stijl-Bewegung sowie der erweiterten des berühmten Künstlerzirkels "Abstraction / Création", der seinerseits bis 1937 in Paris als erste kosmopolitische Vereinigung für die abstrakte Kunst galt. All dies gewann in der "neuen Welt",[4] insbesondere in New York, innovative neue Impulse und Ausrichtungen. Nirgends waren Kunst, Literatur, Theater, Film etc. progressiver in Amerika, als in jenen Jahren des Zweiten Weltkriegs und der Ära unmittelbar danach.

Jack Wilkinson (1913–1974) jedenfalls war seinerseits 1941 aus Paris zurückgekehrt, wo er unter anderem bei Fernand Léger gewesen war. An der Universität von Oregon entwickelte er die ersten Kurse für Design in den Staaten und lehrte die Studenten, "hinter" die zugrundeliegenden Prinzipien zu schauen und sich mehr Imagination in der eigenen Gestaltung zu trauen. Schon sehr bald gilt er als legendärer Lehrer und Vermittler der zeitgenössischen Kunst. Sein Schüler Otto Fried beschrieb seinen wohl als exzessiv empfundenen Unterricht anschaulich: „Since he was a man interested in all subjects, we had discussions in the fields of philosophy, psychology, mathematics, design, and of course, aesthetics. One class started at 9:00 a.m. and continued until 8:00 at night, ten students started out, locations changed, and Jack was still talking and illuminating. The group narrowed to three and then two, with Jack still talking."[5] Wilkinson ist es auch zu verdanken, dass er den Architekten, Philosophen und Vordenker Richard Buckminster Fuller[6] an die Universität von Oregon einlud, der sich später dann anerkennend zu Otto Frieds Kunst äußern sollte.[7] Das Förderprogramm der US-Regierung, die sog. GI Bill, ermöglichte Fried die Finanzierung seines Studiums und auch des Aufenthalts in Europa. Dass Otto Fried seinerseits dann zu Fernand Léger ging, erfolgte auf gezielte Initiative und Empfehlung seines Professors.

Es war definitiv das Bedeutendste, was Otto Fried nach seinem Studium zuteil wurde und er ergriff die Chance, die sich ihm bot, für zwei Jahre nach Europa zurückzukehren, um dort seine künstlerischen Studien weiter auszubauen und neue Erfahrungen in der damals angesagten Kunstmetropole Paris zu gewinnen.[8] Paris war erneut zu einem wichtigen „Hotspot" künstlerischer Avantgarde geworden, da sich gerade hier - nach dem Ende des Zweiten Weltkriegs - all jene jungen Talente trafen, die im neu aufzubauenden Europa ihre Kräfte formieren, Kunst radikal neu erfinden und gestalten wollten. Es war zunächst ein tastendes Anknüpfen an die Zeit vor 1910, als Paris schon einmal Zentrum der europäischen Avantgarde gewesen war, bevor es für kurze Jahre von München abgelöst wurde, weil sich hier der „Blaue Reiter" zu einer kosmopolitischen Größe etablierte. Dieser vermochte es, Dank des intensiven Netzwerkes, das Kandinky, Marc und Macke aufgebaut hatten, Künstler aus vielen Nachbarstaaten für ihre Abstraktionsideen zu gewinnen, mit ihnen gemeinsam zu arbeiten und auszustellen: Robert Delauney, Sonja Delauney-Terk, Ar-

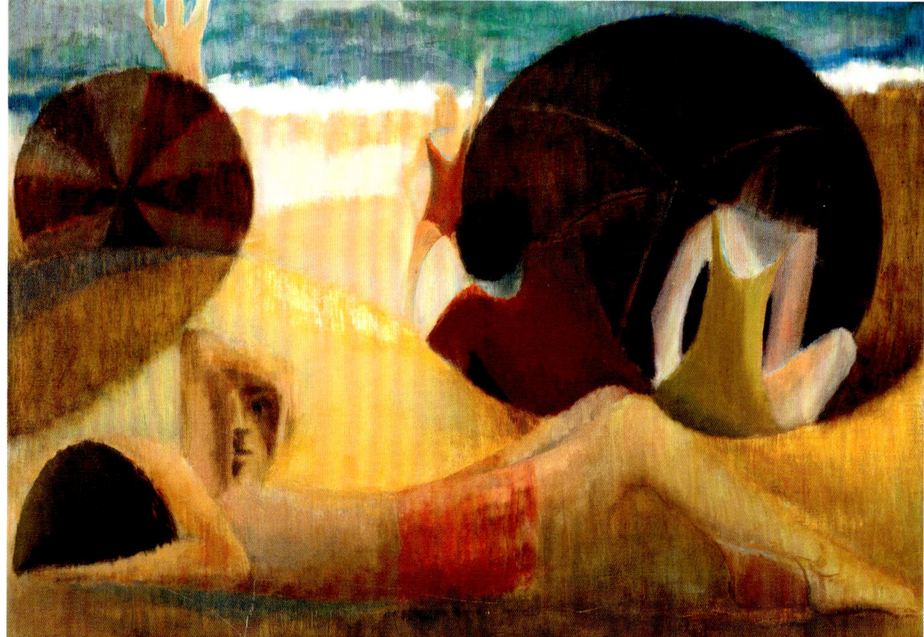

Jones Beach, 1956
Öl auf Leinwand / Oil on canvas
89 x 127 cm
Sammlung des Künstlers /
Collection of the Artist

Europe. World War I destroyed all this, but much of the artistic liberation and innovation continued in the 1920s and early 1930s. It continued also in Paris in the mid-forties, with the presence of well-known names: Pablo Picasso, who had become the most important political voice in the fight against fascism, Fernand Léger, who himself joined the French Communist Party in 1945,[9] and Alberto Giacometti, who had returned from Geneva in 1945. At the same time, however, a younger generation of artists was preparing to revolutionize art again, starting from where art had been branded "degenerate" by the Nazi verdict. They remembered the forms of abstraction of the Blaue Reiter, but at the same time also the freedom of the expressive gesture as founded by Fauves and the Brücke. Many of these young artists then formed the Ecole de Paris (Jean Fautrier, Henri Michaux, Jean-Paul Riopelle and Vieira da Silva) or followed radically individual paths, such as Pierre Soulages and Jean Dubuffet. When Otto Fried arrived in Paris in 1949, he first turned to André Lhôte,[10] in whose Académie de Montmartre he worked; later he moved to Fernand Léger's studio. He was accompanied by his colleague Kenneth Snelson.[11] André Lhôte's painting was clearly more classical than Léger's own view, showed influences from Cézanne and Matisse, and yet Otto Fried's utter search for an ideal landscape can always be traced back to Lhôte's writings and instructions on art. The latter had already organised in 1947 the exhibition "L'influence de Cézanne" in the Galerie de France – which would set the new art standards –, in 1948 written a monograph on Seurat and Cézanne and finally published the *Traité de la figure* in 1950.[12]

In view of Fried's later enthusiasm for experimenting with unusual materials and above all his pronounced willingness towards abstract art, the influence resulting from the encounter with Fernand Léger seems to have been more lasting. In addition to Jack Wilkinson's possible recommendation, the shift was probably due also to the fact that Léger himself had spent his years in exile in New York and had had an enormous influence on the young art scene, including Roy Lichtenstein, Robert Rauschenberg, Ad Held, Ellsworth Kelly and

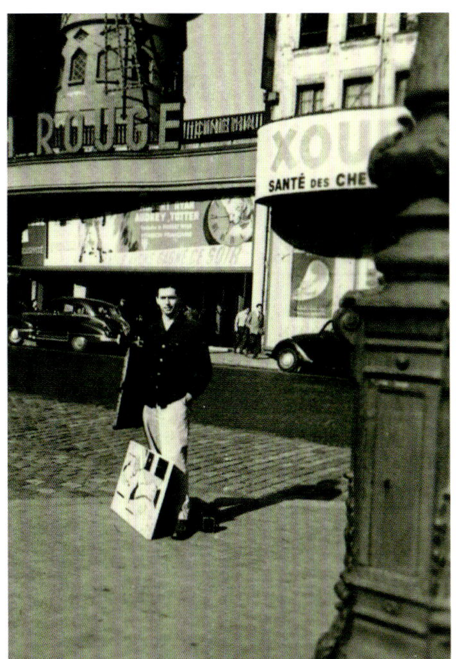

Otto Fried vor dem Moulin Rouge in Paris, um 1950 / Otto Fried in front of the Moulin Rouge, Paris, around 1950

nold Schönberg, Edvard Munch, Malewitch u.a. Durch diese Begegnungen, die sich letztlich fast alle auf Kandinskys revolutionärem Ansatz aus seiner Schrift „Über das Geistige in der Kunst" (1911) beriefen, war eine neue Offenheit der künstlerischen Diskussion und des Austausches entstanden, die es in dieser Breite nie zuvor in Europa gegeben hatte. Der Erste Weltkrieg zerschlug dies auf ernüchternde Weise, aber vieles an künstlerischer Befreiung und Neuerung lebte in den 1920er und Anfangs der 1930er Jahre fort. Im Paris der Mittvierziger Jahre knüpfte man vielfach genau daran an und traf zunächst auf alt bekannte Namen: auf Pablo Picasso, der zur wichtigsten politischen Stimme im Kampf gegen den Faschismus geworden war, auf Fernand Léger, der selbst 1945 in die Kommunistische Partei Frankreichs eintrat[9] sowie auf Alberto Giacometti, der 1945, aus Genf kommend, hierher zurückgekehrt war. Zeitgleich jedoch schickte sich eine jüngere Generation von Künstlern an, die Kunst erneut zu revolutionieren und dabei dort anzusetzen, wo die Kunst durch das Verdikt der Nationalsozialisten als „entartet" gebrandmarkt worden war. Sie besannen sich auf die Abstraktionsformen des Blauen Reiter, zugleich aber auch auf die Freiheit der expressiven Geste, wie sie durch die Fauves und die Brücke begründet worden war. Viele dieser jungen Künstler formten dann die Ecole de Paris (Jean Fautrier, Henri Michaux, Jean-Paul Riopelle sowie Vieira da Silva) oder beschritten radikal individuelle Wege, wie z.B. Pierre Soulages und Jean Dubuffet.

Als Otto Fried 1949 in Paris ankommt, wendet er sich zunächst an André Lhôte,[10] in dessen Académie de Montmartre er arbeitet; später wechselt er dann ins Atelier von Fernand Léger. Begleitet wird er von seinem Studienkollegen Kenneth Snelson.[11] André Lhôtes Malerei war im Vergleich zu Légers eigener Auffassung deutlich klassischer, zeigte Einflüsse von Cézanne und Matisse und doch wird man vermutlich Otto Frieds ausgesprochene Suche nach einem idealen Landschaftsbild immer auch auf Lhôte's Schriften und Anleitungen zur Kunst zurückführen können. So hatte dieser z.B. bereits 1947 die Maßstäbe setzende Ausstellung "L'influence de Cézanne" in der Galerie de France realisiert, sodann 1948 eine Monografie über Seurat sowie über Cézanne verfasst und 1950 schließlich das "Traité de la figure" publiziert.[12]

Mit Blick auf Frieds spätere Experimentierfreude hinsichtlich ungewöhnlicher Materialien und vor allem seiner ausgesprochenen Bereitschaft zur Abstraktion scheint der Einfluss, der aus der Begegnung mit Fernand Léger resultierte, nachhaltiger gewesen zu sein. Sicherlich erfolgte der Wechsel zu ihm nicht zuletzt - neben Jack Wilkinsons möglicher Empfehlung - auch aufgrund der Tatsache, dass Léger selber seine Exiljahre in New York verbracht hatte und hier enormen Einfluss auf die junge Kunstszene gewonnen hatte, darunter Roy Lichtenstein, Robert Rauschenberg, Ad Held, Ellsworth Kelly und Andy Warhol.[13] Das hatte sich herumgesprochen. In gewisser Weise berühren sich hier zwei imaginäre Kreise, bei denen Otto Fried das amerikanische, Fernand Léger hingegen das französische Bindeglied markiert und zu einem fruchtbaren Bruchteil sich diese osmotisch verquicken. Bei Fried, dem Exildeutschen, hat dies eine besondere Tragweite, denn im Grunde ist er hier in doppelter Weise nirgends verankert.

Fried jedenfalls nutzte seinen künstlerisch motivierten Studienaufenthalt in Paris nachhaltig. Eine kleine Léger-Zeichnung, eine Mutter mit ihrer Tochter darstellend, hatte Otto Fried sich ausgesucht, als ihm Léger eine Arbeit schenkte.

Andy Warhol.[13] Word had got around. In a way, two imaginary circles touch here, in which Otto Fried marks the American link, while Fernand Léger marks the French link, and to a fruitful fraction these are osmotically intermingled. To Fried, the exile German, this has a special scope, because he is basically nowhere anchored in a double way.

In any case, Fried made lasting use of his artistically motivated study visit to Paris. He had chosen a small Léger drawing depicting a mother and her daughter when Léger gave him a work as a gift. It seems like the legacy of the famous artist to the young Otto Fried. Some of his drawings from around 1948 suggest that Fried was already anticipating the framework-like structures typical in Cubism and in many works by Léger. Comparable to Léger's drawing style, Fried crosses his only hinted figure with a dominant line structure. In Léger's studio, he would have further developed this for himself. In comparison, there are two famous compositions by Léger from 1950 and 1951,[14] in which he pairs his own shapes with architectural or purely functional structures. For Léger, they meant the direct examination of urban life, which was characterized by skylines and building constructions up to an increasingly dominant industrialization. He interlocked the human being in it as in a narrow, mutually dependent structure of lines, rods, cross struts. Otto Fried does not seem to go that far with his figures and therefore this dependence on modern urbanity is less emphasized. Nevertheless, the two drawings from 1948 clearly show the human figure trapped in lines, which, like architectural struts, become independent of the human figure and clearly overlap it. Humanoid references can only be recognized at a second and third glance. Instead, Otto Fried subtly varies between delicate, thin pencil lines, some of which are duplicated as if to insure oneself, and the vigorously executed darker lines that mark the outermost surface like a further image layer. All the other lines seem to lie underneath and disappear into the barely indicated image space.

From today's perspective, unfortunately only one work can be directly assigned to his time in Paris; other early pictures, which are still in his studio today, date from 1952. Nevertheless, it is more than revealing to see that Fried exhibited at the Jeanne Bucher Gallery in July 1950, as well as on the "Great Exhibition Cycle of Painting" in August in Deauville and in December of the same year attended the "Salon de l'Art Libre" in Paris.[15] Almost immediately after his arrival, the Galerie Jeanne Bucher brought Fried to an illustrious circle of famous artists who she represented for a period of their lives and who had continued to be shown even against the resistance of the Nazis.[16] They included Braques, Nicolas de Staël, Wassily Kandinsky, Otto Freundlich and Paul Klee as well as Fernand Léger, whose class was exhibited by the gallery in the summer of 1950.[17] His first solo exhibition at the American Library in Paris followed in the summer of 1951, before returning to Portland in October. The impressions that the dense, intense art world of Paris had on him can only be guessed at indirectly. The influence that Léger apparently used and therefore Fried obviously patronized is unmistakable.

The painting *Landscape with bridge* from 1951 was probably made in Paris before Fried returned to America. It surprises with its pastel-like colors and the strictly planimetric arrangement of the color fields. Nowhere are perspective indications given, rather a deep landscape is built without organically devel-

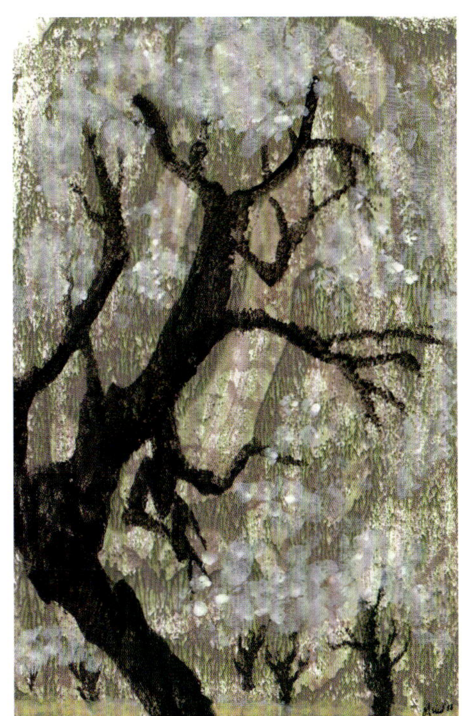

Blossoming Apple Trees, 1958
Monotypie / Monotype
68,7 x 46,7 cm
Mittelrhein-Museum Koblenz

Das erscheint wie das Vermächtnis des berühmten Künstlers an den jungen Otto Fried. Einige seiner Zeichnungen um 1948 lassen ahnen, dass Fried bereits die gerüstartigen Strukturen, wie sie im Kubismus und ebenso in vielen Léger-Werken typisch sind, aufgreift. Vergleichbar mit Légers Zeichenstil verschränkt Fried hier seine nur angedeutete Figur mit einer dominierenden Linienstruktur. Im Atelier von Léger wird er dies weiter für sich entwickelt haben. Vergleichend hierzu bieten sich zwei berühmte Komposition von 1950 und 1951 an,[14] in denen dieser seine eigenen Gestalten mit architektonischen oder rein funktionalen Strukturen paart. Für Léger bedeuteten sie die unmittelbare Auseinandersetzung mit dem urbanen Leben, das von Skylines und Baukonstruktionen, bis hin zu einer immer dominanteren Industrialisierung geprägt war. Er verzahnte den Menschen darin wie in einem engen, sich wechselseitig bedingenden Gefüge aus Linien, Stäben, Querstreben. Otto Fried scheint mit seinen Figuren nicht ganz so weit zu gehen und pointiert deshalb weniger diese Abhängigkeit zur modernen Urbanität. Dennoch zeigen die zwei Zeichnungen von 1948 die menschliche Figur deutlich gefangen in Linienbezügen, die wie architektonisch anmutende Streben sich gegenüber der menschlichen Gestalt verselbständigen und diese eindeutig überlagern. Humanoide Bezüge werden erst auf den zweiten und dritten Blick erkennbar. Stattdessen variiert Otto Fried subtil zwischen zarten, dünnen Bleistiftlinien, die sich teils wie zur eigenen Versicherung doppeln, und den energisch ausgeführten dunkleren Strichen, die wie eine weitere Bildebene die äußerste Oberfläche markieren. Alle übrigen Linien scheinen darunterzuliegen und im kaum angedeuteten Bildraum zu verhallen.

Leider lässt sich aus heutiger Sicht nur ein einziges Werk unmittelbar seiner Pariser Zeit zuweisen; weitere frühe Bilder, die sich heute noch in seinem Atelier befinden, datieren aus dem Jahr 1952. Dennoch ist es mehr als aufschlussreich zu sehen, dass Fried bereits im Juli 1950 in der Galerie Jeanne Bucher ausstellte, sowie an dem "Großen Ausstellungszyklus der Malerei" im August in Deauville und noch im Dezember desselben Jahres am "Salon de l'Art Libre" in Paris teilnahm.[15] Durch die Galerie Jeanne Bucher gelangte Fried fast unmittelbar nach seiner Ankunft in einen erlauchten Zirkel berühmter Künstler, die von ihr Zeit ihres Lebens vertreten und selbst gegen den Widerstand der Nazis weiterhin gezeigt worden waren.[16] Zu ihnen zählten Braques, Nicolas de Staël, Wassily Kandinsky, Otto Freundlich und Paul Klee, sowie eben auch Fernand Léger, dessen Klasse die Galerie im Sommer 1950 ausstellte.[17] Im Sommer 1951 folgt seine erste Einzelausstellung in der Amerika-Bibliothek in Paris, bevor er dann im Oktober nach Portland zurückkehrt. Die Eindrücke, die jene dichte, intensive Kunstwelt von Paris auf ihn genommen hatte, lassen sich nur mittelbar erahnen. Der Einfluss, den Léger offenbar nutzte und deshalb Fried ganz offensichtlich protegierte, ist unverkennbar.

Das Gemälde "Landscape with bridge" von 1951 entstand vermutlich noch in Paris, bevor Fried nach Amerika zurückreiste. Es überrascht durch seine pastellartige Farbigkeit sowie die streng planimetrische Anordnung der Farbfelder. Nirgends werden perspektivische Hinweise gegeben, sondern vielmehr ein tiefer Landschaftsraum gebaut, ohne diesen organisch zu entwickeln. Otto Fried halbiert das große Querformat in der Horizontale geradezu mittels eines Viadukts, das er quer durchs Bild zieht und ordnet Kuben und Bögen dergestalt

oping it. Otto Fried halves the large horizontal format virtually by means of a viaduct that he pulls across the picture, arranging cubes and arches in such a way that the viewer successively opens up the two high bridge arches in the lower half of the picture, each to the sides flanked with cubic house cubes. In the upper half of the picture, on the other hand, the view opens up into a wide, hilly landscape, which is crossed by high masts with overhead lines, both across the upper and lower parts of the picture. The top and bottom halves of the picture each create different perspectives, with the landscape appearing from above and the architecture almost frontally. The separate lines of sight are only related to one another by the overhead cables. This sovereign composition, which is less reminiscent of Fernand Léger than of a fusion between late Cubist compositions and New Objectivity, remains almost singular in Fried's œuvre. The painting *Parisian Window*, 1952, which shows a woman in a window frame, still has a similar diction. She sits behind half-opened window blinds, her hand placed over a cross strut, in a world that appears closed and locked. Here too, Otto Fried emphasizes - without any volume-forming physicality of his figure - the coexistence of surfaces and lines, which turns out to be dominant. The indicated light-shadow ratio, which results from the slits in the open, white shutters and reappears as a shadow on the wall, emphasizes the flat linearity, which Otto Fried clearly cares about. Not nearly as abstract as *Landscape with bridge*, however, this composition also shows his predominant interest in surface references and color combinations beyond any reference to reality, which in turn do not model nuanced volumes, leaving them almost monochrome. As a result, his compositions gain a higher level of abstraction and at the same time sobriety, which goes hand in hand with a melancholy basic chord of his works from this period. A little later, in 1952, Fried settled in New York, where he quickly began to exhibit. Interestingly, Fried turns more and more to the female figure for a short time. He apparently does not take up any of the recent revolution in art, the Abstract Expressionism of the New York School, at least he does not strive to deal with it himself. The former curator of the Portland Art Museum, Kathryn Kanjo, aptly noted in 1999: "Despite living in New York during the heyday of American Abstract Expressionism, the subject and style of Fried's earliest work reveal his European affinity. These easel-sized paintings - including still lifes and mechanical abstractions - engage the language of synthetic cubism as solid passages of color define planes and forms."[18] For the first time, the composition from 1956 reveals hints of the works of his French teacher Lhôte: his *Jones Beach*[19] is reminiscent of his compositions from the late 1930s and after. Unlike Fried, the relationship between figure and landscape played a life-long, dominant role in Lhôte. Fried's painting, on the other hand, is based primarily on a narrative structure, which is, however, broken up essentially by significantly more dominant formal references, almost prefiguring his later circular motif. The six figures on the beach are embedded in the wavy lines of the sand, but are particularly related to each other by two stretched parasols, which only show their circular shape, since they lie on the side of the beach. For the viewer, this results in two "disks", one from the front and one from the rear, the seams or wooden struts of which almost seem to rotate. However, Otto Fried quickly freed himself from the pure figure and concentrated again on the landscape. Although the metropolis must have had an

an, dass der Betrachter sich gleichsam die zwei hohen Brückenbögen in der unteren Bildhälfte sukzessive erschließt, die zu den Seiten hin jeweils mit kubisch angedeuteten Häuserwürfeln flankiert werden. In der oberen Bildhälfte hingegen eröffnet sich der Blick in eine weite, hügelige Landschaft, die von hohen Masten mit Überlandleitungen sowohl quer durch die obere als auch in die untere Bildpartie hinein verschränkt werden. Die obere und untere Bildhälfte erzeugen jeweils unterschiedliche Blickwinkel, wobei die Landschaft von oben, die Architektur hingegen fast frontal erscheint. Die getrennten Sichtachsen sind einzig durch die Überlandkabel miteinander in Beziehung gebracht. Diese souveräne Komposition, die weniger an Fernand Léger als an eine Verschmelzung zwischen spätkubistischen Kompositionen und Neuer Sachlichkeit denken lässt, bleibt jedoch nahezu singulär in Frieds Œuvre. Von ähnlicher Diktion wirkt noch das Gemälde von "Parisian Window", 1952, das eine Frau in einem Fensterrahmen zeigt. Hinter halb geöffneten Fensterblenden sitzt sie, die Hand über eine Querstrebe gelegt, in einer Welt, die verschlossen und abgeriegelt erscheint. Auch hier betont Otto Fried - ohne jegliche volumenbildende Körperlichkeit seiner Figur - das Zueinander von Flächen und Linien, das sich als dominierend erweist. Gerade das angedeutete Licht-Schatten-Verhältnis, das sich durch die Lichtschlitze in dem geöffneten, weißen Blendläden ergibt und als Schatten auf der Wand wieder auftaucht, betont die flächige Linearität, auf die es Otto Fried eindeutig ankommt. Nicht annähernd so abstrakt wie noch "Landscape with bridge" zeigt aber auch diese Komposition sein vorherrschendes Interesse an Flächenbezügen und Farbstellungen jenseits jeglicher Realitätsbezüge, die ihrerseits nicht nuanciert Volumina modellieren, sondern geradezu monochrom aufgetragen werden. Dadurch gewinnen seine Kompositionen einen höheren Grad an Abstraktion und zugleich an Nüchternheit, die einhergeht mit einem melancholischen Grundakkord seiner Arbeiten aus dieser Zeit.
Schon wenig später, noch 1952, lässt Fried sich in New York nieder, wo er rasch auch beginnt, auszustellen. Fried wendet sich hier interessanterweise für kurze Zeit stärker der weiblichen Figur zu. Von der neuerlich stattfindenden Revolution in der Kunst, dem Abstrakten Expressionismus der New York School, nimmt er scheinbar nichts auf, zumindest strebt er keine eigene malerische Auseinandersetzung mit ihr an. Die ehemalige Kuratorin des Portland Art Museum, Kathryn Kanjo, vermerkt 1999 treffend: "Despite living in New York during the heyday of American Abstract Expressionism, the subject and style of Fried's earliest work reveal his European affinity. These easel-sized paintings - including still lifes and mechanical abstractions - engage the language of synthetic cubism as solid passages of color define planes and forms."[18] Die Komposition von 1956 lässt erstmals Anklänge an die Werke seines französischen Lehrmeisters Lhôte sichtbar werden: Sein "Jones Beach"[19] erinnert an dessen Kompositionen aus den späten 1930er Jahren und danach. Anders als bei Fried spielte bei Lhôte das Verhältnis von Figur und Landschaft zeitlebens eine dominierende Rolle. Frieds Gemälde hingegen beruht vordergründig auf einer narrativen Struktur, die jedoch ganz wesentlich aufgebrochen wird durch deutlich dominantere formale Bezüge, die geradezu sein späteres Kreismotiv präludieren. Die sechs Figuren am Strand sind eingebettet in die Wellenlinien des Sandes, aber besonders miteinander in Beziehung gesetzt durch zwei aufgespannte Sonnenschirme, die nur ihr Kreisrund erkennen lassen, da sie seitlich lagernd auf dem Strand aufliegen. Für den Betrachtenden ergeben sich daraus zwei

influence on him and he grasped its dynamism, he is now turning his attention to landscapes that open up to merge into the spherical. It is still a long development until the purely abstract compositions of the 1970s and subsequent decades, but you can feel that Fried is not aiming for a landscape in the conventional sense, but rather for the sublimation of nature. This is clearly illustrated also in the monotype that Otto Fried produced in 1958 and is now in the Mittelrhein-Museum in Koblenz. At the invitation of the United States Information Service in Germany, Otto Fried exhibited some of his works in three German cities that year. Curiously, the first presentation of his works took place in the Deutschherrenhaus, which at that time was still the office for the regional road administration, after it had been used temporarily as a hospital during the war. In any case, the monotype *Blossoming Apple trees* (1958) shows an abstract composition, with a clear all-over of bright spots of color, which are only interrupted by a very distinctive tree trunk and its extensive branches.[20] Only when you take a closer look do you see other, much smaller tree trunks in the lower image strip. The composition celebrates also spring, this exuberant nature, which proves itself in an almost overwhelming bloom. Otto Fried, however, clearly replaces this from purely narrative telling, does not lose himself in the exact details of the representation, but rather "floods" the picture area with a play of colors made of light spots on a gray background of leaves. You might think of Piet Mondrian's different versions of an apple tree.[21] Just like with Mondrian, Fried achieved a complete abstraction from nature and landscape a few years later. When Otto Fried turned completely to the circular form in its infinite variations from the 1970s, he finally reached abstraction. Among other things, he had been inspired by a very intensely felt trip to Japan, which gave him an approach to Asian spirituality and reduction of forms in art.[22] His circles and disks as a fundamental design element of his subsequent creative decades are nonetheless inconceivable without his always clear re-rassurance into nature. Fried often lets waves or clouds ring through his circular disks and thus often connects the floating cosms purely formally. He is always concerned with a symbol of the eternal cycle, the one in all, the connection between earth and universe.[23] His cosmic circular constellations are inconceivable without his early pictures of nature and his deep preoccupation with Expressionism – in his abstract-sublime formal language of Kandinsky, Delauney, Marc, Klee. But his late compositions once again detach themselves from the individual gesture and sublimate nature and cosmos in a few, eternally valid signs that seem to come from a deep calm of their own self.

Otto Fried, who fled Germany and was artistically trained in exile, has always experienced the landscape as a reliable constant in his life and felt its eternal cycle in the interplay of nature. That reconciled him, always a friendly and cheerful person, also with his home. Portland, New York and Paris have become the stations of his cosmopolitan life. However, he found his inner self in an internalized nature. Because beyond the metropolises, for Otto Fried it is only the landscape that became the universal parable of creation and which he sees lifted in the cosmic universe.[24]

"Scheiben", eine von vorne, eine von hinten zu erkennen, deren Nähte bzw. Holzstreben beinahe zu rotieren scheinen.

Vom reinen Figurenbild löst sich Otto Fried jedoch rasch und konzentriert sich wieder ganz auf das Landschaftliche. Wenngleich die Metropole Einfluss auf ihn genommen haben muss und er sich ihrer Dynamik nicht entzogen haben wird, wendet er nun sein Augenmerk auf Landschaften, die ihm einen Weg eröffnen, um ins Sphärische einzumünden. Noch ist es eine lange Entwicklung bis zu den rein abstrakten Kompositionen der 1970er und nachfolgenden Jahrzehnten. Aber es ist zu spüren, dass Fried keine Landschaft im herkömmlichen Sinne anstrebt, sondern vielmehr eine Sublimierung der Natur. Anschaulich wird dies u.a. auch in der Monotypie, die Otto Fried 1958 fertigt, welche sich heute im Mittelrhein-Museum in Koblenz befindet. Auf Einladung des United States Information Service in Deutschland wird Otto Fried in diesem Jahr in drei deutsche Städte eingeladen und stellt hier einige seiner Werke aus. Kurioserweise erfolgte die erste Präsentation seiner Werke im Deutschherrenhaus, das zum damaligen Zeitpunkt noch als Amt für die Landestraßenverwaltung eingerichtet war, nachdem es im Krieg vorübergehend als Lazarett genutzt worden war. Die Monotypie "Blossoming Apple trees" (1958) jedenfalls zeigt eine abstrahierte Komposition, mit einem deutlichen all-over an hellen Farbtupfen, die nur durch einen sehr markanten Baumstamm und seinen ausgreifenden Ästen unterbrochen werden.[20] Erst bei genauerem Hinschauen werden weitere, deutlich kleinere Baumstämme im unteren Bildstreifen sichtbar. Die Komposition feiert gleichsam den Frühling, diese überbordende Natur, die sich in einer geradezu überwältigenden Blütenpracht erweist. Otto Fried löst dies jedoch deutlich vom rein narrativen Erzählen ab, verliert sich nicht in genauen Darstellungsdetails, sondern "überschwemmt" die Bildfläche mit einem Farbspiel aus hellen Tupfen auf grauen Blattgrund. Entfernt mag man an Piet Mondrians verschiedenen Bildfassungen eines Apfelbaumes denken.[21] Ebenso wie bei Mondrian gelangt Fried wenige Jahre später zu einer vollkommenen Abstraktion von Natur und Landschaft.

Als Otto Fried sich ab den 1970er Jahren gänzlich der Kreisform in ihren unendlichen Variationen zuwendet, ist er endgültig in der Abstraktion angekommen. Angeregt dazu hatte ihn u.a. eine sehr intensiv empfundene Reise nach Japan, die ihm eine Annäherung an die asiatische Spiritualität und Reduktion von Formen in der Kunst vermittelt.[22] Seine Kreise und Scheiben als fundamentales Gestaltungsmoment seiner nachfolgenden Schaffensjahrzehnte sind gleichwohl nicht denkbar ohne seine stets deutliche Rückversicherung in der Natur. Vielfach lässt Fried Wellen oder Wolken in seinen Kreisscheiben durchklingen und verbindet so oftmals rein formal die schwebenden Kosmen. Immer geht es ihm um ein Versinnbildlichen des ewigen Kreislaufs, des Einem im Allen, des Zusammenhangs von Erde und Universum.[23] Seine kosmischen zirkularen Konstellationen sind ohne seine frühen Naturbilder und seine tiefe Beschäftigung mit dem Expressionismus - in seiner abstrakt-sublimen Formensprache von Kandinsky, Delauney, Marc, Klee - nicht denkbar. Aber seine späten Kompositionen lösen sich noch einmal von der individuellen Geste und sublimieren Natur und Kosmos in wenigen, ewig gültigen Zeichen, die aus einer tiefen Ruhe des eigenen Selbst zu kommen scheinen.

Otto Fried, geflohen aus Deutschland und im Exil künstlerisch ausgebildet, hat die Landschaft immer als eine verlässliche Konstante in seinem Leben er-

1 Gallery 291 hosted numerous international exhibitions between 1905 and 1917. Stieglitz started again after the First World War with his exhibition activities, increasingly connecting the European with the American avant-garde. Please refer: https://de.wikipedia.org/wiki/Galerie_291#cite_note-SG277-57; accessed on May 3, 2020.

2 Exh.-Cat. Mittelrhein-Museum Koblenz 1978, w. p.

3 Britta Buhlmann, Annette Reich, Karen Wilkin, *Hans Hofmann: Magnum Opus, 9 March – 16 June 2013*; Museum Pfalzgalerie Kaiserslautern.

4 It was founded in 1931 by Georges Vantangerloo in Paris, who replaced the "Cercle et Carré" association founded by Michel Seuphor, operating only in 1930.

5 portlandartmuseum.us/mwebcgi/mweb.exe?request=record;id=7405;type=701; accessed on May 2, 2020.

6 Ibid.

7 Kurt Eitelbach, in Exh.-Cat. Mittelrhein-Museum Koblenz 1978.

8 In this catalogue: *Metal Relief Sculptures. Otto Fried interviewed by Kenneth Snelson*, p. 64 ff.

9 He joined the French Communist Party after returning from the exile in America.

10 https://andre-lhote.org/academy; accessed on May 2, 2020.

11 In this catalogue: *Lisa Forrell: Otto Fried - A personal tribute*, p. 53 ff.

12 https://andre-lhote.org/academy; accessed on May 2, 2020.

13 Fernand Léger, *Paris – New York*, catalogue for the homonymous exhibition at the Fondation Beyeler 2008.

14 See *Big Julie*, that was created in New York as *The Bycicliste*, both: 1951 (Metropolitan Museum, New York).

15 In his interview with Kenneth Snelson, Otto Fried enthusiastically mentions Lawrence Margolis. They worked together; paintings by Otto Fried illustrated for example Margolis's booklet *WE 3*, published in Paris in 1950; see also: Catalog of Copyright entries, Vol. 4, Part 1A, Books, Jan.-June 1950, Library of Congress, Washington 1950, p. 439.
https://books.google.de/books?id=okIhAQAAIAAJ&pg=PA439&lpg=PA439&dq=Laurence+Margolis,+Paris,+1950ies&source=bl&ots=oH4tl8nrp4&sig=ACfU3U13x9F0-igO69MsZghshG9NGtQy-A&hl=de&sa=X&ved=2ahUKEwiego61l5jpAhVH2KQKHSszBGoQ6AEwAHoECAUQAQ#v=onepage&q=Laurence%20Margolis%2C%20Paris%2C%201950ies&f=false

16 Jhttp://jeannebucherjaeger.com/about/jeanne-bucher/, accessed on May 24, 2020.

17 From 15 to 31 July 1950 Atelier Fernand Léger, in: *Fernand Léger. The Museum of Modern Art*, New York 1998, p. 297.

18 Kathryn Kanjo, *Variation on a theme*, in: *Otto Fried - Recent Work*, Portland Art Museum, Portland 1999, p. 5.

19 Jones Beach is part of the nearby recreation area of New Yorkers, who like to spend their free time here, towards Long Island.

20 It was purchased by Otto Fried in 1959 via the U.S. Embassy in Bonn for the Mittelrhein-Museum.

21 Piet Mondrian, *Abend*, 1908, Kunstmuseum Den Haag.

22 In addition, Otto Fried was fascinated by the large space programs of NASA, the moon landing and the exploration of space.

23 Cfr. on this aspect *Flowering Atmosphere*, 1973, p. 45, as well as *Expansion*, 1979, p. 51.

24 Even more than his paintings, the drawings reveal how Otto Fried has always linked forms and structures closely, and thus nothing appears singularly in empty spaces.

fahren und im Wechselspiel der Natur ihren ewigen Kreislauf empfunden. Das hat ihn, den stets freundlichen und heiteren Menschen, versöhnt - auch mit seiner Heimat. Portland, New York und Paris sind die Stationen seines kosmopolitischen Lebens geworden. Sein inneres Selbst jedoch fand er in einer verinnerlichten Natur. Denn jenseits der Metropolen ist es für Otto Fried einzig die Landschaft, die ihm zum Universalgleichnis der Schöpfung wurde und die er im kosmischen Universum aufgehoben sieht.[24]

1 Die Gallery 291 richtete zwischen 1905 und 1917 zahlreiche internationale Ausstellungen aus. Stieglitz setze nach dem I. Weltkrieg mit seinen Ausstellungsaktivitäten erneut an, verband zusehends die europäische mit der amerikanischen Avantgarde. Siehe: https://de.wikipedia.org/wiki/Galerie_291#cite_note-SG277-57; abgerufen am 3. Mai 2020.

2 Ausst.-Kat. Mittelrhein-Museum Koblenz 1978, o.S.

3 Britta Buhlmann, Annette Reich, Karen Wilkin: Hans Hofmann: Magnum Opus, 9 März – 16 Juni 2013; Museum Pfalzgalerie Kaiserslautern.

4 Gegründet wurde sie 1931 von Georges Vantangerloo in Paris, der die von Michel Seuphor gegründete Vereinigung „Cercle et Carré" ablöste, die ihrerseits nur 1930 bestanden hatte.

5 portlandartmuseum.us/mwebcgi/mweb.exe?request=record;id=7405;type=701; abgerufen am 2.5.2020

6 Ebenda.

7 Kurt Eitelbach, in Ausst.-Kat. Mittelrhein-Museum Koblenz 1978.

8 In diesem Katalog: „Metal Relief Sculptures. Otto Fried interviewt von Kenneth Snelson", S. 65 ff.

9 Eintritt in die Kommunistische Partei in Frankreich nach seiner Rückkehr aus dem amerikanischen Exil.

10 https://andre-lhote.org/academy; abgerufen am 2. Mai 2020.

11 In diesem Katalog: „Lisa Forrell: Otto Fried - Eine persönliche Würdigung", S. 53 ff.

12 https://andre-lhote.org/life-and-works, abgerufen am 2. Mai 2020.

13 Fernand Léger: „Paris – New York", Katalog zur gleichnamigen Ausstellung in der Fondation Beyeler 2008.

14 Vgl. „Big Julie", das in New York entstanden war sowie „The Bycicliste", beide: 1951 (Metropolitan Museum, New York).

15 In seinem Interview mit Kenneth Snelson erwähnt Otto Fried begeistert Lawrence Margolis. Sie arbeiteten zusammen; Gemälde von Otto Fried illustrieren beispielsweise Margolis' 1950 in Paris erschienenes Büchlein „WE 3"; siehe auch: Catalog of Copyright entries, Vol. 4, Part 1A, Books, Jan.-June 1950, Library of Congress, Washington 1950, S. 439. https://books.google.de/books?id=okIhAQAAIAAJ&pg=PA439&lpg=PA439&dq=Laurence+Margolis,+Paris,+1950ies&source=bl&ots=oH4tI8nrp4&sig=ACfU3U13x9F0-igO69MsZghshG9NGtQy-A&hl=de&sa=X&ved=2ahUKEwiego61I5jpAhVH2K-QKHSszBGoQ6AEwAHoECAUQAQ#v=onepage&q=Laurence%20Margolis%2C%20Paris%2C%201950ies&f=false

16 http://jeannebucherjaeger.com/about/jeanne-bucher/, abgerufen am 24. Mai 2020.

17 Vom 15. bis 31. Juli 1950 Atelier Fernand Léger, in: „Fernand Léger. The Museum of Modern Art", New York 1998, S. 297.

18 Kathryn Kanjo, „Variation on a theme", in: „Otto Fried - recent work", Portland Art Museum, Portland 1999, S. 5.

19 Jones Beach zählt zum nahen Erholungsbereich der New Yorker, die gerne Richtung Long Island hier ihre Freizeit verbringen.

20 Es wurde 1959 von Otto Fried über die U.S. Botschaft in Bonn für das Mittelrhein-Museum erworben.

21 Piet Mondrian, „Abend", 1908, Kunstmuseum Den Haag.

22 Darüber hinaus war Otto Fried fasziniert von den großen Raumfahrtprogrammen den NASA, der Mondland und der Erforschung des Alls.

23 Siehe hierzu „Flowering Atmosphere", 1973, S. 45, sowie „Expansion", 1979, S. 51.

24 Mehr noch als seine Gemälde verdeutlichen die Zeichnungen, dass Otto Fried Formen und Strukturen immer eng mit einander verkettet und somit nichts singulär im leeren Raum erscheint.

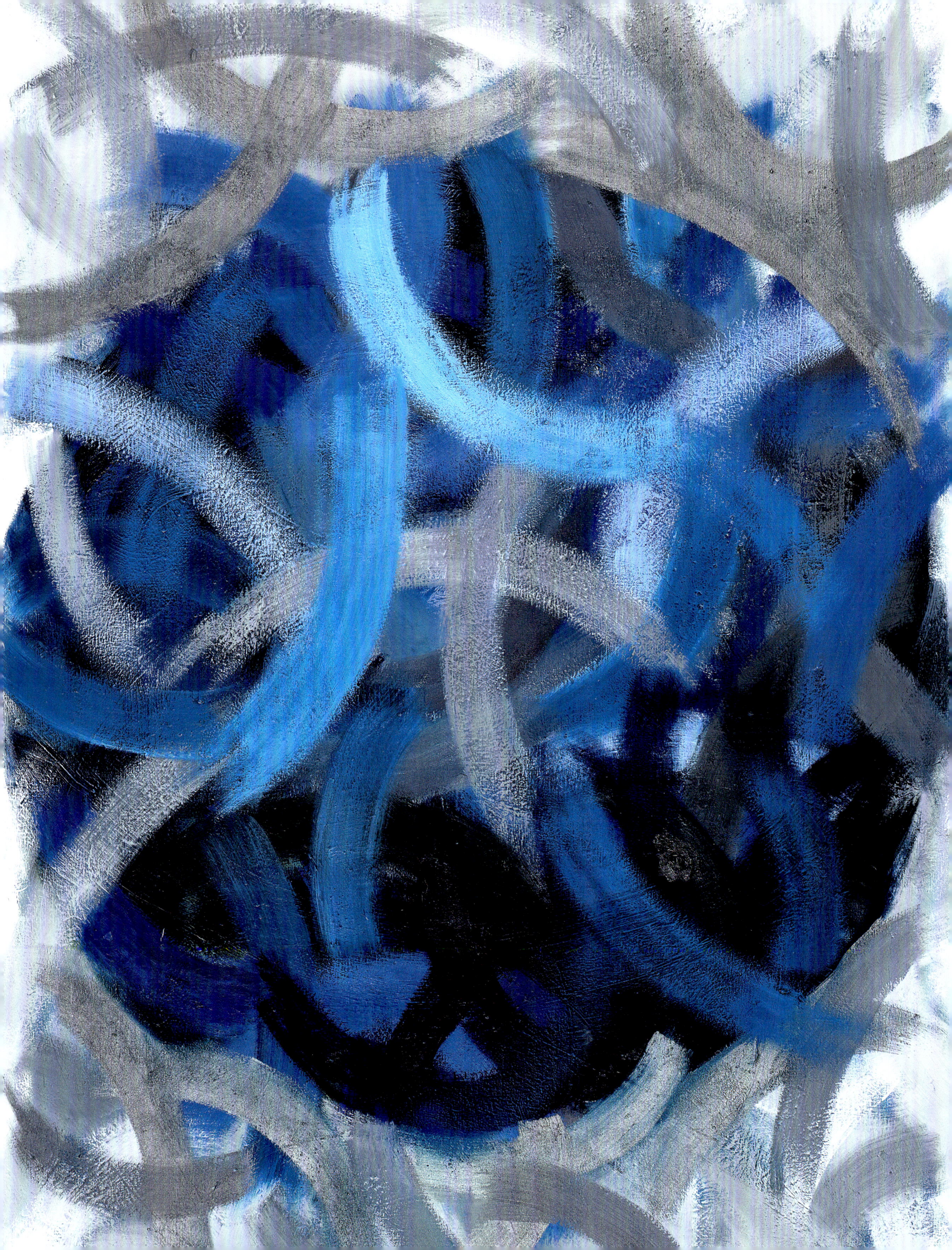

LARISSA WESP

"FLOWERING ATMOSPHERES"

ABSTRAKTION UND KREIS IN DEN GEMÄLDEN OTTO FRIEDS

„Kreise und Sphären beschreiben Anfänge, die in kontinuierlicher Bewegung auf das Ende zu tanzen, wie die Reise eines Samenkorns, das zu einem jahrhundertealten Rotholzriesen heranwächst und schließlich zurückkehrt, um die Erde zu regenerieren."[1] - Otto Fried

Otto Frieds Œuvre beginnt Ende der Vierziger Jahre mit impressionistisch anmutenden Landschaftsbildern, die sowohl den Geist der amerikanischen Landschaftsmalerei der Hudson River School als auch des europäischen Impressionismus in sich tragen. Andere frühe Zeichnungen und Gemälde, die Fried zwischen 1948 und 1950 anfertigte, zeugen wiederum von einer Beschäftigung mit dem Kubismus und beispielsweise Marcel Duchamps Werk „Akt, eine Treppe herabsteigend, Nr. 2" (1912), einem Versuch, einen Bewegungsablauf in einem Bild wiederzugeben (Vgl. Frieds Zeichnung „Untitled" 1948–50, Abb. S. 39). Einzelne Gemälde wie „Parisian Window" und „Landscape with

LARISSA WESP

"FLOWERING ATMOSPHERES"

ABSTRACT ART AND CIRCLES IN THE PAINTINGS BY OTTO FRIED

"Circles and spheres describe beginnings dancing towards endings in continuous movement, like the journey of a seed, as it grows to become a centuries-old redwood giant, and finally returns to regenerate the earth."[1] - Otto Fried

Otto Fried's œuvre began at the end of the 1940s with landscape paintings which hinted at Impressionism and contained both the spirit of American landscape painting of the Hudson River School and European Impressionism. Further early drawings and paintings made by Fried between 1948 and 1950 testify to his interest towards Cubism and for example Marcel Duchamp's work *Nu descendant un escalier, no. 2* (*Nude Descending a Staircase, no. 2*, 1912), an attempt to reproduce a sequence of movements in a picture (see Fried's drawing *Untitled*, 1948-1950, fig. p. 39). Individual paintings such as *Parisian Window* and *Landscape with Bridge*, which Fried created in his Parisian days

Greved Tao
Detail
1982 / 1983
Öl auf Leinwand / Oil on canvas
130 x 195 cm
Sammlung des Künstlers /
Collection of the Artist

at Fernand Léger's, are part of this encounter with avant-garde art. The Parisian woman who looks through the open shutters in a pink dress can be read like an interpretation of the painting *Cape Cod Morning* painted by Edward Hopper two years earlier, shaped by Fried's impressions of European modernism in Paris. Nevertheless, his paintings remained moulded by Oregon landscapes until the 1970s. However, in 1972 Fried turned away from landscape painting and, focusing on the central figure of the circle from then on, gave life to a completely new visual language from which he would develop his own style in the following decades.[2]

With his first circular compositions, Fried continued with landscape painting in an abstract form. He painted overlapping circles on one-color primed canvases, which he filled with vivid painting from horizontally flowing, veiled areas of color (*Untitled*, 1973, fig. p. 44). Like mountain ranges, these superimposed areas run through the individual circles, the colors develop from earthy brown and red tones to blue gray to white and can be associated with mountainous, foggy landscapes. The circles seem to offer views of a distant landscape - for example through the round glass of a telescope. However, these landscapes quickly become more abstract, the circle comes to the fore ever more clearly and manifests itself as a central figure. What remains of his enthusiasm for nature and landscape are the subject areas of sea or water and air, which are reflected in the blue color spectrum, primarily used by Fried.[3] Color veils draw horizontally through the circles like thickening seas of clouds, the shapes of inflated ship sails seem ever cloudier and more abstract between them. In the mid-1970s, of these landscape impressions remain only the abstract, veil-like color areas, which Fried now designs in their shift from light to dark tones. In this way, the circle becomes increasingly three-dimensional and no longer appears as a framework for views of landscapes, but as a body floating on the picture surface. Spatial references are created through the front and side by side placing of the circles. Planetary constellations seem to draw their paths in pictures like "overlapping temperatures". The light blue color spectrum gives way, instead Fried from now on uses more dark, earthy tones. Together with the imagery, also the titles become more abstract. While titles such as *Mount Hood* (1973) or *White Green Spinnaker* (1972) still refer to the landscape and seafaring, others like *Overlapping Temperatures* (1975), *Flowering Atmosphere* (1976), *Sphären* (1976) no longer provide any concrete information about the image content, but rather appear to be chosen associatively.

At the beginning of the 1980s, other shapes appeared in Fried's paintings in addition to the circle. There was a considerable development in the style of his painting. Fried no longer designs the background of his paintings as empty space, but fills it with semicircles, areas and bands that form the background or run through the image space. Occasionally, he places shades in the background, giving the impression of a tangible space. Fried fills the compositions with their contained surfaces and bodies through sweeping brushstrokes, applied so precisely to the colored primer that they combine into a network-like structure. At the same time, Fried succeeds in giving the figures their own three-dimensionality through the use of color gradients, which he uses both in the underlying primer and in the line weave. There are moments of tension on the surface, where Fried uses contrasting color gradients to give the impression of convex and concave arches in adjacent areas, but also between the three-dimensional spheres and the flat painting that surrounds them (*Summer Raga*, 1985). By incorporating organically curved bodies and lines, Fried broke up his geometrically oriented repertoire of forms during the

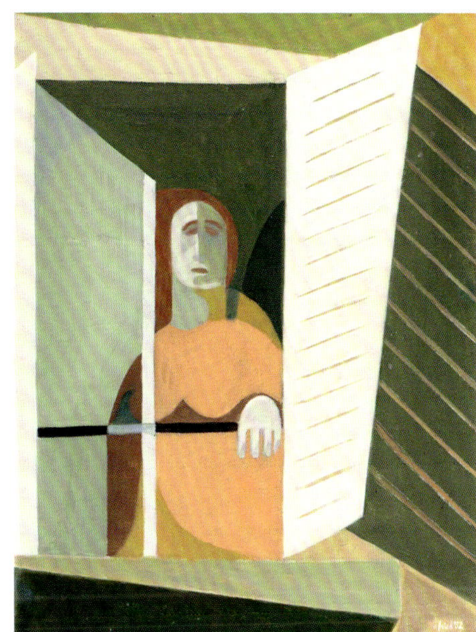

Parisian Window, 1952
Öl auf Leinwand / Oil on canvas
60 x 40 cm
Sammlung des Künstlers / Collection of the Artist

Bridge", die Fried in seiner Pariser Zeit bei Fernand Léger schuf, reihen sich in diese Begegnung mit Kunst der Avantgarde ein. Die Pariserin, die im rosa Kleid durch die geöffneten Fensterläden blickt, lässt sich wie eine Interpretation des Gemäldes „Cape Cod Morning", welches Edward Hopper zwei Jahre zuvor gemalt hatte, beeinflusst von Frieds Eindrücken der europäischen Moderne in Paris, lesen. Dennoch bleibt seine Malerei bis in die siebziger Jahre geprägt von den Landschaften Oregons. 1972 wendet sich Fried jedoch von der Landschaftsmalerei ab und entwickelt, basierend auf der fortan konstant zentralen Figur des Kreises, eine vollkommen neue Bildsprache, aus der er in den folgenden Jahrzehnten seinen ganz eigenen Stil entwickeln wird.[2]

Fried führt mit seinen ersten Kreiskompositionen die Landschaftsmalerei in abstrahierter Form fort. Auf einfarbig grundierten Leinwänden malt er einander überschneidende Kreise, die er mit belebter Malerei aus horizontal fließenden, schleierartigen Farbflächen füllt („Untitled" 1973, Abb. S. 44). Wie Berglandschaften ziehen sich diese übereinander liegenden Flächen durch die einzelnen Kreise, die Farben entwickeln sich von erdigen Braun- und Rot-Tönen über Blaugrau bis ins Weiß und lassen sich mit nebelverhangenen Landschaften assoziieren. Die Kreise scheinen hierbei Ausblicke auf eine entfernte Landschaft zu gewähren – beispielsweise durch das runde Glas eines Fernrohrs. Schnell werden diese Landschaften jedoch abstrakter, der Kreis tritt immer deutlicher in den Vordergrund und manifestiert sich als zentrale Figur. Von seiner Begeisterung für die Natur und Landschaft bleiben die Themenfelder Meer bzw. Wasser und Luft, die sich in dem blauen Farbspektrum wiederfinden, welches Fried vorrangig verwendet.[3] Wie sich verdichtende Wolkenmeere ziehen Farbschleier horizontal durch die Kreise, immer trüber und abstrakter scheinen die Formen von aufgeblähten Schiffssegeln zwischen ihnen hindurch.

Mitte der Siebzigerjahre bleiben von diesen Eindrücken nur die abstrakten, nebelschleierartigen Farbflächen, die Fried nun im Verlauf von hellen zu dunklen Tönen gestaltet. Der Kreis erhält auf diese Weise zunehmend Dreidimensionalität und erscheint nicht länger als Rahmen für Ausblicke auf Landschaften, sondern wird zu einem auf der Bildfläche schwebenden Körper. Durch das Vor- und Nebeneinander der Kreise, werden räumliche Bezüge hergestellt – planetenhafte Konstellationen scheinen in Bildern wie „overlapping temperatures" ihre Bahnen umeinander zu ziehen. Das hellblaue Farbspektrum weicht, stattdessen verwendet Fried fortan mehr dunkle, erdige Töne. Mit der Bildsprache werden auch die Titel abstrakter. Während Titel wie „Mount Hood" (1973) oder „White Green Spinnaker" (1972) noch auf die Landschaft und Seefahrt verwiesen, lassen Titel wie „Overlapping Temperatures" (1975), „Flowering Atmosphere" (1976), „Sphären" (1976) keine konkreten Hinweise zum Bildinhalt mehr zu, sondern scheinen vielmehr assoziativ gewählt.

Mit Beginn der Achtzigerjahre treten neben dem Kreis weitere Formen in Frieds Gemälden auf und es findet eine erhebliche Entwicklung im Stil seiner Malerei statt. Den Hintergrund seiner Gemälde gestaltet Fried nicht länger als leeren Raum, sondern füllt ihn mit Halbkreisen, Flächen und Bändern, die den Hintergrund bilden oder sich durch den Bildraum ziehen. Vereinzelt setzt er Schattierungen in den Hintergrund, sodass der Eindruck eines greifbaren Raumes entsteht. Die Kompositionen mit ihren darin enthaltenen Flächen und Körpern füllt Fried mit schwungvollen Pinselstrichen, die er so präzise auf die farbige Grundierung aufträgt, dass sie sich

1980s. Curved, wavy and helical lines wander through the image space. Crystalline shapes such as those in *Fourth Zone* (1988, fig. p. 32) are reminiscent of the radiant rendering of light, as developed in Rayonism by Mikhail Larionov around 1913. However, it is difficult to trace the development of Fried's style in these years back to concrete influences or to assign it to contemporary art movements. The compositions of shapes and figures floating freely in space are only remotely reminiscent of the works of Constructivism, in which geometric shapes are placed in the free space. But the three-dimensional curvatures and the recognizable brushstrokes break with this flat style and rather bring to mind the cubic forms of the works of Fried's teacher Fernand Legér. Nevertheless, Fried's compositions are reduced to a few bodies standing in the center that float in an abstract space, while in Legér's compositions there is a close juxtaposition of surfaces and bodies.

A short break from the focusing on the circle as the central form is brought about by a new group of works that Fried created between 1989 and 1990 and stands out from his previous œuvre. *Ecriture d'un monde à part* (1990, fig. p. 34), from the exhibition at the Ludwig Museum Koblenz, is one of the pictures in this series. Fried painted here on thick paper napkins,[4] which he had previously folded and divided into an area of two by two square fields. The napkins, painted with four small compositions, were then applied to the canvas in a tile-like arrangement next to and on top of one another. Depending on the size of the image frame, the works in this series are divided into different numbers of squares, thus forming their own grid, in which Fried in turn places individual, self-contained compositions, resulting then in the context of the whole picture as a self-contained context of mutually referring colors and formulas.
At the center of each field in these paintings is Fried's classic motif of the circle, which, like in his paintings from the late 1980s, is in dialogue with the curved lines and bodies arranged around it. Unlike in his previous paintings, the works on canvas are flat because they absorb the applied paint. A hint of depth only takes place through the superimposition of the individual composition elements. Within each cloth – in a grid of two by two fields – Fried always used the same or similar forms, but in different arrangements and colors. With this structure, the artist creates various nested picture spaces, each of which is laid out independently and in relation to one another: the smallest unit is the single square field, filled with a self-contained composition, arranged around the motif of a circle. Viewed as a single picture, it corresponds to the structure of the paintings of the 1980s. This is followed by the image space within an applied cloth, in which four different compositions are created, distributed in two by two fields. Finally, there is the entire painting as a large pictorial space, in which the aforementioned pictorial spaces are assembled. The individual fields are often grouped together according to their color scheme in such a way that they all pursue one subject. For example, *Ecriture d'un monde à part* boasts a completely uniform blue, while in other pictures of the series the hue of the individual fields results in a color gradient developing through the picture. The sequence of the individual compositions in the paintings has an analytical effect. All possibilities of the constellations around the circle seem to be played out and contrasted. "[...] the artist has chosen the incertitude of a rambling alphabet. Alphabet distributed on surfaces covered with equal, con-

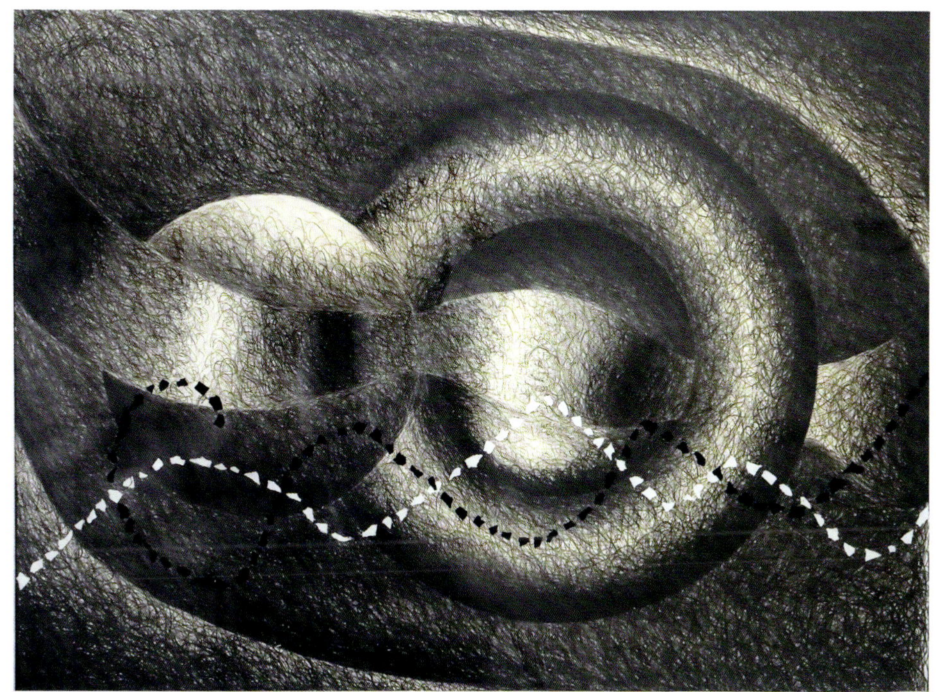

Ohne Titel / Untitled, 1987
Collage, Bleistift, Papiercollage auf Papier / Collage, pencil and paper collage on paper
71 x 99 cm
Privatsammlung / Private collection

netzartig zu flächigen Strukturen verbinden. Gleichzeitig gelingt es Fried durch Farbverläufe, die er sowohl in der unterliegenden Grundierung als auch in den Strichgeflecht einsetzt, den Figuren eine eigene Dreidimensionalität zu verleihen. Es entstehen Spannungsmomente auf der Bildfläche, sowohl dort wo Fried gegensätzliche Farbverläufe nutzt, um in nebeneinander liegenden Flächen den Eindruck konvexer und konkaver Wölbungen entstehen zu lassen, als zwischen den dreidimensionalen Kugeln und der flächigen Malerei, die diese umgibt („Summer Raga", 1985, Abb. S. 73). Durch die Aufnahme organisch geschwungener Körper und Linien bricht Fried im Laufe der Achtzigerjahre sein bisher geometrisch ausgerichtetes Formenrepertoire auf. Geschwungene, wellen- und helixförmige Linien wandern durch den Bildraum. Kristalline Formen wie in "Fourth Zone" (1988, Abb. S. 32) erinnern an die strahlenhafte Wiedergabe von Licht, wie sie zuvor im Rayonismus von Michail Larionow um 1913 entwickelt wurden. Nur schwer lässt sich Frieds Stilentwicklung dieser Jahre jedoch auf konkrete Einflüsse zurückführen oder zeitgenössischen Kunstströmungen zuordnen. Die Zusammensetzung der Kompositionen aus frei im Raum schwebenden Formen und Figuren erinnern lediglich entfernt an Werke des Konstruktivismus, in denen geometrische Formen im freien Bildraum platziert sind. Die dreidimensionalen Wölbungen und die erkennbaren Pinselstriche brechen jedoch mit diesem flach angelegten Stil, vielmehr rufen sie die kubischen Formen der Werke von Frieds Lehrer Fernand Legér ins Gedächtnis. Gleichwohl sind Frieds Kompositionen auf wenige im Zentrum stehende Körper reduziert, die in einem abstrakten Raum schweben, während in Legérs Kompositionen ein dichtes Nebeneinander von Flächen und Körpern herrscht.

Einen kurzzeitigen Bruch in der Konzentration auf den Kreis als zentrale Bildform bringt eine neue Gruppe von Werken, die Fried zwischen 1989 und 1990 schafft und die aus seinem bisherigen Œuvre heraussticht. „Ecriture d'un monde à part" (1990, Abb. S. 34) aus der Ausstellung im Ludwig Museum Ko-

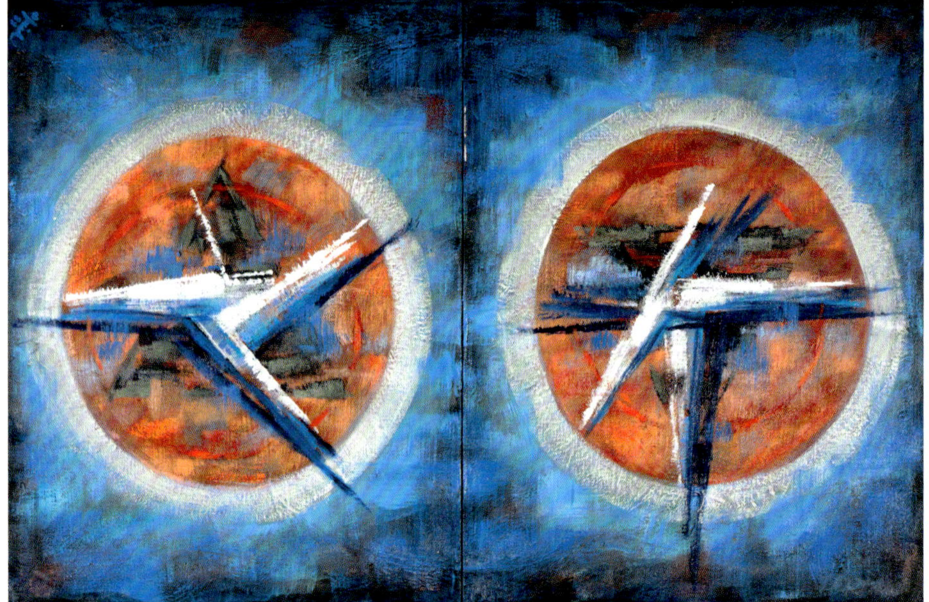

Fourth Zone, 1988
Öl auf Leinwand /
Oil on canvas
2 Teile / 2 parts:
je / each 66 x 102,5 cm
Sammlung des Künstlers /
Collection of the Artist

tinuous squares with alternate chromaticisms, where manoeuvres contrasting different interests, different options, are carried out."[5] The grid-like division into the many separate fields ensures stability and tranquility in the otherwise open image space. It forms the framework that gives structure to the empty image space, but at the same time creates a constant tension between the form of the circle, the organically curved bodies and the straight shape of the square.

What significantly distinguishes the series of paintings from Fried's other works is, however, not only the formal structure, but, as already said, the special materiality and the resulting structure of the surface. Instead of applying the cloths smoothly on the canvas, Fried allowed a strong drapery. The folds create an uneven surface structure, which comes into play to different degrees, depending on the light. They do not seem to follow any order and are in no way only to be assessed as part of the image carrier. Rather, they appear as a deliberately used design element, so strong is their presence when viewing the pictures. In an interview with Kenneth Snelson,[6] Fried emphasizes the importance he gives to the texture of applied paint, for example. He creates different patterns on the smooth surfaces of his metal reliefs by applying acid. In his monotypes, which make up a significant part of Fried's artistic œuvre, the drapery of the paper from which the impression was made creates different grains in the color areas. Since the structure of the color application on the cloths is lost, Fried uses the drapery of the fabric to give the surface a special structure. What is interesting is the emphasis on the material and the surface, which, depending on the incidence of light on the canvas, comes to the fore so much that the painted content of the picture is overshadowed, shifting behind the folds and structures of the fabric.

The images stand out from Fried's painterly œuvre both materially – by using the napkins – and compositionally – by emphasizing the square and the tension between it and the organic forms. The surprising inclusion of the square in this series of pictures and the associated division of the picture area show parallels to works by contemporary artists of the late 1950s and 1960s. Men-

blenz ist eines der Bilder dieser Reihe. Fried malt hier auf dicke Papier-Servietten[4], die er zuvor faltete und so in eine Fläche von zwei mal zwei quadratischen Feldern teilte. Diese, mit vier einzelnen kleinen Kompositionen bemalten Tücher, appliziert er in kachelartige Anordnung neben und übereinander auf die Leinwand. Abhängig von der Größe des Bildträgers werden die Werke dieser Serie so in eine unterschiedliche Zahl von quadratischen Flächen geteilt, die somit in eigenes Raster bilden, in das Fried wiederum einzelne, in sich geschlossene Kompositionen setzt. Diese ergeben im Zusammenhang des Bildganzen einen in sich geschlossenen Kontext von aufeinander verweisenden Farben und Formeln.

Im Zentrum jedes einzelnen Felds dieser Gemälde steht Frieds klassisches Motiv des Kreises, der, wie auch in seinen Gemälden der späten Achtzigerjahre, im Dialog mit den darum angeordneten, geschwungenen Linien und Körpern steht. Anders als in seinen vorausgehenden Gemälden ist die Malerei auf den Tüchern flächig, da diese die aufgetragene Farbe aufsaugen. Eine Andeutung von Tiefe findet nur durch die Überlagerung der einzelnen Kompositionselemente statt. Innerhalb eines jeden Tuches – in einem Raster von zwei mal zwei Feldern – hat Fried stets dieselben oder einander ähnelnde Formen verwendet, jedoch in variierenden Arrangements und Farbgebungen. Mit diesem Aufbau erzeugt Fried verschiedene ineinander verschachtelte Bildräume, die jeweils eigenständig als auch im Verhältnis zueinander angelegt sind: Die kleinste Einheit ist das einzelne quadratische Feld, gefüllt mit einer in sich geschlossenen Komposition, angelegt um das Motiv eines Kreises. Als alleinstehendes Bild betrachtet, entspricht es dem Aufbau Frieds Gemälde der Achtzigerjahre. Es folgt der Bildraum innerhalb eines applizierten Tuches, in dem auf zwei mal zwei Feldern verteilt vier verschiedene Kompositionen realisiert sind, die miteinander in Beziehung stehen. Zuletzt gibt es das gesamte Gemälde als großen Bildraum, in dem die zuvor genannten Bildräume versammelt sind. Häufig sind die einzelnen Felder in Ihrer Farbgebung so zueinander gruppiert, dass sie in Ihrer Gesamtheit ein Thema verfolgen. So ist „Ecriture d'un monde à part" beispielsweise vollständig in einheitlichem Blau gehalten, in anderen Bildern der Serie ergibt sich aus der Farbgebung der einzelnen Felder ein Farbverlauf, der sich über das Bild entwickelt. Die Aneinanderreihung der einzelnen Kompositionen in den Gemälden wirkt analytisch. Alle Möglichkeiten der um den Kreis angelegten Konstellationen scheinen durchgespielt und einander gegenübergestellt zu werden. „[...] the artist has chosen the incertitude of a rambling alphabet. Alphabet distributed on surfaces covered with equal, continuous squares with alternate chromaticisms, where manoeuvres contrasting different interests, different options, are carried out."[5] Die rasterhafte Aufteilung in die vielen voneinander abgetrennten Felder sorgt für Stabilität und Ruhe im sonst offen gelassenen Bildraum. Sie bildet jenes Gerüst, das dem leeren Bildraum Struktur verleiht, gleichzeitig entsteht jedoch ein stetiges Spannungsverhältnis zwischen der Form des Kreises, den organisch geschwungenen Körpern und der geradlinigen Form des Quadrates.

Was die Bildserie erheblich von Frieds übrigen Gemälden unterscheidet, ist jedoch nicht allein der formale Aufbau, sondern, wie bereits angedeutet, die besondere Materialität und die dadurch bedingte Struktur der Oberfläche. Anstatt die Tücher glatt auf der Leinwand zu applizieren hat Fried einen starken Faltenwurf zugelassen. Die Falten sorgen für eine unruhige Oberflächenstruk-

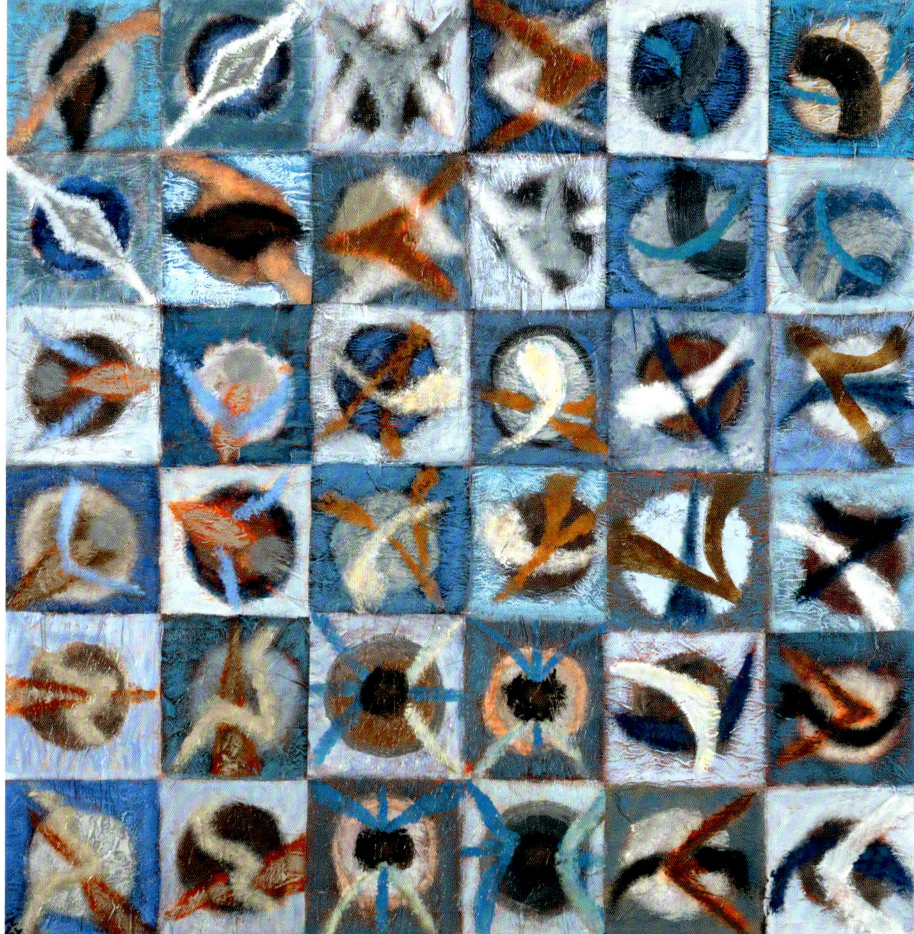

Ecriture d'un monde á part, 1990
Collage: Öl auf Papier-Servietten applizierte auf Leinwand / Collage: Oil on paper napkins laid down on canvas
128 x 128 cm
Sammlung des Künstlers / Collection of the Artist

tion may be made here to the *Color Chart Paintings* by Jim Dine, to Gerhard Richter's color charts, the black paintings by Ad Reinhardt or Jasper Johns' *Alphabet* paintings. All of these works pursue different ideas, but their image structure is characterized by the division of the image area into a grid of rectangles, used to create an order system in which different elements – be it color tones, letters of the alphabet, or different composition possibilities, as with Fried – are lined up like a table, a chart. With regard to the assembly-like application of the napkins, which are both image carriers and creative means, parallels can also be found in early Pop Art works – by Robert Rauschenberg or Jasper Johns – as well as in Yves Klein's assemblages, in which the structure of the used material is an essential element of the monochrome image compositions.

Fried's series of works goes hand in hand with a new turning point in his paintings, from which the central motif of the circular body floating in the image space dissolves ever more into abstract arrangements of round lines. In his compositions from 1989, Fried completely renounces to three-dimensionality allusions. He places his network of broad brushstrokes over monochrome, flat-primed painting (*Coreoptic*, 1995, fig. p. 99). By adding pigment, he creates a matt, pastel-like color application in which the brush stroke remains recognizable. The circle – as in the individual fields of the paintings in the *Napkin Series* – is increasingly taking a back seat, which is surrounded and overshadowed by

tur, die je nach Lichteinfall unterschiedlich stark zur Geltung kommt. Sie scheinen keiner Ordnung zu folgen und sind keinesfalls nur als Teil des Bildträgers zu bewerten. Vielmehr erscheinen sie als gezielt eingesetztes Gestaltungselement, so stark ist ihre Präsenz beim Betrachten der Bilder. Im Interview mit Kenneth Snelson betont Fried, wie viel Bedeutung er beispielsweise der Textur aufgetragener Farbe beimisst.[6] Auf den glatten Flächen seiner metallenen Reliefs erzeugt er verschiedene Muster, indem er Säure aufträgt. In seinen Monotypien, die einen erheblichen Anteil in Frieds künstlerischem Œuvre ausmachen, erzeugt der Faltenwurf des Papiers, von welchem der Abdruck gemacht wurde, unterschiedliche Maserungen in den Farbflächen. Da die Struktur des Farbauftrags auf den Tüchern verloren geht, nutzt Fried den Faltenwurf des Stoffs, um der Oberfläche eine spezielle Struktur zu verleihen. Interessant ist die Betonung des Materials und der Oberfläche, die je nach Lichteinfall auf die Leinwand so sehr in den Vordergrund tritt, dass der gemalte Inhalt des Bildes überschattet wird und hinter die Falten und Strukturen des Stoffs tritt.

Sowohl materiell – durch die Verwendung der Tücher – als auch kompositorisch – durch die Betonung des Quadrates und das Spannungsverhältnis desselben zu den organischen Formen – stechen die Bilder aus Frieds malerischem Œuvre heraus. Die überraschende Einbeziehung des Quadrats in dieser Bildserie und die damit einhergehende Einteilung der Bildfläche zeigen Parallelen zu Werken zeitgenössischer Künstler der späten Fünfziger und Sechzigerjahre. Erwähnen lassen sich hier die „Color Chart Paintings" von Jim Dine, Gerhard Richters Farbtafeln, die schwarzen Gemälde Ad Reinhardts oder Jasper Johns' *Alphabet*-Gemälde. All diese Werke verfolgen zwar unterschiedliche Ideen, sind jedoch in ihrem Bildaufbau geprägt durch die Eintei-

Bladed Caverns,
2000
Öl / Acryl auf Leinwand /
Oil / acryl on canvas
27 x 46 cm
Privatsammlung / Private
collection

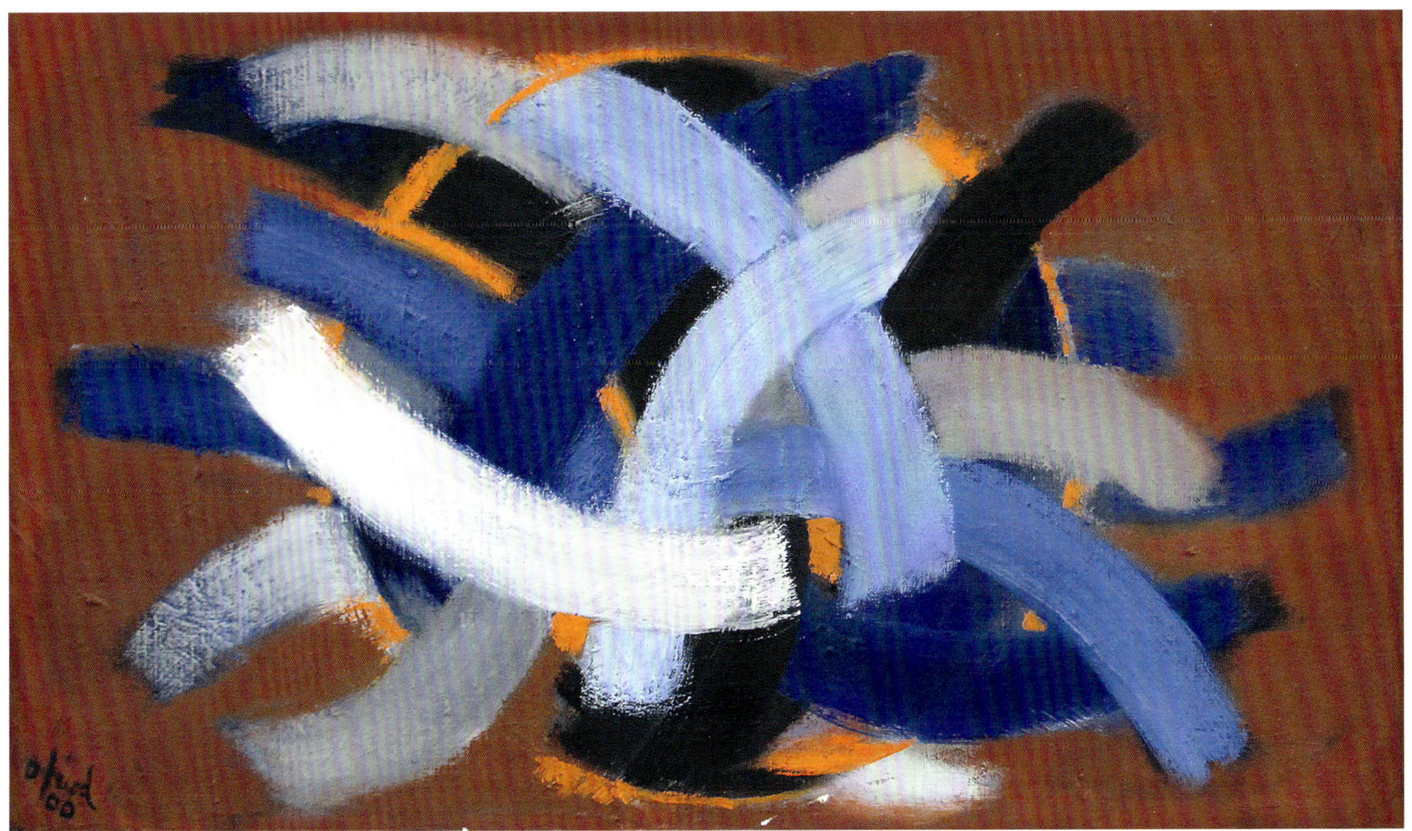

organic lines and shapes. The curved line takes its place as a design element from which Fried assembles his increasingly abstract compositions. These vivid circular lines, from which works such as *Greved Tao* (1987, fig. p. 26) are composed, are reminiscent of the division of the circles in Robert Delaunay's works, one could almost think that the lines from Delaunay's works had started to move and wander now confused by the pictorial space of Otto Fried's works. In 1997 Fried painted the largest painting of his entire œuvre (*Untitled*, 1998, fig. p. 104–105). The circle almost completely disappears in the numerous overlapping lines of the composition. At the same time, it is present in the curved lines, which, like fragments of the circle, are distributed over the image space. The lines are no longer laid out as an interwoven network across the image surface, but rather appear as living organisms that "dance" through the image space "in continuous movement".

1 Otto Fried, quoted from Thomas West 1995, p. 11.
2 Thomas West dates the change to abstract painting in 1972. Lisa Forrell proposes in her essay the same year for the change in Fried's style and cites as the first example of his circular compositions the invitation card to her wedding, which Fried designed with two semicircles. See Thomas West 1995, p. 7; see also the essay by Lisa Forrel in this cataloguel: *Otto Fried - A personal tribute*, p. 56.
3 See Thomas West 1995, p. 7.
4 Used by Fried in his studio to clean his brushes.
5 Claude Bouyeure 1990, w. p.
6 See the essay *Metal Relief Sculptures. Otto Fried interviewed by Kenneth Snelson*, p. 66, in this catalogue.

lung der Bildfläche in ein Raster aus Rechtecken, welches genutzt wird um ein Ordnungssystem herzustellen, in welchem unterschiedliche Elemente – seien es Farbtöne, Buchstaben des Alphabets, oder wie bei Fried verschiedene Kompositionsmöglichkeiten – tabellenartig aufgereiht werden. Bezüglich der assemblageartigen Applikation der Tücher, die gleichzeitig Bildträger als auch gestalterisches Mittel sind, lassen sich ebenfalls Parallelen in frühen Werken der Pop Art – bei Robert Rauschenberg oder Jasper Johns – finden, aber auch in den Assemblagen von Yves Klein, bei denen die Struktur des genutzten Materials maßgeblicher Teil der monochromen Bildkompositionen sind.

Die Werkreihe Frieds geht einher mit einem erneuten Wendepunkt in seinen Gemälden, von dem an sich das bisher zentrale Motiv des im Bildraum schwebenden Kreiskörpers mehr und mehr in abstrakten Anordnungen runder Linien auflöst. In seinen Kompositionen ab 1989 verzichtet Fried vollständig auf Andeutungen von Dreidimensionalität. Über einfarbig flächig grundierte Malerei setzt er sein Geflecht aus breiten Pinselstrichen („Coreoptic", 1995, Abb. S. 99). Durch die Beisetzung von Pigment erzeugt er einen matten, pastellartigen Farbauftrag, in dem der Strich des Pinsels erkennbar bleibt. Der Kreis tritt – wie auch in den einzelnen Feldern der Gemälde der „Tuch-Serie" – immer mehr in den Hintergrund, der von organischen Linien und Formen umgeben und überschattet ist. An seine Stelle tritt die geschwungene Linie als Gestaltungselement, aus dem Fried seine immer abstrakteren Kompositionen zusammensetzt. Diese lebendigen kreisförmigen Linien, aus denen sich Werke wie „Greved Tao" (1987, Abb. S. 26) zusammensetzen, erinnern an die Zerteilung der Kreise in den Werken Robert Delaunays, fast könnte man meinen, die Linien aus Delaunays Werken hätten sich in Bewegung gesetzt und wanderten nun durcheinander durch den Bildraum der Werke Otto Frieds. 1997 malt Fried das größte Gemälde seines Gesamtœuvres („Untitled", 1998, Abb. S. 104–105). Der Kreis verschwindet beinahe vollständig in den zahlreichen sich überlagernden Linien der Komposition. Gleichzeitig ist er in den geschwungenen Linien gegenwärtig, die wie übrig gebliebene Bruchstücke des Kreises über den Bildraum verteilt sind. Die Linien sind nicht länger als ineinander verwobenes Netz über die Bildfläche angelegt, sondern erscheinen vielmehr als lebendige Organismen, die „in kontinuierlicher Bewegung" durch den Bildraum „tanzen".

1 „Circles and spheres describe beginnings dancing towards endings in continuous movement, like the journey of a seed, as it grows to become a centuriers-old redwood giant, and finally returns to regenerate the earth," Otto Fried, zitiert nach Thomas West 1995, S. 11.

2 Thomas West datiert den Wechsel zur abstrakten Malerei in das Jahr 1972, auch Lisa Forrell führt in ihrem Aufsatz dasselbe Jahr für den Umbruch in Frieds Stil an und nennt als erstes Beispiel seiner Kreiskompositionen die Einladung zu Ihrer Hochzeit, die Fried mit zwei Halbkreisen gestaltete. Vgl. Thomas West 1995, S. 7; Vgl. Beitrag von Lisa Forrell: „Otto Fried - Eine persönliche Würdigung", in diesem Katalog, S. 57.

3 Vgl. Thomas West 1995, S. 7.

4 Diese nutzte Fried in seinem Atelier gewöhnlich zum Reinigen seiner Pinsel.

5 Claude Bouyeure 1990, o. S.

6 Vgl. Beitrag in diesem Katalog: „Metal Relief Sculptures. Otto Fried interviewt von Kenneth Snelson", S. 67.

WERKE WORKS 1948–1979

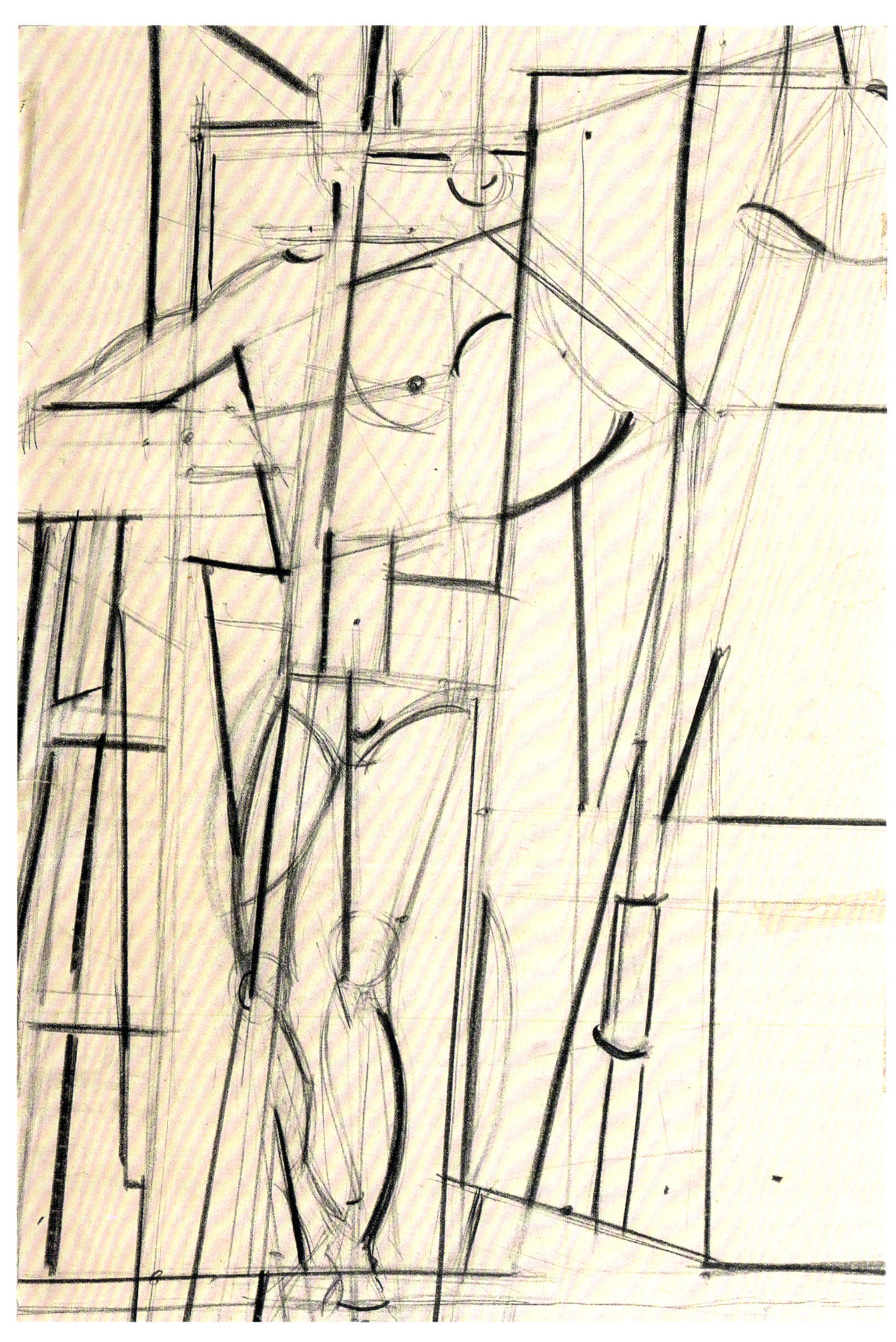

OHNE TITEL / UNTITLED
1948–1950
Grafit auf Papier / Graphite on paper

OHNE TITEL / UNTITLED
1948–1950
Grafit auf Papier / Graphite on paper

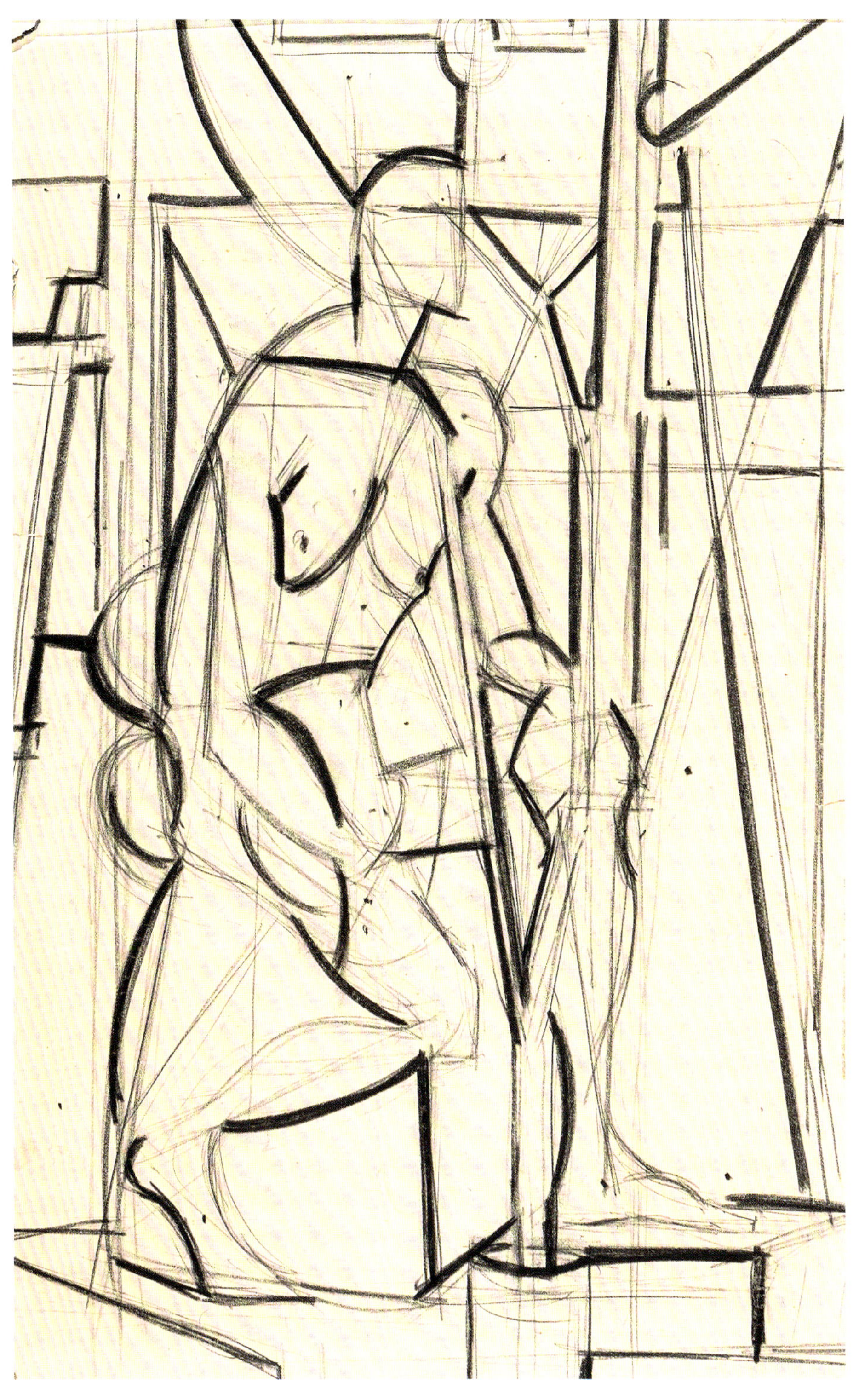

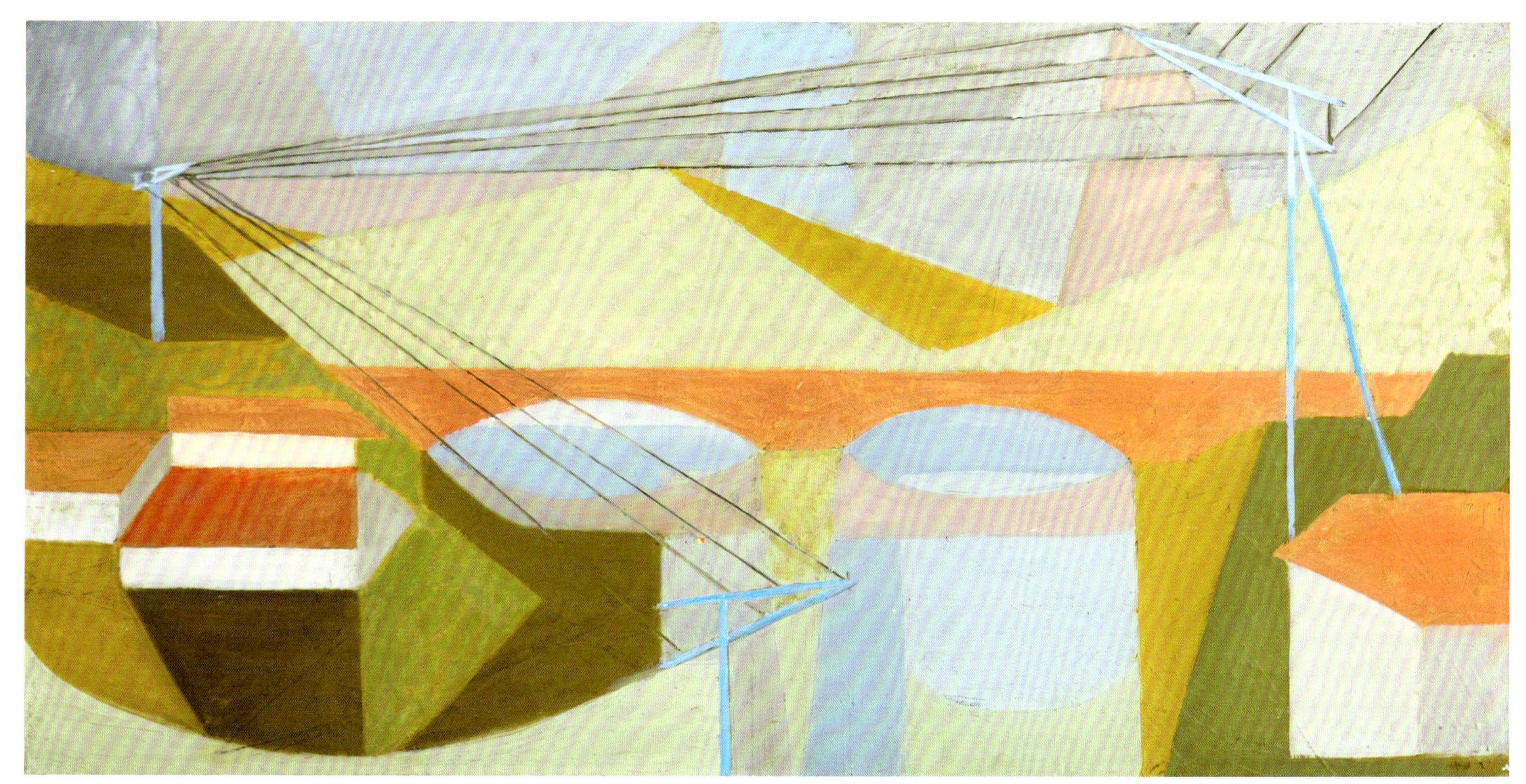

LANDSCAPE WITH BRIDGE
1951
Öl auf Leinwand / Oil on canvas

PARISIAN WINDOW
1952
Öl auf Leinwand / Oil on canvas

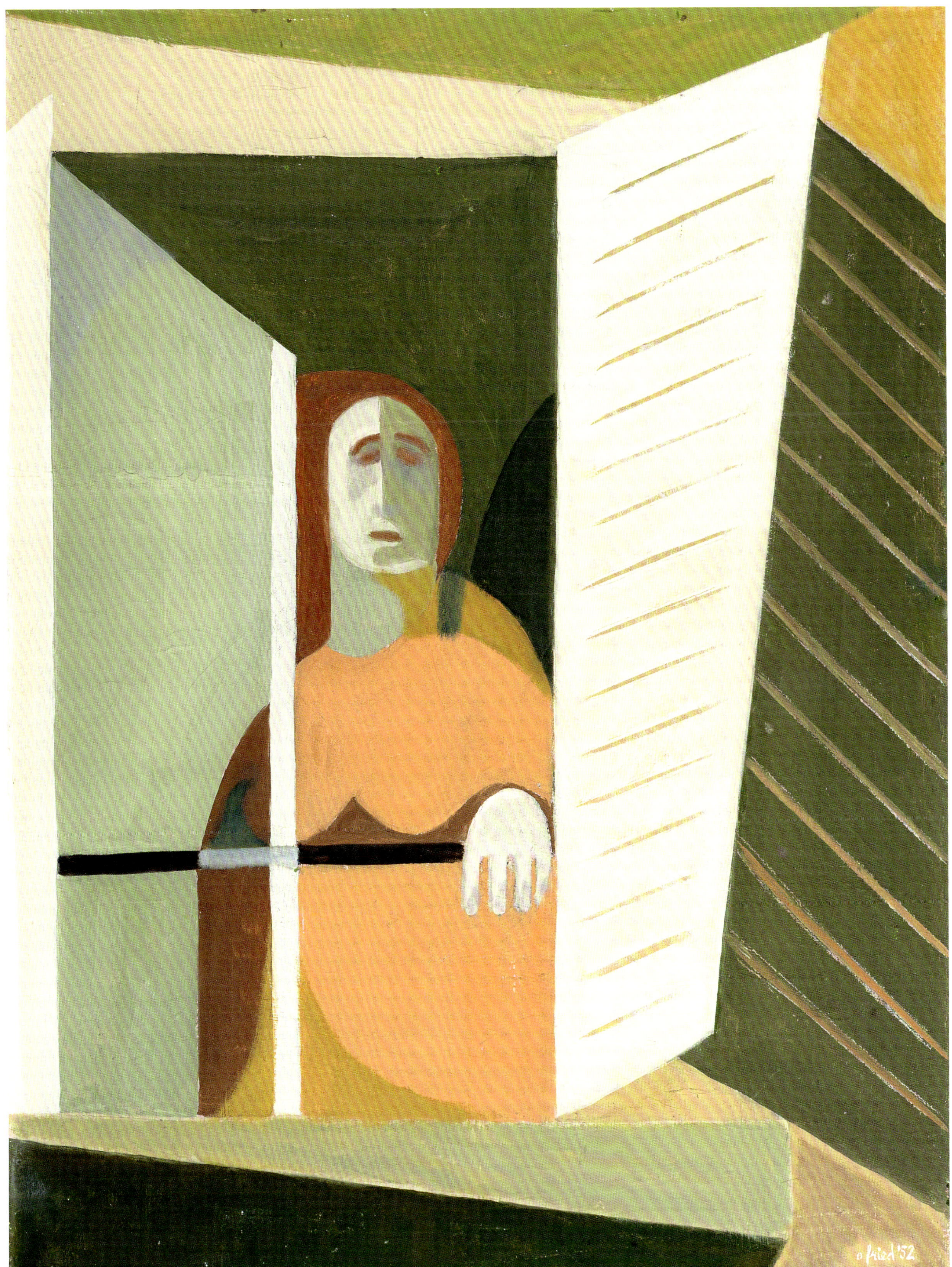

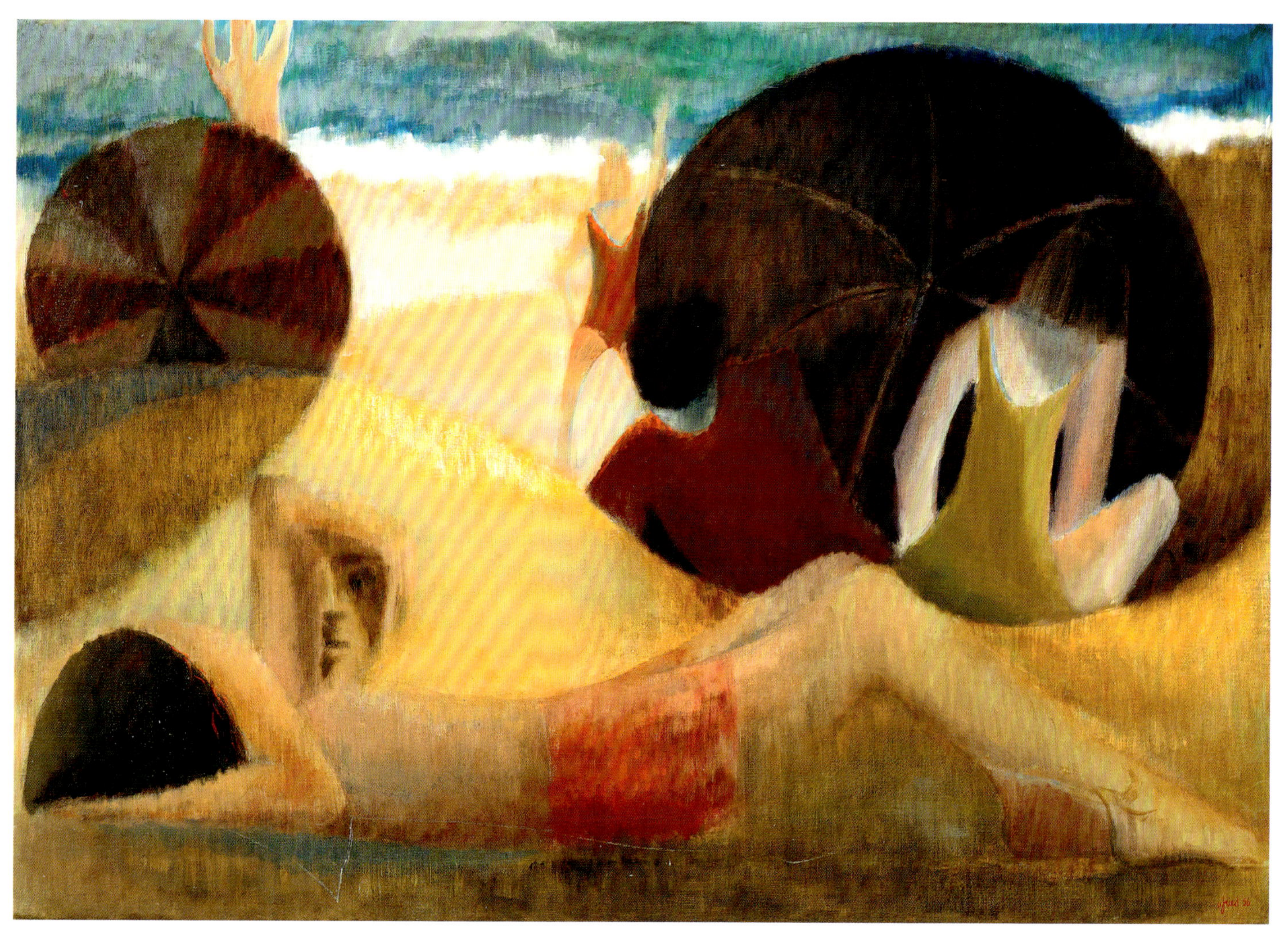

JONES BEACH
1956
Öl auf Leinwand / Oil on canvas

BLOSSOMING APPLE TREES
1958
Monotypie / Monotype

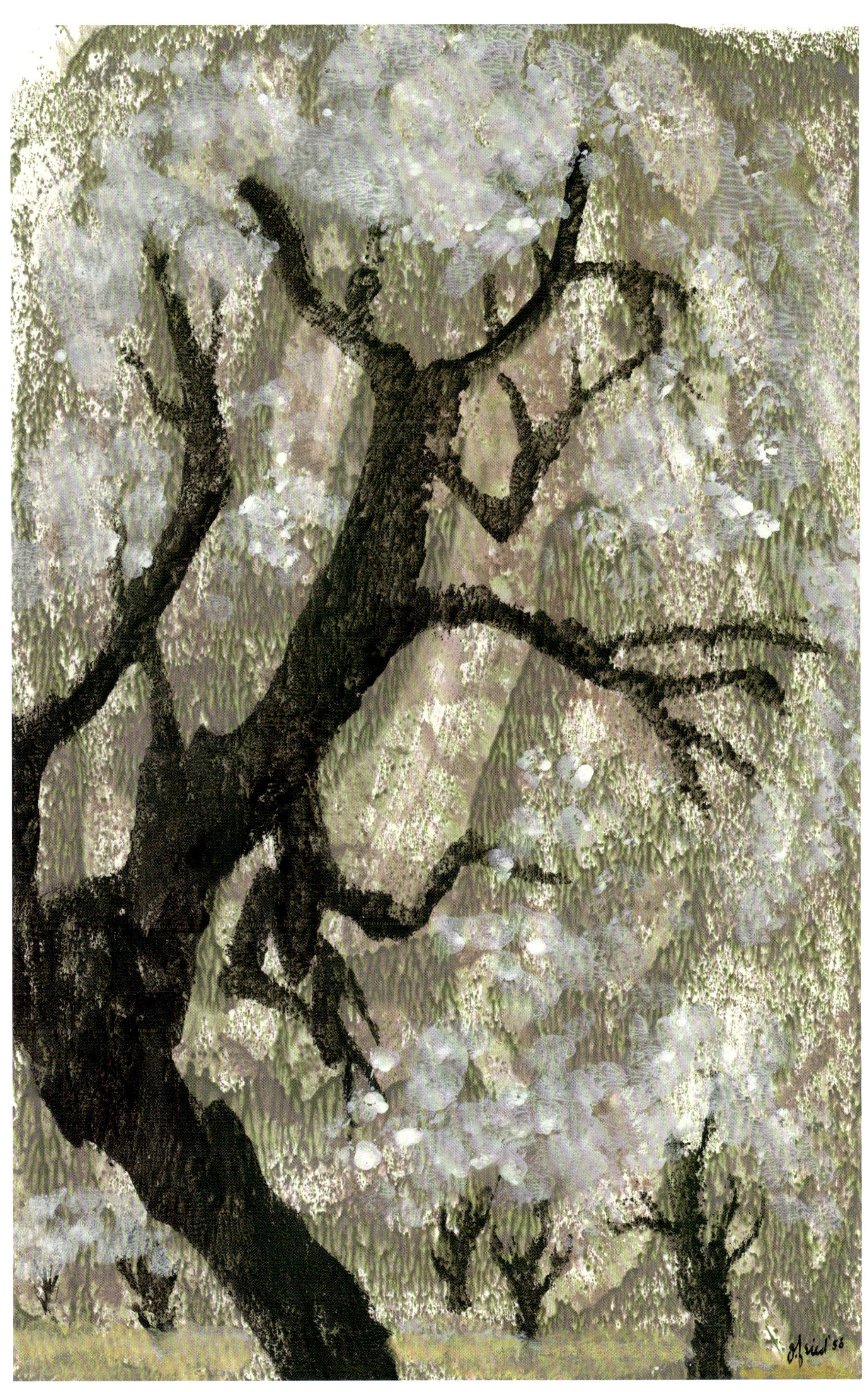

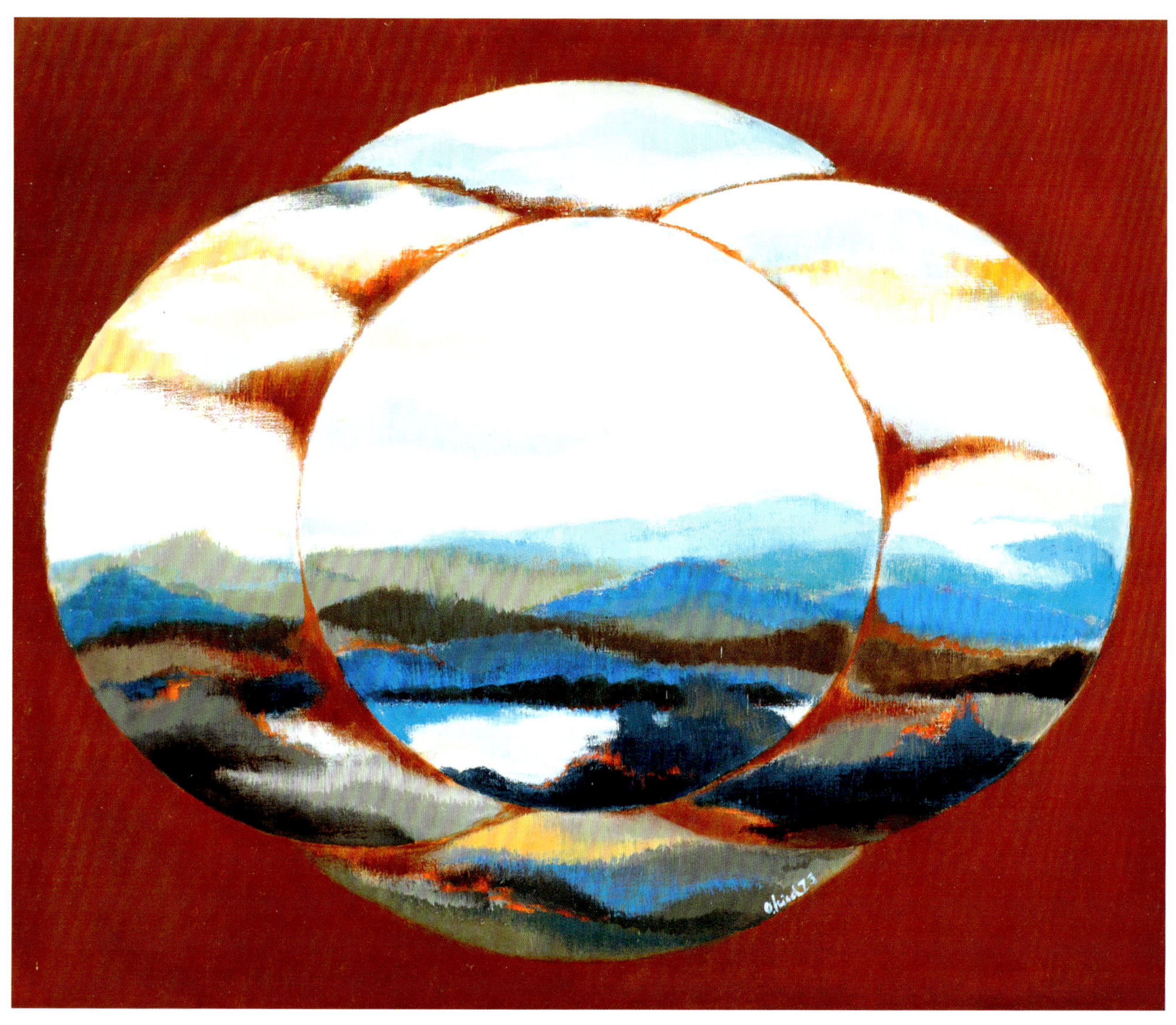

OHNE TITEL / UNTITLED
1973
Öl auf Leinwand / Oil on canvas

OVERLAPPING TEMPERATURES
1975
Öl auf Leinwand / Oil on canvas

FLOWERING ATMOSPHERE
1976
Öl auf Leinwand / Oil on canvas

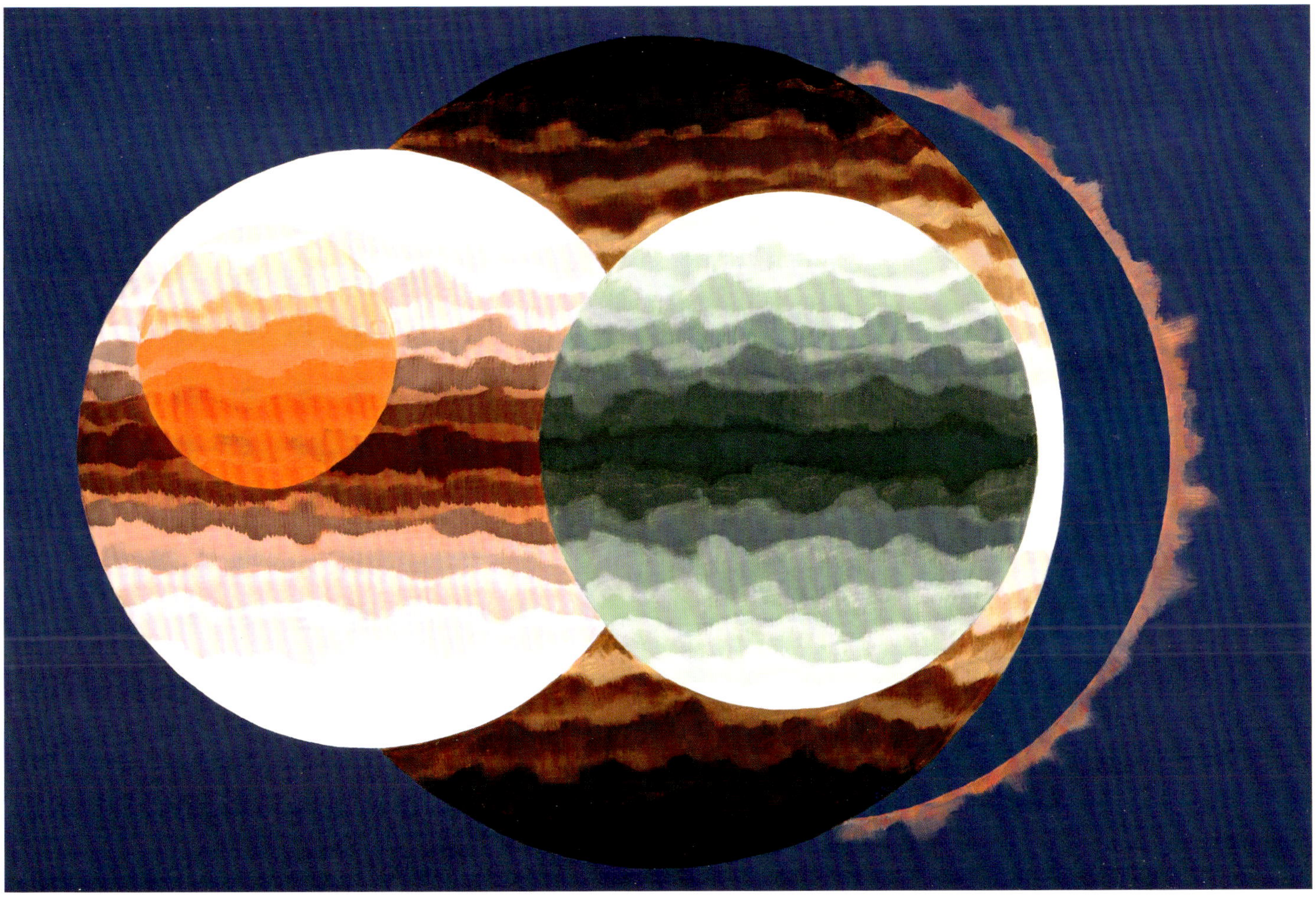

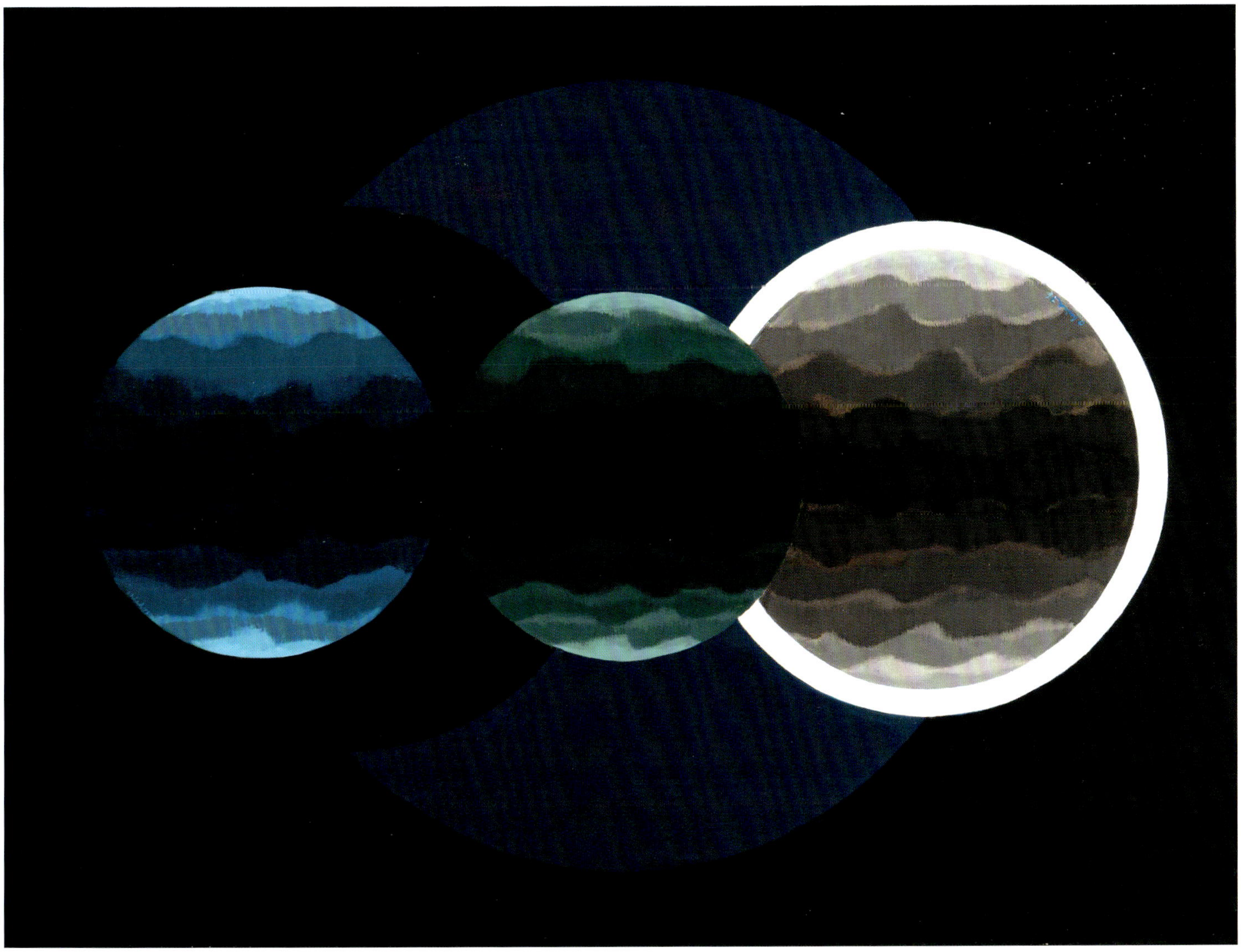

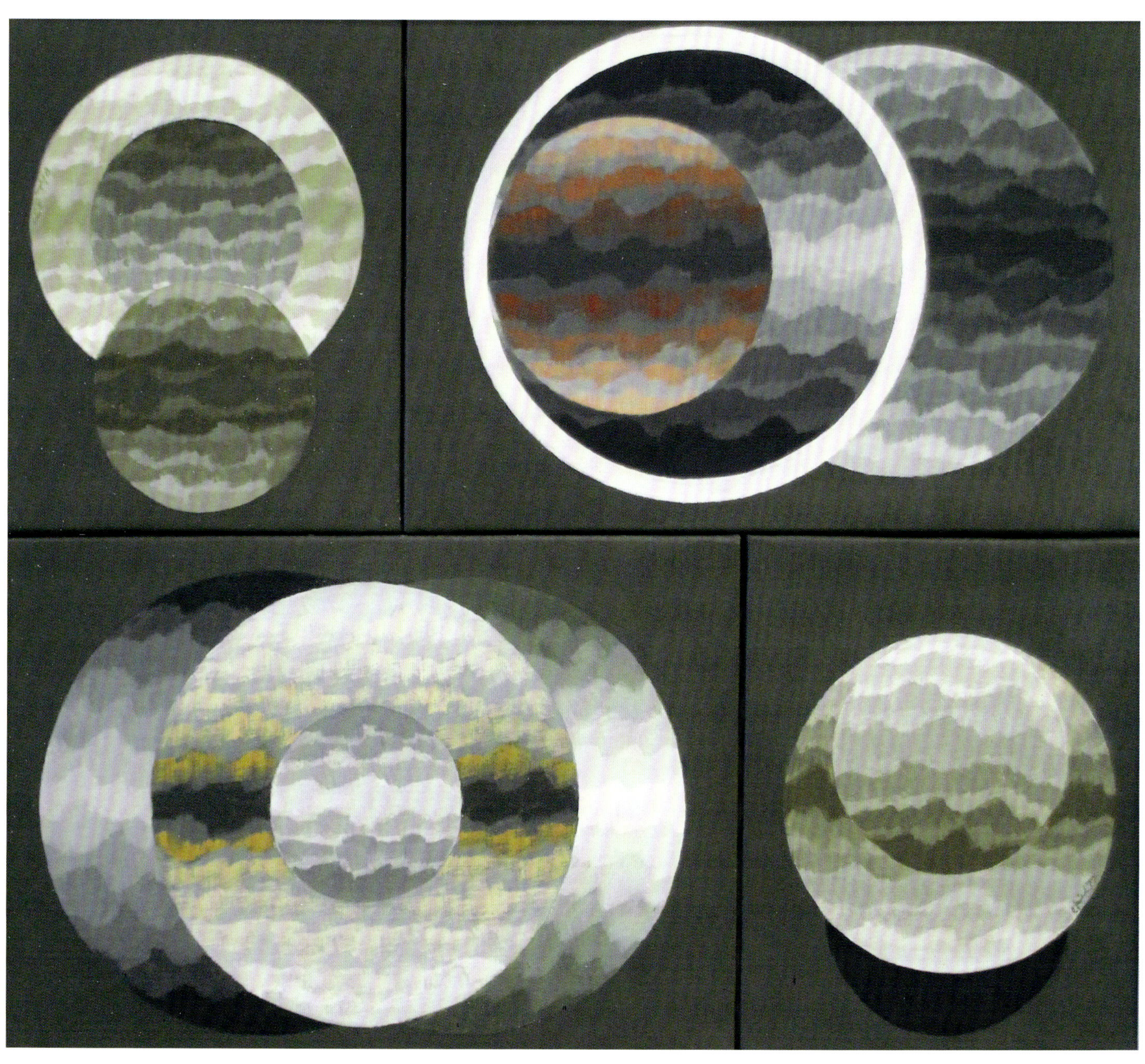

OHNE TITEL / UNTITLED
Circa 1975-1978
Öl / Acryl auf Leinwand / Oil / acryl on canvas

SPHÄREN
1976
Bleistift auf Papier / Pencil on paper

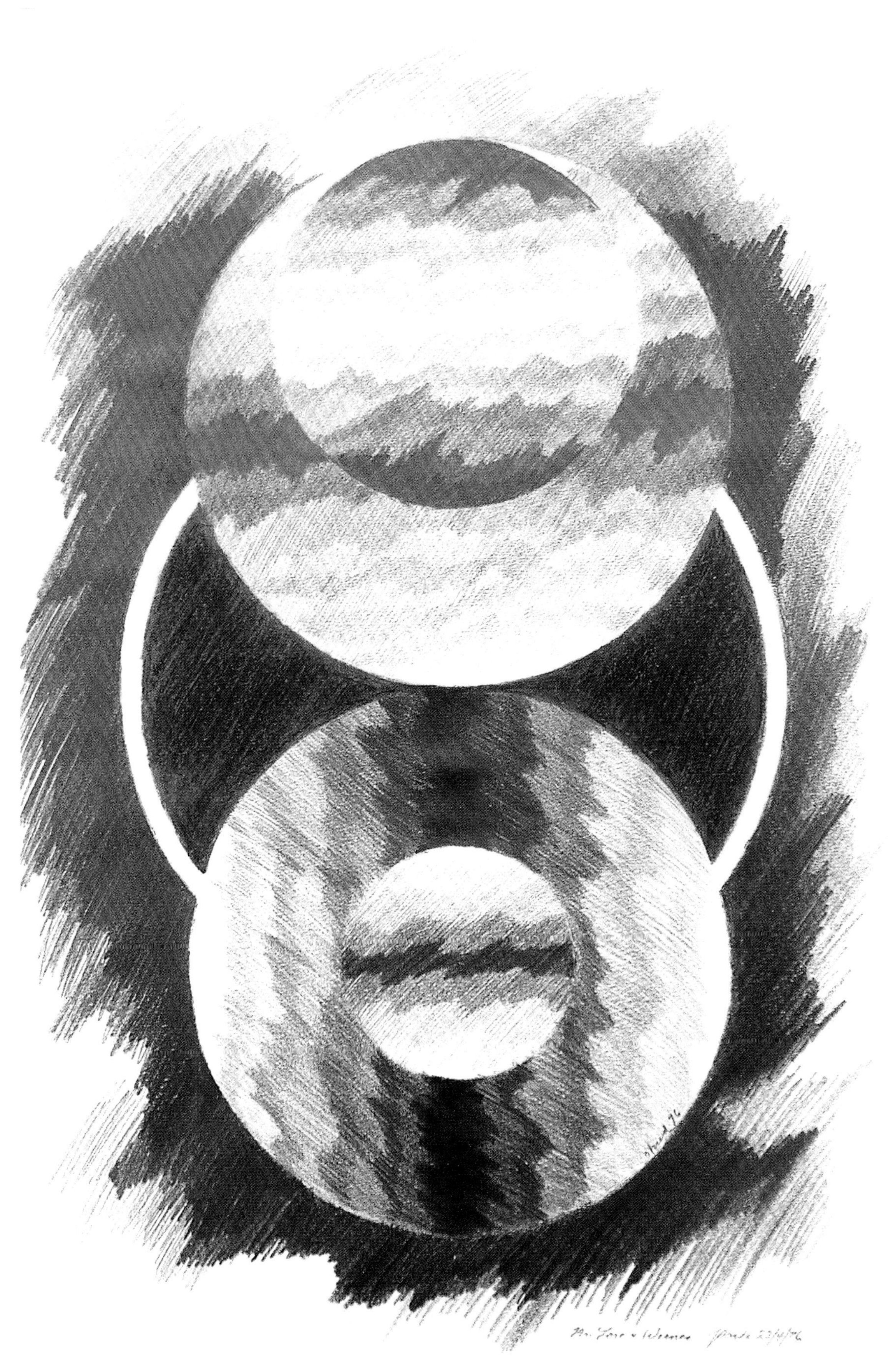

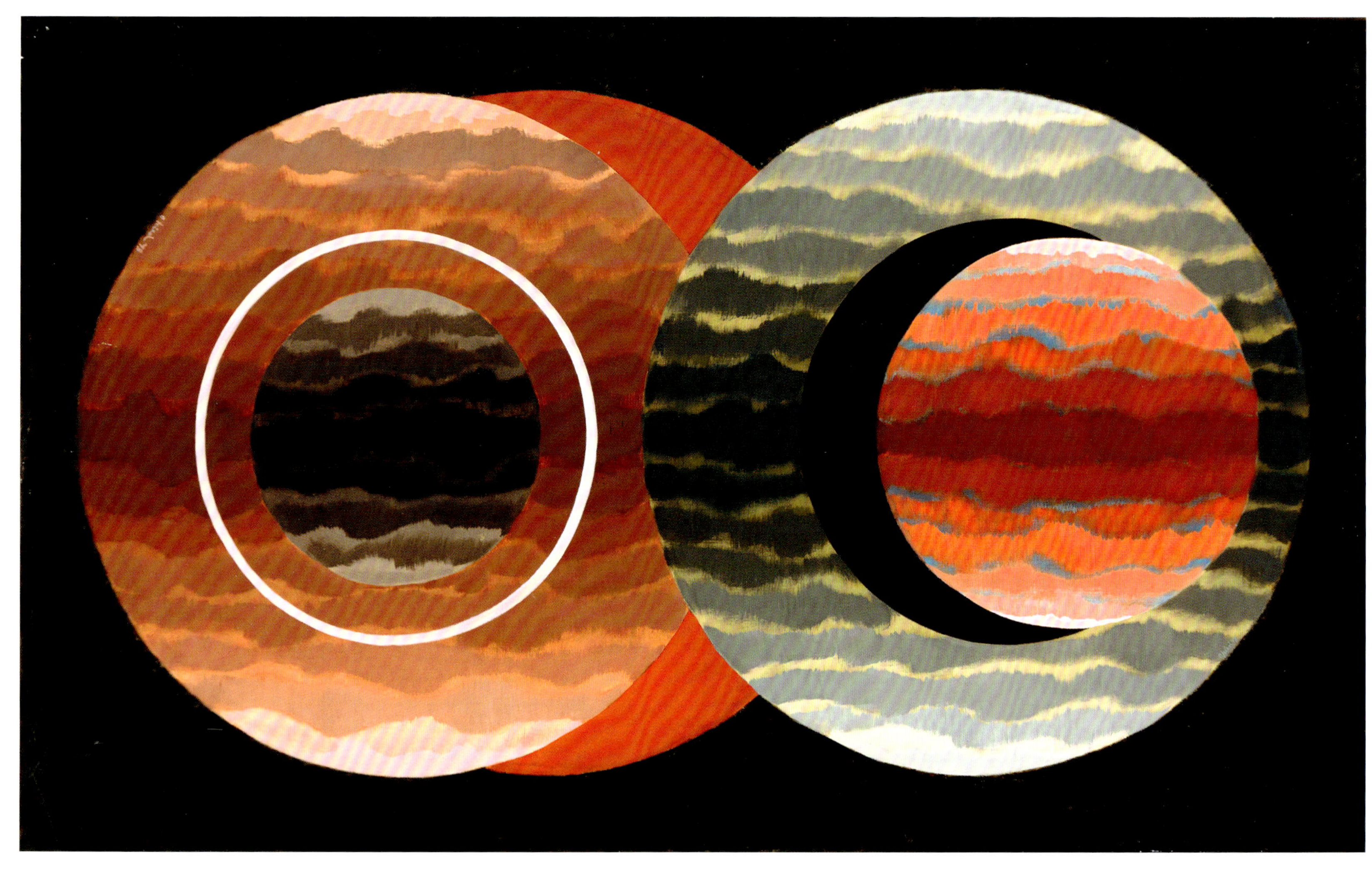

JACKHAMMER BLUES
1978
Öl auf Leinwand / Oil on canvas

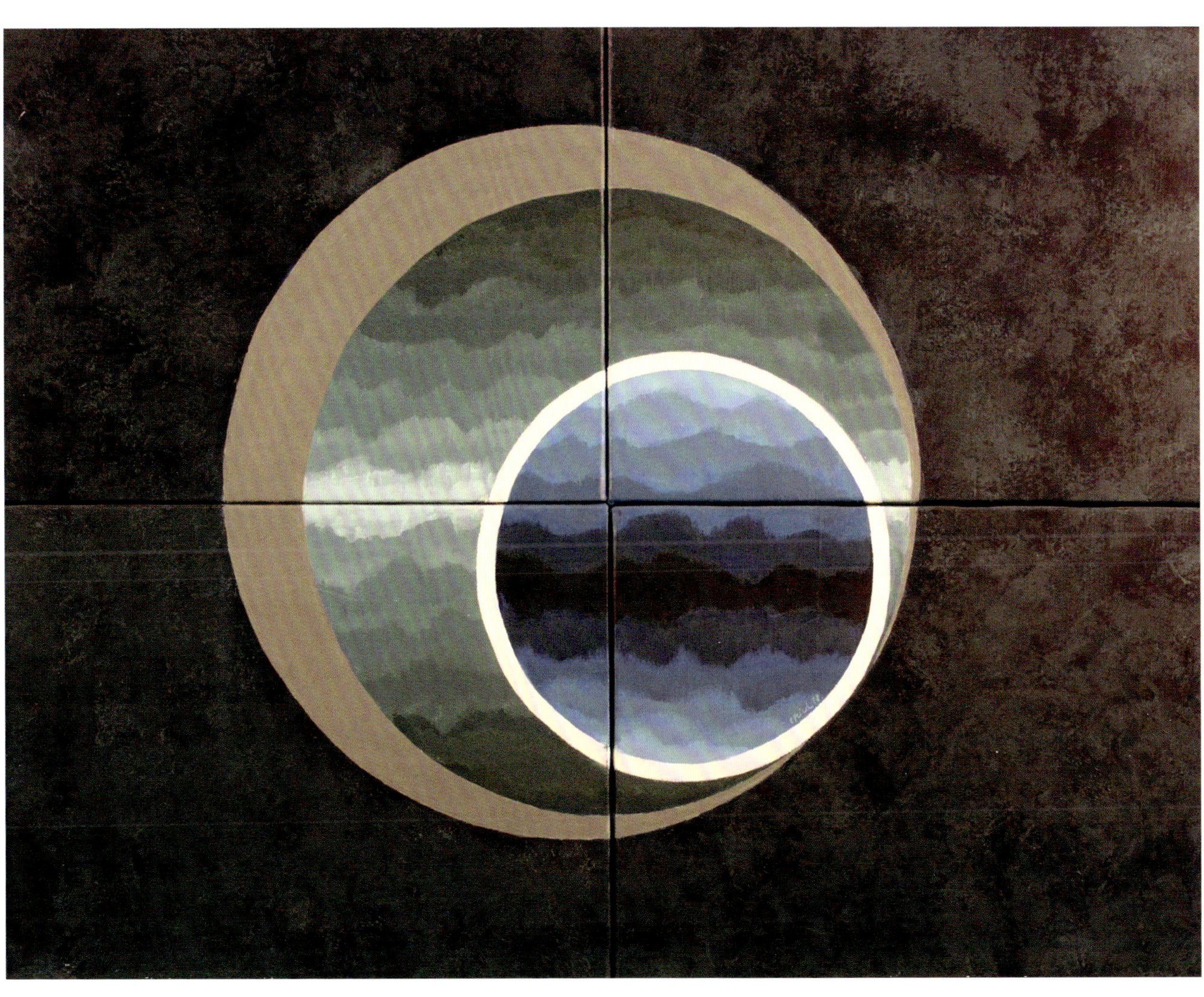

FEINES ATTESTAT
1978
Öl auf Leinwand / Oil on canvas

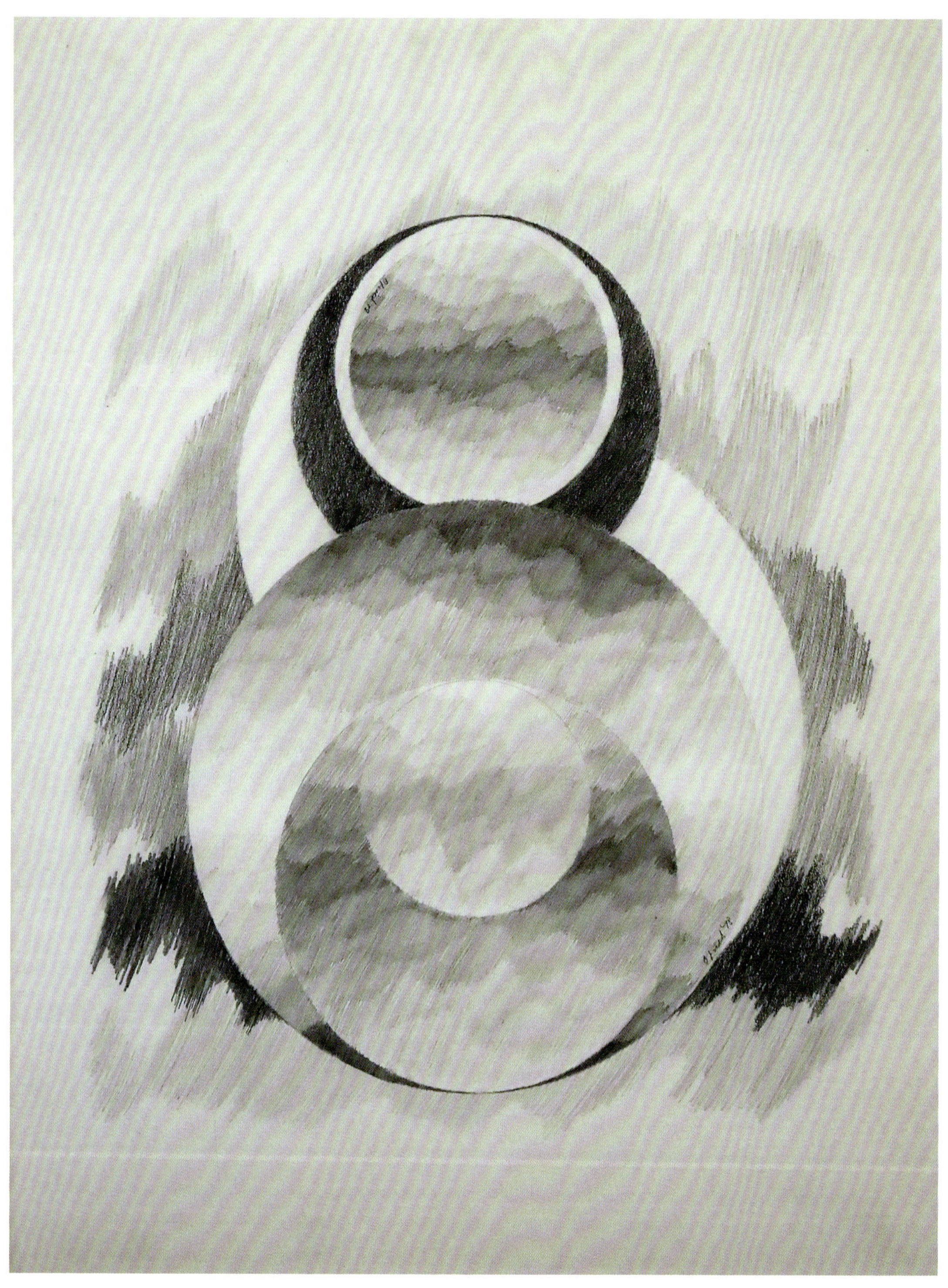

RUHE BITTE
1976
Bleistift auf Papier / Pencil on paper

EXPANSION
1979
Öl auf Leinwand / Oil on canvas

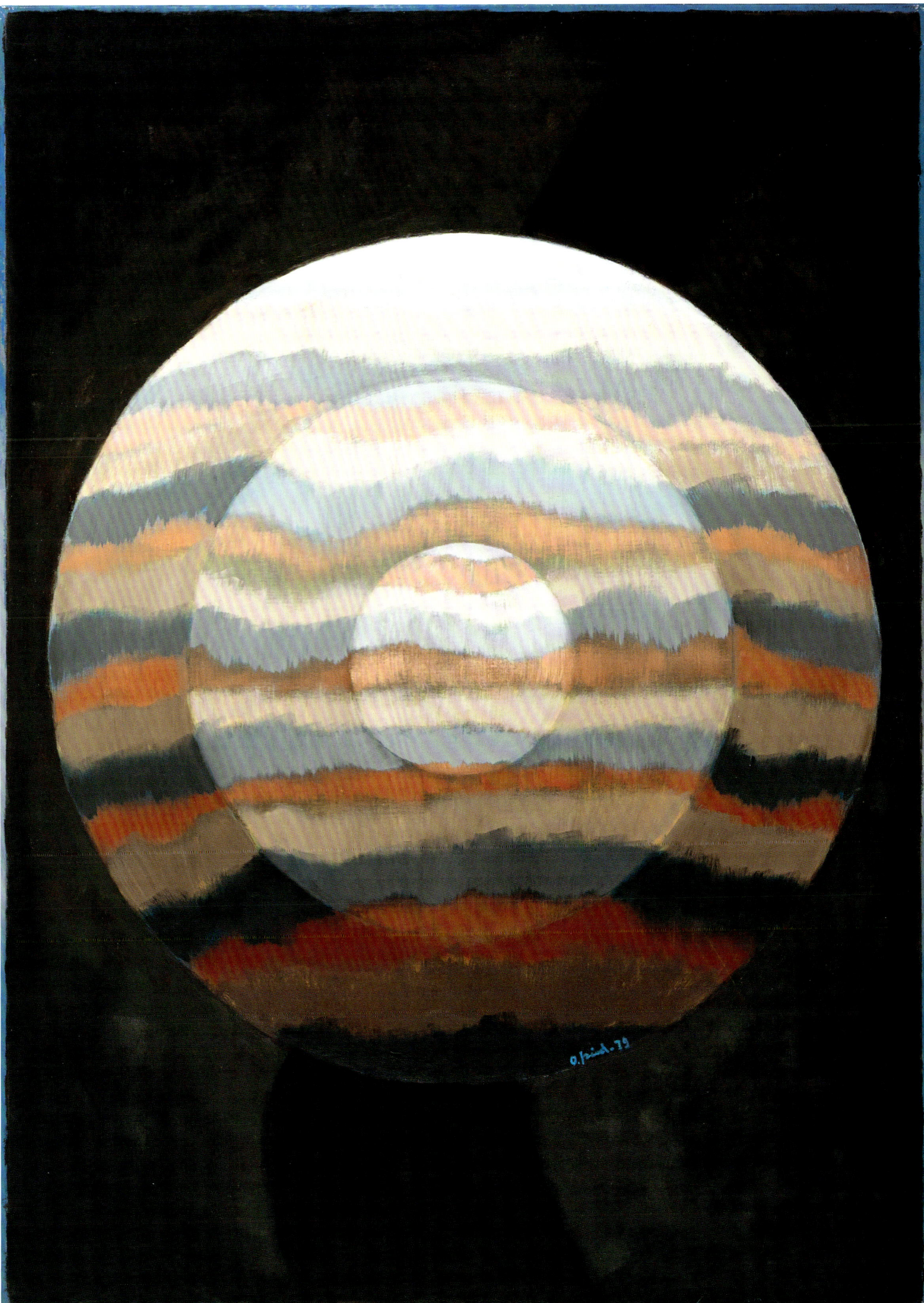

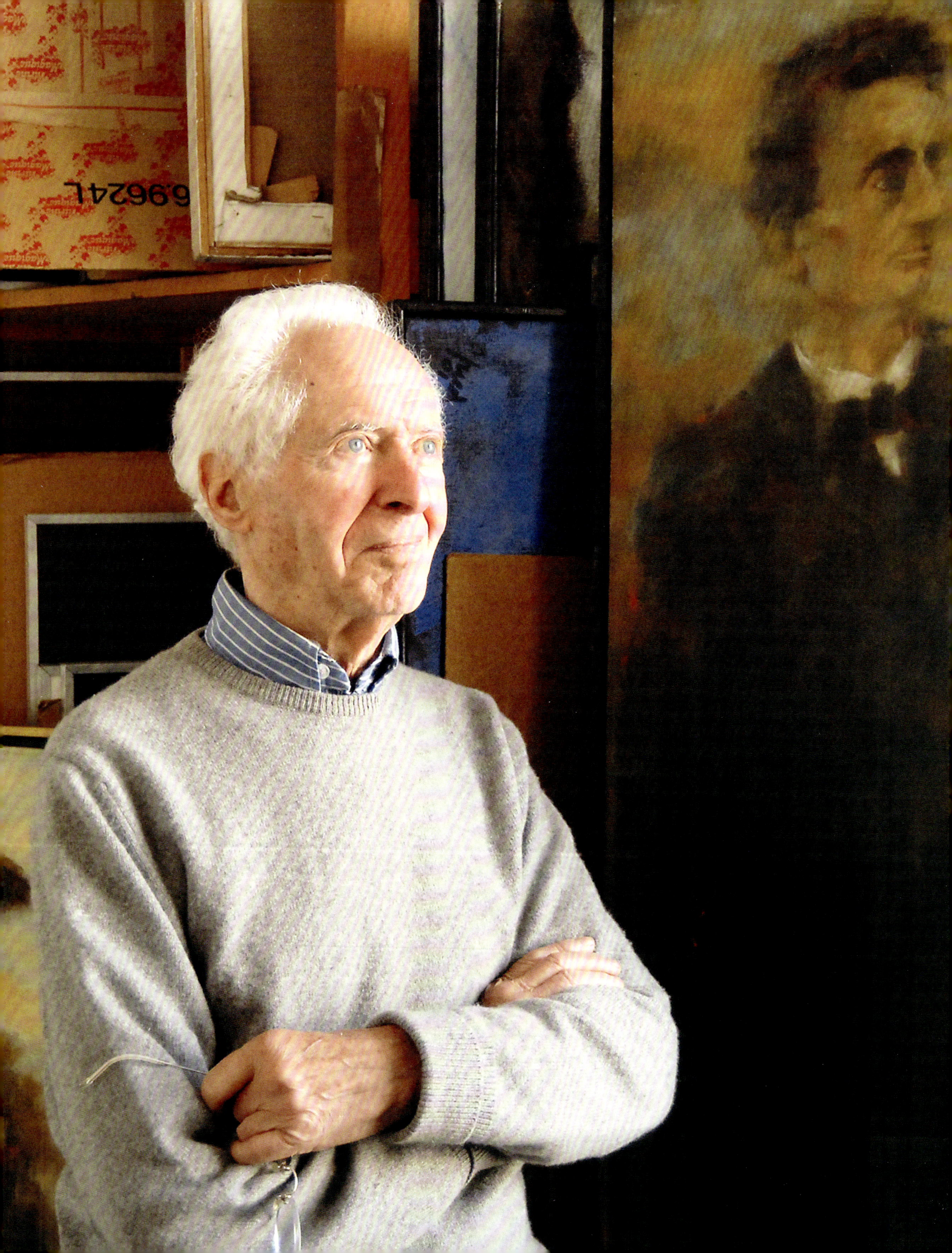

LISA FORRELL

Otto Fried Eine persönliche Würdigung

Es gab nie eine Zeit, in der ich Otto nicht kannte. Ich kenne ihn durch seine Bilder, seine Objekte, seine Geschichten, sein Lachen, seinen unbekümmerten Blick auf die Welt und vor allen Dingen kenne ich ihn durch all das, was ich von ihm gelernt habe. Er hatte wohl den größten und einen tiefgreifenden Einfluss auf mein Leben.

Als Otto aus Portland, Oregon, wo für ihn „Zuhause" war, nach New York kam, lernte er meine Eltern kennen. Sie haben mehr oder weniger zu der Bohemeszene gehörten. Mein Vater war Komponist und meine Mutter Filmeditorin. Sie lebten in den Künstlerkreisen der fünfziger Jahre umgeben von avantgardistischen Malern, Bildhauern, Musikern und Filmleuten. Ich weiß nicht, wie sie sich kennengelernt haben; als ich geboren wurde, war Otto schon da. Er wohnte damals in einem kleinen Raum im fünften Stock in der Third Avenue. Das Zimmer diente als Schlafraum und Atelier

LISA FORRELL

Otto Fried A Personal Tribute

There was never a time I didn't know Otto. I know him through his paintings, his *objets*, his stories, his laughter, his devil-may-care view of the world, and most of all, because of everything he taught me. He is arguably the greatest and most profound influence on my life.

As soon as Otto arrived in New York from Portland Oregon, the place he called 'home', he met my bohemian parents. My father was a composer and my mother then a film editor. They travelled in artistic circles of the Fifties, surrounding themselves with the composers, visual artists and filmmakers who were all part of the *avant-garde*. I don't know how they met, because once I was born, Otto was always there. He lived in a small room in a fifth floor walkup on Third Avenue. The room doubled as a bedroom and an artist's studio, with a tiny kitchen in the corner. He hardly cooked, as he had little money for food, and so spent a great deal of time eating with us.

Otto Fried in seinem Atelier in Paris, 2006 / Otto Fried in his studio in Paris, 2006

As a young child, I became fascinated by him, his deep blue eyes, his insightful views of the world, his difficult history. He had come from Germany, yet he would always identify himself as a proud American. For us, Portland seemed far further away than Germany as New York was then inundated with surviving German and other Jews after the war. He would tell us of his young life in Horchheim, near Koblenz, where his father was a butcher, and the family had lived for around 200 years, until the horrors of Hitler and the Nazi party infected the country with its inhumane disease. He told us of his brother who died under terrible circumstances and the concentration camp where his father was sent. He told us of his flight to South America and onwards to Oregon where a lawyer cousin, a long-lost relative, provided him with papers and a home while he waited for his parents to come. And they did, quite miraculously. Today, in his old age, and with all pretenses thrown to the wind, he spends much time showing the photographs of the Horchheim butcher shop, his parents, his brother Ernst.

Until now, and all throughout his life, Otto never ever wore his pain on his sleeve. Life, for Otto, was too precious and had to be embraced – whatever the pain of the past. Perhaps this is the greatest lesson he taught me. It was art and art alone that got him through. He has an endearing habit of repeatedly telling me that all he knows how to do is to paint.

The persistent rain in Portland creates an extraordinary landscape of beauty – high, tall trees – magnificent greens of all hues – the way the clouds form high above the canopy, and the mist descends into the valleys – as Otto described. I had always thought that high art would emerge out of this landscape, but bizarrely, it never spawned many great painters. Perhaps the landscape is just too overwhelming, not human enough. Portland however, delivered to Otto the most profound love of nature and a life-long friend in Kenneth Snelson, a recognized and prolific American sculptor who went on to study with Otto in Léger's Paris studio.

Once Otto arrived in New York, the greatest influence on his work was not the landscape painters of the vast country – neither the 19th century painters such as Arthur Reginald Smith or the more modern, Mark Keathly who paint great swathes of color and movement of the demanding and sometimes terrifying landscape, nor of the Hudson River school whose meanderings through the gentle *paysage* of the East had been hailed as a 'movement'.

Although Otto had studied at Léger's studio in Paris after the war, the modernist movement was not his to follow. Instead, the tremendous influences for Otto were 19th century European, and, during his 'first' period, Impressionism. Above the piano in my parents' apartment hung a man and a boy in a rowboat, with gentle waves in a misty but unclear distance. The boy turns his head, the man continues rowing. The colors are muted, soft, dulled, but evocative of so much feeling. The feeling of longing for a place to go. Is it Otto in that boat?

Each year that my parents made a bit more money, they would first spend it on purchasing Otto's paintings. *The Rowboat* was the first in 1963. It hangs in my living room now. For years after that my parents continued to purchase... one after the other. An impressionistic view of the mountains, again, unmistakably the Alps, hardly the wild Rockies, and another, a bursting blaze of orange and yellow colors – an impressionistic view of a sunset. It became so that our apartment was filled to bursting with Otto. He became our family artist and made our home resplendent.

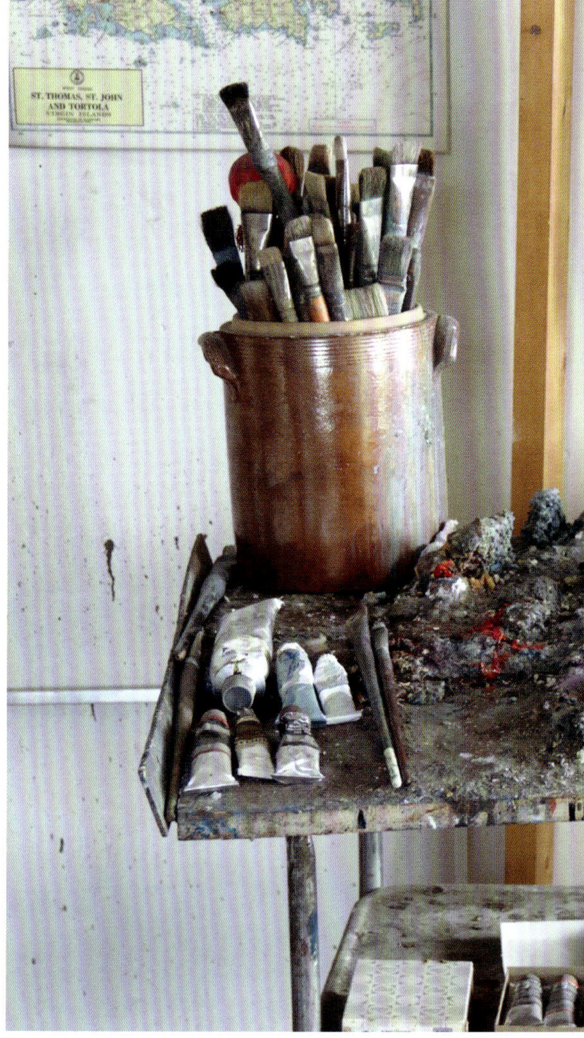

Otto Frieds Atelier in Paris, 2006 /
Otto Fried 's studio in Paris, 2006

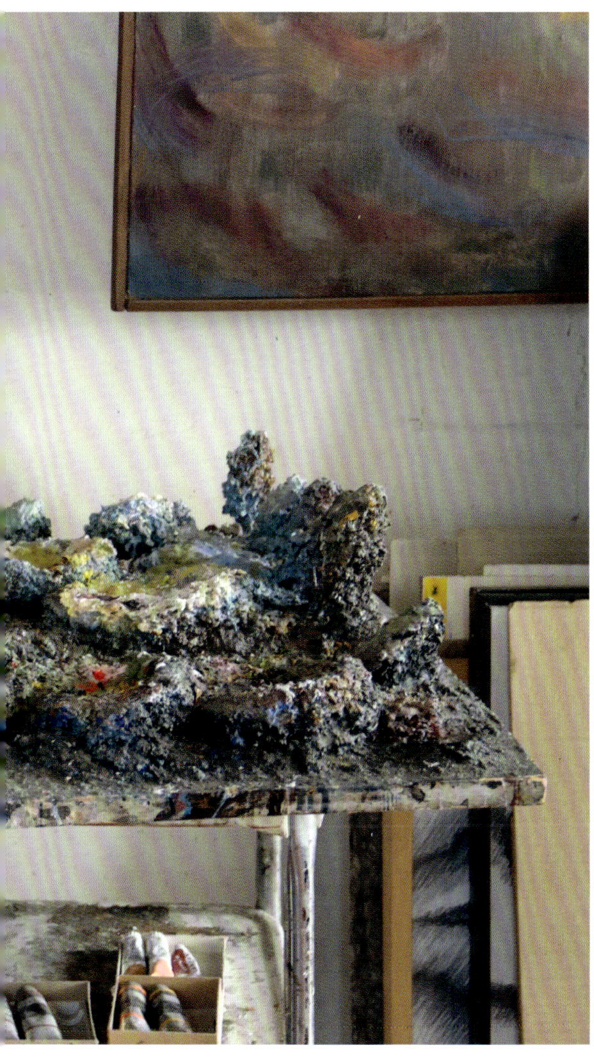

mit einer winzigen Küche in einer Ecke. Er kochte kaum, denn er hatte kaum Geld für Lebensmittel und aß oft bei uns.

Als kleines Kind war ich fasziniert von ihm, seinen tiefblauen Augen, seinen klugen Ansichten von der Welt, seiner schwierigen Geschichte. Er war aus Deutschland gekommen, verstand sich aber immer als stolzer Amerikaner. Für uns schien Portland weiter entfernt zu sein als Deutschland, da New York nach dem Krieg voll von überlebenden deutschen und anderen Juden war. Er erzählte uns von seiner Jugend in Horchheim bei Koblenz, wo sein Vater Metzger war und die Familie mehr als 200 Jahre gelebt hatte, bis die Schrecken Hitlers und der Nazis das Land mit einer inhumanen Krankheit infizierten. Er erzählte uns von seinem Bruder, der unter schrecklichen Umständen starb, und dem Konzentrationslager, wohin sein Vater geschickt wurde. Er erzählte uns von seiner Flucht über Mittelamerika und weiter nach Oregon, wo ihm ein wiedergefundener Cousin und Anwalt zur Einbürgerung und einem Zuhause verhalf, während er darauf wartete, dass seine Eltern kamen. Und das taten sie – was an ein Wunder grenzte. Heute, in seinem hohen Alter, zeigt er sehr gern die Fotos der Metzgerei in Horchheim, seiner Eltern und seines Bruders Ernst.

Bis jetzt, und sein ganzes Leben lang, hat Otto sich seinen Schmerz nie anmerken lassen. Zu kostbar ist das Leben für Otto und es muss ausgekostet werden – vergiss den Schmerz der Vergangenheit! Vielleicht ist dies die größte Lektion, die er mir beigebracht hat. Es war die Kunst und die Kunst allein, die ihn durchbrachten. Ich mag es, wenn er mir immer wieder sagt, alles was er kann sei malen.

Der ständige Regen in Portland bringt eine außergewöhnliche Landschaft von großer Schönheit hervor – hohe Bäume – prächtiges Grün in allen Tönen –, die Art und Weise, wie sich die Wolken hoch oben zu einem Baldachin ballen und der Nebel in die Täler hinabsteigt – so hat es Otto beschrieben. Ich dachte immer, dass aus dieser Landschaft doch hohe Kunst hervorgegangen sein müsste, aber erstaunlicherweise hat sie nicht viele große Maler hervorgebracht. Vielleicht ist die Landschaft einfach zu überwältigend, nicht menschlich genug. Oregon bescherte Otto jedoch eine tiefe Liebe zur Natur und einen lebenslangen Freund in Kenneth Snelson, einem anerkannten und produktiven amerikanischen Bildhauer, der später mit Otto zum Studium bei Léger nach Paris ging.

Als Otto in New York ankam, hatten nicht die Landschaftsmaler des riesigen Landes den größte Einfluss auf seine Arbeit – weder die Maler des 19. Jahrhunderts, wie Arthur Reginald Smith, noch der modernere Mark Keathly, die alle große Farbflächen und Bewegungen der fordernden und manchmal beängstigenden Landschaft malen, noch die Hudson River Schule, deren Mäandern durch die sanfte Landschaft des Ostens als „Bewegung" gefeiert worden war.

Obwohl Otto nach dem Krieg in Légers Atelier in Paris studiert hatte, war die Moderne nicht die Bewegung, der er sich anschloss, es waren vielmehr die Europäer des 19. Jahrhunderts – und während seiner 'ersten Periode' – die Impressionisten, die enormen Einfluss auf Otto hatten. Über dem Klavier in der Wohnung meiner Eltern hing ein Bild von einem Mann und einem Jungen in einem Ruderboot, auf sanften Wellen in einer nebligen, aber unklaren Entfernung. Der Junge dreht den Kopf, der Mann rudert weiter. Die Farben sind gedämpft, weich, matt, aber sie rufen so viel Gefühl hervor. Das Gefühl, sich nach einem Ort zu sehnen, an dem man bleiben kann. Ist das Otto da in dem Boot?

Als meine Eltern etwas mehr Geld verdient hatten, gaben sie es erst einmal für den Kauf eines von Ottos Gemälden aus. „The Rowboat" war das erste. Es hängt

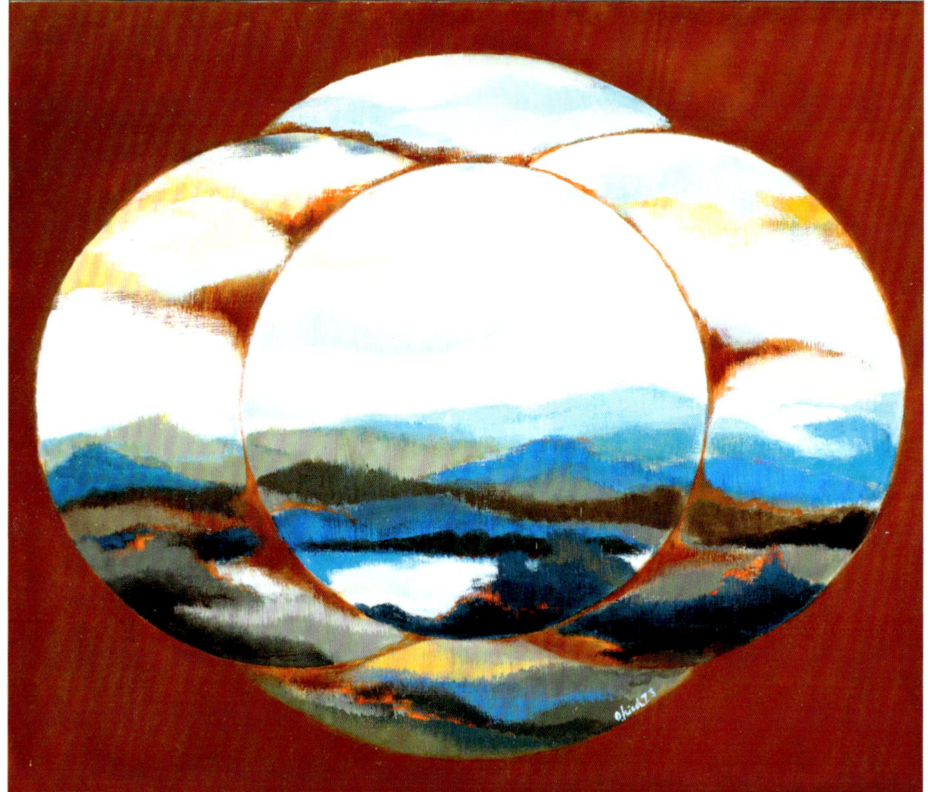

Ohne Titel / Untitled, 1973
Öl auf Leinwand / Oil on canvas
50 x 75 cm
Privatsammlung / Private collection

But Otto was not only a painter of oil on canvas. Almost everything he touched, he painted. He would sit in a restaurant and draw on the napkins... then return to the studio to varnish the crayon markings. Painted napkins, for a period, were everywhere. I often thought he saw more in the napkins than in the conversation surrounding him! He'd paint stones he collected on the beaches, and sticks and natural objects. Now he redesigns food on plates in the kitchen and makes paper sculptures out of tissues and his trousers. He drew in pencil, in pen, in ink, made gouaches, aquarelles, shaped metal and would use any material immediately available.

For my first marriage, Otto drew our wedding invitation. Two semi circles rounded and crossing each other. The symbolism was clear, simple and perfect.

As a wedding gift, he gave us a painting in four parts, of a yacht moving through soft blue water, the sails shimmer in limpid light; all in slightly different versions. It is a happy painting with joy in movement and sits by my desk to this day.

The semi-circles of the wedding invitation in 1972 were an indication of Otto's next period. The Circle Period. For at least a decade he drew circles of all kinds, a deep and profound exploration of the shape. At first they were colored in impressionistically, and then became more abstract in movement and application. The colors were deep browns and blues, with tinges of a gold/yellow, until Otto settled on a blue as his, then, signature color. Blue became the basis, the fundament. The raison d'être. Blue is all things to all men... the color of sadness, the 'blues', the lightness of the sky, the heavens, linked to the sun, happiness. Otto worked not only on one signature blue à la Yves Klein, but a study of all blues; always mixed, always changing.

From the blue circle period Otto branched out into more abstract forms. Gone were the perfect circles, encapsulating studies in color, and in came what I call

jetzt in meinem Wohnzimmer. Jahr für Jahr haben meine Eltern das so gemacht und eins nach dem anderen erworben: Eine impressionistische Ansicht der Berge, wieder einmal und unverkennbar die Alpen, wohl kaum die wilden Rockies und ein anderes, eine berstende Flamme orange- und gelbfarbig – eine impressionistische Ansicht eines Sonnenuntergangs. So füllte sich allmählich unser Apartment mit ‚Ottos'. Er wurde unser Familienkünstler, der unsere Wohnung immer mehr zum Strahlen brachte.

Otto war aber nicht nur ein Öl-auf-Leinwand-Maler. Fast alles, was er berührte, bemalte er. Er saß in einem Restaurant und zeichnete auf die Papierservietten. Dann kehrte er ins Studio zurück, um die Buntstiftmarkierungen zu lackieren. Eine Zeit lang waren in seinem Atelier überall bemalte Servietten. Ich dachte oft, er interessiere sich mehr für die Servietten, als für die Unterhaltungen um ihn herum! Er bemalte Steine, die er an den Stränden gesammelt hatte, Stöcke und andere Dinge. Er zeichnete mit Bleistift, Feder, Tinte, fertigte Gouachen und Aquarelle und formte Metall und verwendete jedes gerade verfügbare Material.

Als ich heiratete, zeichnete Otto unsere Hochzeitseinladung. Zwei Halbkreise gerundet und einander kreuzend. Die Symbolik war klar, einfach und perfekt. Als Hochzeitsgeschenk schenkte er uns ein vierteiliges Gemälde einer Yacht, die sich durch weiches blaues Wasser bewegt. Die Segel schimmern in klarem Licht. Alles in leicht unterschiedlichen Versionen. Es ist ein fröhliches Gemälde mit Freude an der Bewegung; es hat bis heute seinen Platz an meinem Schreibtisch.

Die Halbkreise der Hochzeitseinladung von 1972 waren schon ein Hinweis auf Ottos nächste Periode. Die Kreisperiode. Mindestens drei Jahrzehnte lang zeichnete er Kreise aller Art - eine tiefe und tiefgreifende Erforschung der Form. Zuerst waren sie impressionistisch eingefärbt, dann wurden sie abstrakter in Bewegung und Form. Ihre Farben bestanden aus tiefen Brauns und Blaus mit einem Hauch von Gold/Gelb, bis Otto sich für ein Blau als damals für ihn charakteristische Farbe entschied. Blau war die Basis, das Fundament. Die *raison d'être*. Blau ist alles für alle Menschen... die Farbe der Traurigkeit, der „Blues", aber auch die Leichtigkeit des Himmels, verbunden mit der Sonne, Glück. Otto arbeitete nicht nur an einem *Signature*-Blau wie Yves Kleins, sondern an einer Studie über alle Blaus; immer gemischt, immer wechselnd.

Von der Periode des blauen Kreises aus, schlug Otto eine neue Richtung ein, hin zu abstrakteren Formen. Vorbei waren die perfekten Kreise, die ganze Reihen von Farbstudien in sich bargen, und herein kamen die Tränen, wie ich sie nenne. Ein Getröpfel, vor allem blau. Es skandalisiert das sonst so ansprechende Gemälde. Eine neue Richtung und eine Veränderung wie keine andere zuvor. Ärgerlicher, emotionaler. Weniger weich und zugänglich. Lange Zeit weinten sich diese Tränen durch viele Gemälde, wurden größer und bedeutender. Und als sie wuchsen, wuchs auch die Abstraktion. Kreise sind nie ganz verschwunden, aber die wurden umgeformt und formten sich in unvorstellbarer Weise. Und so wurden seine Bilder immer mehr zu Erkundungen in einer verstörenden Realität.

Weil Otto sich so für die Natur in all ihren Formen interessierte, begann er mit der Idee zu spielen, die Ölgemälde unter Verwendung verschiedener Metalle, die auf seltsame Weise geformt und auf die Gemälde geklebt wurden, in Montagen umzuwandeln. Die Tränen verhärteten sich. Es war, als hätte sich etwas Beunruhigendes in sein Leben eingeschlichen, mit tränenbefleckten Tropfen, eine Vergegenständlichung. Wenn ich Otto danach fragte, antwortete er, er sei „auf Ent-

the tears. A drip drop of largely blue scandalizing the otherwise pleasing painting. A branching out and change like no other. Angrier, more emotional. Less soft and accessible. For a long period these tears wept through many a painting, growing larger and more significant. And as they grew, so did the abstraction. Circles never completely left, but were reshaped and formed in unimaginable ways. And so his paintings became more of an exploration into the disturbing reality.

Because Otto was so interested in nature in all its forms, he began playing with the idea of transforming the oil paintings into montages with the use of various metals shaped in strange ways and glued on to the paintings. The tears of old became metallic and harsh. It was as if something troubling had crept into his life with tear stained drops leading to metallic presentations. When I asked Otto about this, he would reply that he was 'on a voyage of exploration'. Perhaps the underlying anger in Léger's work (or so I believe) had finally inhabited him.

Brancusi, whose beauty in form is self-evident, was especially influential. Instead of making huge sculptures, Otto began making fireside objects, log holders and andirons. He marveled at the word "andirons" meaning the implement that holds the wood, and started to sculpt them. A fireplace never quite looked so charming. From metalwork for fireplaces came other practical and purely aesthetic sculptures, much of which harked back to the movement of circles. The circles morphed into a new form.

Unlike some artists who stick to their single (often successful) visions, Otto changed and moved and explored all the time. Nothing was static, all was an exploration. In this way he was daring, allowing change to occur without fear – not only stylistic changes but also material. Many others have done the same, like Gauguin, Braque and, of course, Picasso. They were all fearless, as is Otto. Otto lives, breathes and works his art. He said there was 'nothing else for him to do'. But that is not entirely the case.

We are in Otto's studio in his Parisian apartment that he shares with his second wife, Micheline de Haardt. He met her at a dinner in New York in the late Sixties. She worked in the international fashion industry in a big way and was a great lover of art (and an excellent draughtswoman herself). He moved to join her in the late Sixties, and I moved to Berlin, Paris and finally London in the early Seventies. I know my move away from America was in part guided by Otto. I never wanted to be too far from him, so great was the breadth of his influence. He had the time, and over time, I became his charge, the person to whom he gave all that he might have given to the child he never had.

The studio has blinds on the windows to slightly dampen the (sometimes) harsh Parisian light. Objects are scattered, collected here and there: cut up bits of paper, mini drawings, photos of his parents (looking so elegant, content and well dressed before the war), and, most especially, a placemat.

This placemat is of the tourist variety, covered in plastic. It depicts the map of St. John, an island in the Caribbean, and part of the U.S. Virgin Islands. It has pride of place in Otto's studio. Next to it sits a large shell, graded and rubbed by the salt water and sea, and next to that is a stone, finely chiseled and smooth on its surface.

St. John was the place where Otto retreated in the Fifties. I don't remember for how long, but he lived, or so he told me, in a beach hut. He looked at nature intensely and alone. That island was especially magnificent, at least before mass tourism. The beaches were pristine white, with soft sand and stunning coral

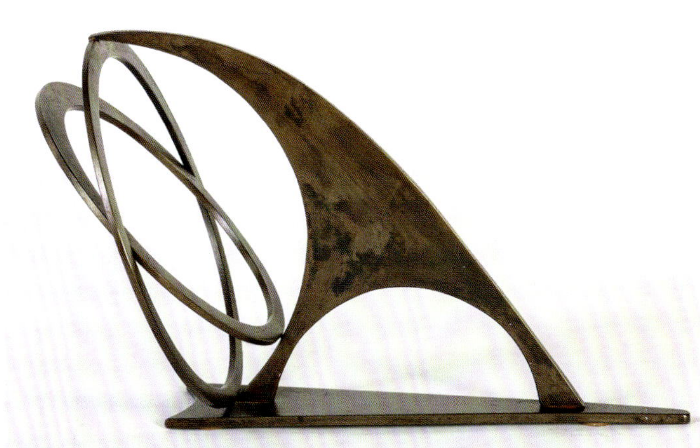

Amitiés, 1996
Bronze mit Patina /
Patinated bronze
31 x 48 x 29 cm
Privatsammlung /
Private collection

deckungsreise". Vielleicht hatte die Wut, die in Légers Werk steckt (das glaube ich zumindest), ihn endlich ergriffen.
Besonders einflussreich war Brancusi. Form und Schönheit ist hier evident. Anstatt riesige Skulpturen zu machen, begann Otto, Kaminobjekte, Holzhalter und „Andirons" herzustellen. Er staunte über das Wort „Andirons", mit dem das Gerät bezeichnet wird, das die Holzscheite hält, und begann, diese Dinge zu formen. Ein Kamin hat noch nie so bezaubernd ausgesehen! Aus Metallarbeiten für Kamine entwickelten sich andere praktische und rein ästhetische Skulpturen, von denen viele auf die Bewegung der Kreise zurückgingen. Die Kreise verwandelten sich in eine neue Form.
Im Gegensatz zu einigen Künstlern, die an ihren einzelnen (oft erfolgreichen) Visionen festhalten, hat sich Otto ständig verändert, er hat sich bewegt und experimentiert. Nichts war statisch, alles war eine Erkundung. Er hatte den Mut, Veränderungen ohne Angst zuzulassen – nicht nur stilistische Veränderungen, sondern auch materielle. Viele andere haben das auch so gemacht, Gauguin, Braque und natürlich Picasso. Sie waren alle furchtlos, genau wie Otto. Otto lebt, atmet seine Kunst. Er sagte, es gäbe „nichts anderes für ihn zu tun".
Das ist aber nicht ganz der Fall.
Wir sind in Ottos Atelier in seiner Pariser Wohnung, die er mit seiner zweiten Frau, Micheline de Haardt, teilt. Er lernte sie bei einem Abendessen in New York kennen. Sie arbeitete an maßgeblicher Stelle in der internationalen Modebranche und war eine große Kunstliebhaberin (und selbst eine ausgezeichnete Zeichnerin). Er zog Anfang der sechziger Jahre zu ihr, und ich zog Anfang der siebziger Jahre nach Berlin, Paris und schließlich nach London. Ich weiß, dass bei meinem Wegzug aus Amerika nicht zuletzt auch Otto eine Rolle spielte. Ich wollte nie allzu weit von ihm weg sein, so groß war sein Einfluss. Er hatte die Zeit, und im Laufe der Jahre übernahm er Verantwortung für mich; ich wurde die Person, der er alles gab, was er dem Kind gegeben haben mochte, das er nie hatte.
Das Atelier hat Jalousien an den Fenstern, um das (manchmal) harte Pariser Licht leicht zu mildern. Gegenstände liegen herum, hier und dort sind sie auch gesammelt: Papierschnipsel, winzige Zeichnungen, Fotos seiner Eltern (die so gut gekleidet, elegant und zufrieden aussahen) und etwas ganz besonderes – ein Platzset aus St. John. Ein touristisches Souvenir mit Plastiküberzug zum Schutz der Karte dieser Karibikinsel, die Teil der US-amerikanischen Jungferninseln ist. Es ist ein Gegenstand hohen Ranges in Ottos Atelier. Daneben liegt

reefs. The coconut palms spread out like eagles against the ever-present breeze. The mangrove swamps allow for fascinating study and the peaceful sun always sets against the backdrop of the other Virgin islands. I know, since most of our family holidays were spent on that island, thanks to Otto. That is the place he was most blissful as a young person, where he kept body and soul as one.

Look at the form of a flower, a simple leaf, varieties of sand and you will get all you need to know, Otto explained, while I sat on the stool in his studio. He would bring me any item he had purloined from beaches, fields, *promenades*. My first Otto lesson was that "no artist can create anything more beautiful than what nature produces".

Otto was a terrific swimmer and mountain climber. In this way, he was very much a German child of the Thirties. No other European country produced such fit and sporty citizens at that time... and he followed suit. He loved his mountains and walking in the clean pure air. When he moved to Paris, he often returned to Germany to be with his 'cousins' and do just that. Perhaps his Alpine walks reminded him of his childhood or even Portland. Another profound lesson is to go out among nature and breathe it in. Never doubt its power. I like to think of Otto as an early ecologist.

His marriage to Micheline changed his fortunes. She had inherited a home in Mittainville, a country house not far from Paris in the *Forêt de Rambouillet*. There he planted apple orchards and worked in a garden as though he were a life-long laborer. In my early adulthood, before I had children, I would spend part of my summers there, watching Otto adoringly observing the trees, the bushes, the branches. For years he made a fantastic Calvados out of his apples. He branded the bottles with his own drawing of apples and proudly labeled each bottle as "Otto's Calva". He would gift it to most visitors and I regret to this day not keeping a bottle, if only for the beauty of the label. Everything became art and art was everything.

Otto, the consummate European, but always claiming to be American, made me sensitive and appreciative. He made me European; he made me understand elegance, beauty, and art. He made me speak languages, and pushed me to speak perfect French and German, continuing to correct me until well into his eighties. These were his three languages and I adopted them as mine too. Otto claimed not to speak any language without an accent, which is true, so that whichever language he speaks, there is a hint of the other two. To this day he moves seamlessly between all three and all three have enriched his life. Along with swimming and hiking, he is extraordinarily well read. Early on, as a teenager in New York, he gave me a treasured photograph of himself, but written on the back is an extract from a poem by de Musset. He told me to keep the photo, not for himself, but for the poem. He had, in my memory, more of a penchant for French literature, and was influenced by the enlightened Voltaire and his sense of freedom. Otto was liberal and all embracing. For years he received a magazine called 'The Progressive', published in America. That was the extent of his political activity, except to abhor injustice wherever he saw it.

His musical taste is classical, pure and simple. He and Micheline went often to the opera. They would spend an evening with music at home, so happily. They were at ease giving dinners and travelled through *le tout Paris* easily. But he always kept up with his friends in America, and wrote a huge amount of letters, always in his elegant hand, describing what he might have observed – whether a

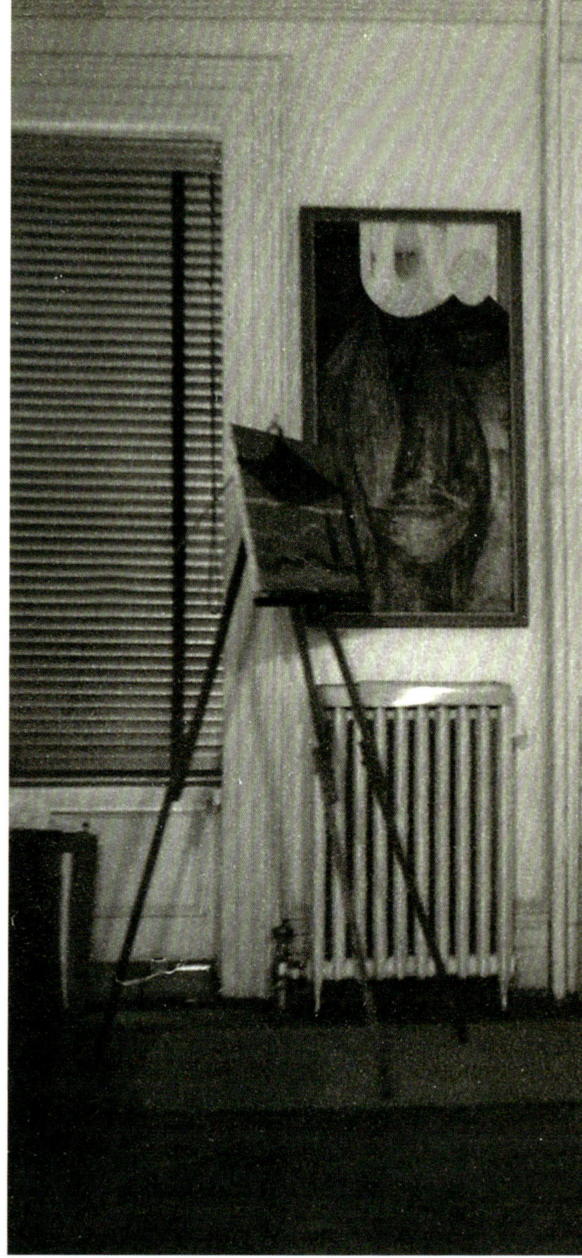

Otto Frieds Atelier um 1950 /
Otto Fried's studio in the 1950s

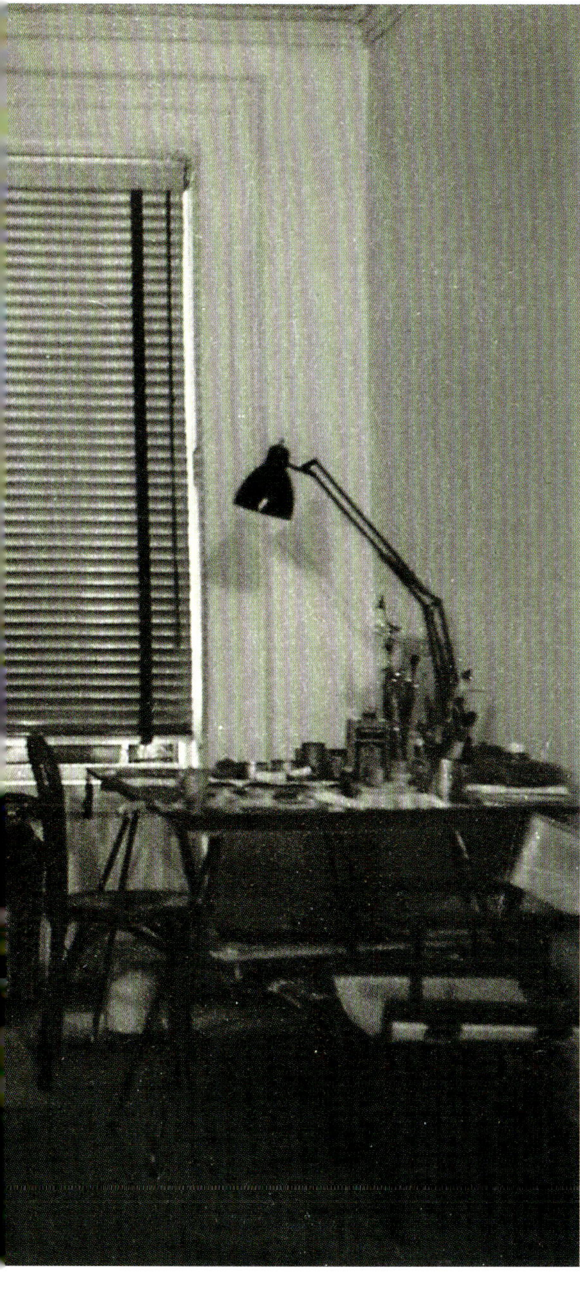

eine große Muschel, die vom Salzwasser und vom Meer ausgeblichen und abgerieben ist, und daneben ein Stein, fein gemeißelt mit glatter Oberfläche.
St. John war der Ort, an den sich Otto in den fünfziger Jahren zurückzog. Ich erinnere mich nicht, wie lange, aber er lebte, wie er es mir erzählte, in einer Strandhütte. Er betrachtete die Natur, ganz intensiv und allein. Diese Insel war besonders großartig, zumindest vor dem Massentourismus. Die Strände – makellos weiß mit weichem Sand und atemberaubenden Korallenriffen. Die Kokospalmen breiten sich wie Adler gegen die allgegenwärtige Brise aus. Die Mangrovensümpfe erlauben die faszinierendsten Studien und die anderen Jungferninseln bilden die Kulisse für einen friedlichen Sonnenuntergang. Ich weiß, wir haben es Otto zu verdanken, dass wir die meisten unserer Familienferien auf dieser Insel verbringen konnten. Dies ist der Ort, an dem er als junger Mensch am glücklichsten war, an dem er Körper und Seele zusammenhalten konnte.
„Schau Dir die Form einer Blume, ein einfaches Blatt oder verschiedene Arten von Sand an und Du hast alles, was Du wissen musst", erklärte Otto, während ich auf dem Hocker in seinem Atelier saß. Er brachte mir dann alle möglichen Objekte, die er an Stränden, auf Feldern und Wegen gefunden hatte. Meine erste Lektion bei Otto war, dass „kein Künstler etwas Schöneres schaffen kann als das, was die Natur hervorbringt".
Otto war ein großartiger Schwimmer und Bergsteiger. In dieser Hinsicht war er ein deutsches Kind der dreißiger Jahre geblieben. Kein anderes europäisches Land hat zu der Zeit so fitte und sportliche Bürger hervorgebracht... und er tat es ihnen gleich. Er liebte seine Berge und ging gern in der sauberen, reinen Luft spazieren. Nachdem er nach Paris gezogen war, kehrte er oft nach Deutschland zurück, um seine Cousine und seinen Cousin und auch seine Koblenzer Freunde wiederzusehen. Vielleicht erinnerten ihn diese Wanderungen an seine Kindheit oder an seine Touren in Portland. Eine weitere Lektion, die ich lernte, war, in die Natur hinauszugehen und sie ein- und auszuatmen. Zweifle niemals an ihrer Kraft! Ich sehe Otto deshalb als einen frühen Ökologen.
Seine Ehe mit Micheline erweiterte seine Möglichkeiten. Sie hatte ein Haus in Mittainville geerbt, ein Landhaus unweit von Paris im *Forêt de Rambouillet*. Dort pflanzte er Apfelbäume und arbeitete in einem Garten, als wäre er nie etwas anderes als ein Landarbeiter gewesen. Im frühen Erwachsenenalter, bevor ich Kinder hatte, verbrachte ich oft einen Teil meines Sommers dort und sah, wie gern Otto Bäume, Büsche und Zweige beim Wachsen beobachtete. Aus seinen Äpfeln machte er jedes Jahr einen fantastischen Calvados. Er hatte da seine eigene Marke: Stolz etikettierte er die Flaschen mit seinen eigenen Zeichnungen von Äpfeln und dem Namen „Ottos Calva". Er schenkte den meisten Besuchern eine davon, und ich bedauere, dass ich bis heute keine Flasche behalten habe, schon allein wegen der Schönheit der Etiketten. Alles wurde Kunst und Kunst war alles.
Otto, der vollendete Europäer, der aber immer behauptete, Amerikaner zu sein, machte mich sensibel und dankbar. Er machte mich zur Europäerin. Er brachte mir sein Verständnis von Eleganz, Schönheit und Kunst nahe. Er brachte mich dazu, Sprachen zu sprechen, und drängte mich, perfektes Französisch und Deutsch zu sprechen, indem er mich bis weit in seine achtziger Jahre hinein korrigierte. Dies waren seine drei Sprachen und ich nahm sie auch als meine an. Otto behauptete, keine Sprache ohne Akzent zu sprechen, was stimmt, so dass, welche Sprache er auch immer spricht, da auch immer ein Hauch der

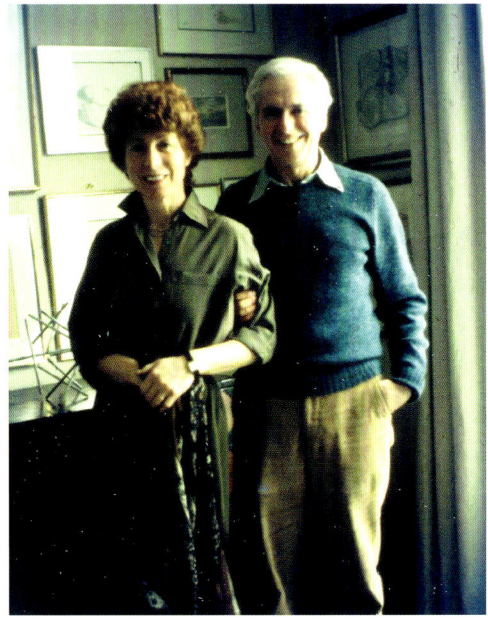

Otto und seine Frau Micheline in ihrer Wohnung in Paris, März 1981 / Otto and his wife Micheline in their home in Paris, March 1981

simple flower or a grand exhibition, but rarely how he felt. Feelings and emotion came through paintings and art. He never complained, never became enraged, never was sick, never made demands. He taught me too to maintain elegance when all might be crumbling around.
Above all, he made me understand how to come through adversity without dwelling on the horrors of the world. How to charm the world and be charmed by it. He is a consummate literate artist, brimming with health, humble in the extreme, elegant, generous spirited, yet very private.
He would say "I am the paintings, there is little else to say about me."

Post-scriptum

I write during the corona virus epidemic and hence have not been able to see Otto for my monthly encounters with him in Paris. I miss him. Even though he may only now have a vague inkling of the pandemic facing us all, I wonder what he would do, if he were fully aware, in the current isolation. My view is that he would be content. He would paint, he would read, listen to music, he would play with his objects, he would contemplate beauty.
Perhaps that is a lesson for us all.

Remerciements

There are two people whom I would like to recognize in the life of Otto and my own.
The first is Marie-Laure Pannier, Micheline's goddaughter. I met Marie-Laure when I first came to Europe and we have been close for nearly 50 years ever since. She too loves Otto, and the two of us are their daughters in spirit. I think of her as part of *ma grande famille.*
The second is Barbara Wolbert, whom I only recently met, but whose devotion to Otto is remarkable and life-affirming. I am indebted to her for this opportunity to celebrate Otto and his work together.

Lisa Forrell, 05.30.2020
Otto's goddaughter

beiden anderen zu hören ist. Bis heute bewegt er sich nahtlos zwischen allen drei Sprachen. Alle drei haben sein Leben bereichert.
Er ist außerordentlich belesen. Als Teenager in New York gab er mir schon früh ein Foto von sich, das ich wie einen Schatz hüte. Auf die Rückseite hat er Zeilen eines Gedichts von de Musset geschrieben. Er sagte mir, ich solle das Foto nicht wegen des Bildes von ihm sondern wegen des Gedichts aufbewahren. Er hatte in meiner Erinnerung eher eine Vorliebe für französische Literatur und war von dem aufgeklärten Voltaire und dessen Freiheitsgefühl beeinflusst. Otto war liberal und offen für alles. Jahrelang erhielt er eine in Amerika veröffentlichte Zeitschrift namens „The Progressive". Das war sein Maß an politischer Aktivität, außer Ungerechtigkeit zu verabscheuen, wo immer er sie wahrnahm. Sein Musikgeschmack ist klassisch. Er und Micheline gingen oft in die Oper. Sie verbrachten auch manche Abende voller Glück mit Musik zu Hause. Unangestrengt gaben sie Abendessen und bewegten sich ganz selbstverständlich durch *Le tout Paris*. Aber er blieb immer auf dem Laufenden wie es seinen Freunden in Amerika gerade ging und schrieb - immer in seiner eleganten Handschrift – unzählige Briefen, in denen er beschrieb, was er beobachtet hatte – ob eine einfache Blume oder eine große Ausstellung – aber selten, wie er sich fühlte. Gefühle und Emotionen kamen durch Malerei und Kunst. Er beschwerte sich nie, wurde nie wütend, war nie krank, stellte nie Forderungen. Er brachte mir auch bei, Eleganz zu bewahren, wenn alles zusammenbricht.
Vor allem hat er mir verständlich gemacht, wie ich durch mancherlei Widrigkeiten kommen kann, ohne viel über die Schrecken der Welt nachzudenken. Wie man die Welt bezaubert und sich von ihr verzaubern lässt. Er ist ein vollendeter, gebildeter Künstler voller Gesundheit, äußerst bescheiden, elegant, großzügig, temperamentvoll und doch sehr privat.
Er würde sagen: „Ich bin die Bilder, es gibt wenig anderes über mich zu sagen".

Post-Scriptum

Ich schreibe während der Corona-Virus-Epidemie und konnte Otto daher nicht wie sonst einmal im Monat in Paris besuchen. Ich vermisse ihn. Auch wenn er vielleicht jetzt erst eine vage Ahnung von der Pandemie hat, mit der wir alle konfrontiert sind, frage ich mich, was er in der gegenwärtigen Isolation wohl tut. Ich denke, er wird zufrieden sein. Er wird malen, er wird lesen, er wird Musik hören, er wird mit den Dingen spielen, die ihn umgeben und sich Gedanken über Schönheit machen. Vielleicht ist das eine Lehre für uns alle.

Dankausgang

Es gibt zwei Menschen im Leben von Otto und meinem eigenen, die ich erwähnen möchte. Die erste ist Marie-Laure Pannier, Michelines Patentochter. Ich habe Marie-Laure kennengelernt, als ich zum ersten Mal nach Europa kam und seitdem sind wir uns sehr nahe. Auch sie liebt Otto, und wir beide sind im Geiste ihre Töchter. Ich denke an sie als Teil von *ma grande famille*.
Die zweite ist Barbara Wolbert, die ich erst kürzlich kennengelernt habe, deren Zuwendung zu Otto jedoch bemerkenswert und lebensbejahend ist. Ich bin ihr zu Dank verpflichtet für diese Gelegenheit, sowohl Otto als auch sein Werk zu feiern.

Lisa Forrell, 30.05.2020
Ottos Patentochter

Metal Relief Sculptures.
Otto Fried Interviewed by Kenneth Snelson, Summer 1991

Introduction

Otto Fried and the American artist Kenneth Snelson met in 1947 while studying in the painting class of artist Jack Wilkinson. In 1951 the two young artists went to Paris after their studies, where they worked in the studio of Fernand Léger. Snelson, who attended a summer course at Black Mountain College during his studies, where he assisted the inventor R. Buckminster Fuller, arranged Fried's meeting with Buckminster Fuller in New York in 1952. Although the two artists had a completely differently evolution, they remained close throughout their lives, with regular exchanges.

In December 1991 Otto Fried exhibited his *Metal Relief Sculptures* in the Achim Moeller Fine Art Gallery in New York. The works – shaped by geometric, cubist forms that protrude from the picture space in relief – are reminiscent of Pablo Picasso's collages and assemblages, while representing really a translation of Fried's abstract circular compositions from the previous years into a new, three-dimensional medium. Kenneth Snelson interviewed his friend Otto Fried about these artworks in the summer of 1991 and talked to him about matters, technique, technology, inspiration, influences, artistic development and the time they spent studying together...

Interview

Kenneth Snelson: As I recall, we met in the spring of 1947, both on the GI Bill, at the University of Oregon, in Jack Wilkinson's painting class. Then we were in Paris in 1951. If memory serves, I recall that you turned up regularly at Fernand Léger's Académie Montmartre. I mostly played hookey, photographing Paris. Well, including our years in New York, we've been talking about art for some forty-four years.

Otto Fried: We've certainly had our share of creative experiences, and these have been at the heart of our conversations. I still believe that the GI Bill was the single greatest present we ever got. It opened up a world for anyone wanting to take advantage of its untold opportunities. Jack Wilkinson was also a boon on us, at the university. We were lucky to have him stir us up through his challenges of all our ideas, about visual art and the life of the mind. Paris meant another large step in my meeting the post-philosopher Lawrence Margolis, who has enlarged my world considerably ever since.

KS: I have seen your paper works in three dimensions and now you are developing these pieces in metal. Does the change in material have a substantial influence in these later works?

OF: I suppose there is a continued give-and-take with all new steps. My earlier paper work, which was first flat then led into shaped constructions, is definitely related to my metal shapes, and the textural qualities are continued with a variety of new results. It is the fragility of the Kraft paper that natural led me into metal.

KS: These three-dimentional pieces aren't exactly a revolution for you, since you've often explored sculptural ideas, but how long have you been working on these new deep-relief pieces and how did they develop?

OF: As you may remember, in Jack Wilkinson's design classes we explored a variety of materials, in particular paper and cardboard, to develop our understanding of their formal properties. So these forms have been part of my life ever since, but I had never produced these in a really concerted effort until the summer of 1987, when I became fascinated by the color of Kraft paper. I had been commissioned to do a large piece for a terrace and realized, of course, that the paper would not withstand the wind. I used metal sheets, essentially aluminum and lead, that I could handle almost as easily as paper.

KS: Are there any particular influences — say, of the French school, the Cubists or Constructivists — which you think of, when working on these pieces?

OF: In 1950 I learned a French proverb: "One is always the son of someone," and of course I remember well the multimedia constructions of the Cubist movement which I first saw in 1947. I believe though that my present involvement is a new variation. Each time I pick up a new piece of metal, I am uncertain of the shape it will take. Metal seems to have a life of its own. It has a recalcitrant quality, and I try to take advantage of this as an ever-renewing source.

KS: Am I correct in characterizing them as deep reliefs? Or do you prefer to think

Metal Relief Sculptures.

Otto Fried interviewt von Kenneth Snelson, Sommer 1991

Einleitung

Otto Fried und der amerikanische Künstler Kenneth Snelson lernten sich 1947 im Rahmen ihres Studiums in der Malereiklasse des Künstlers Jack Wilkinson kennen. 1951 gingen die beiden jungen Künstler im Anschluss an ihr Studium nach Paris, wo sie im Atelier des Künstler Fernand Léger arbeiteten. Snelson, der während seines Studiums einen Sommerkurs am Black Mountain College besuchte, bei welchem er dem Erfinder R. Buckminster Fuller assistierte, arrangierte 1952 ein Treffen Frieds mit Buckminster Fuller in New York. Gleichwohl sich beide Künstler völlig unterschiedlich entwickeln, bleiben sie zeitlebens durch eine enge Freundschaft und den regelmäßigen Austausch verbunden.

Im Dezember 1991 stellt Otto Fried seine "Metal Relief Sculptures" in der Galerie Achim Moeller Fine Art in New York aus.[1] Die Werke – geprägt durch geometrische, kubistische Formen, die reliefartig aus dem Bildraum ragen – erinnern an Collagen und Assemblagen Pablo Picassos, sind jedoch vielmehr eine Übersetzung Frieds abstrakter Kreiskompositionen der vorausgehenden Jahre in ein neues, dreidimensionales Medium. Über ebendiese Werke interviewte Kenneth Snelson seinen Freund Otto Fried im Sommer 1991 und sprach mit ihm über Material, Technik, Inspiration, Einflüsse, künstlerische Entwicklung und die gemeinsame Zeit des Studiums…

Interview

Kenneth Snelson: Wenn ich mich recht erinnere, trafen wir uns im Frühjahr 1947, an der Universität von Oregon in Jack Wilkinsons Malklasse, beide gefördert durch das GI-Gesetz. Dann waren wir 1951 in Paris. Wenn ich mich recht erinnere, bist du regelmäßig in Fernand Légers Académie Montmartre aufgetaucht. Ich habe meist geschwänzt und Paris fotografiert. Nun, einschließlich unserer Jahre in New York haben wir vierundvierzig Jahre lang über Kunst gesprochen.

Otto Fried: Wir haben gewiss unsere kreativen Erfahrungen miteinander geteilt, und diese standen im Mittelpunkt unserer Gespräche. Ich glaube immer noch, dass das GI-Gesetz das größte Geschenk war, das wir je bekommen haben. Es eröffnete eine Welt für jeden, der seine unzähligen Möglichkeiten nutzen wollte. Jack Wilkinson war auch ein Segen für uns an der Universität. Wir hatten das Glück, dass er uns durch seine Herausforderungen in Bezug auf all unsere Ideen, über visuelle Kunst und das Leben des Geistes, aufrüttelte. Paris bedeutete für mich einen weiteren großen Schritt bei der Begegnung mit dem Post-Philosophen Lawrence Margolis, der meine Welt seither erheblich erweitert hat.

KS: Ich habe deine dreidimensionalen Papierarbeiten gesehen, und nun überträgst du diese Arbeiten in Metall. Hat die Veränderung des Materials einen wesentlichen Einfluss auf diese späteren Arbeiten?

OF: Ich nehme an, dass es bei allen neuen Schritten ein ständiges Geben und Nehmen gibt. Meine früheren Papierarbeiten, die zuerst flache, dann dreidimensionale Konstruktionen waren, stehen definitiv mit meinen Metallkonstruktionen in Verbindung, und die texturalen Qualitäten werden darin mit einer Vielzahl neuer Ergebnisse fortgesetzt. Es ist die Fragilität des Kraftpapiers, die mich auf natürliche Weise zum Metall geführt hat.

KS: Diese dreidimensionalen Werke sind für dich genau genommen keine Revolution, da du dich oft mit skulpturalen Ideen beschäftigt hast, aber wie lange arbeitest du schon an diesen neuen Tiefreliefarbeiten und wie haben sie sich entwickelt?

OF: Wie du dich vielleicht erinnerst, haben wir in Jack Wilkinsons Design-Kursen eine Vielzahl von Materialien, insbesondere Papier und Karton, untersucht, um Verständnis für ihre formalen Eigenschaften zu entwickeln. Diese Formen sind seither Teil meines Lebens, aber ich hatte sie nie in einem wirklich konzertierten Versuch verwendet, bis zum Sommer 1987, als ich von der Farbe des Kraftpapiers fasziniert wurde. Ich hatte den Auftrag erhalten, ein großes Werk für eine Terrasse zu machen, und natürlich erkannte ich, dass das Papier dem Wind nicht standhalten würde. Ich verwendete Metallbleche, im Wesentlichen Aluminium und Blei, die ich fast so leicht handhaben konnte wie Papier.

KS: Gibt es besondere Einflüsse – etwa der französischen Schule der Kubisten oder Konstruktivisten –, an die du bei der Arbeit an diesen Stücken denkst?

OF: 1950 lernte ich ein französisches Sprichwort: „Man ist immer der Sohn

of them as sculptures which are seen through 180° rather than 360°? Can you experience them equally off to the side, or is the frontal view the essential one?

OF: Honestly, I can't think of my structures as sculpture. I believe a sculpture involves a visual experience that allows form and light that move in all 360°. It needs to be seen from all angles and, as happens in your own work, even from underneath, if possible. I think of my work as high or deep reliefs that should be seen essentially from the front.

KS: To what extent are you concerned with familiar issues, subject matter, symbolism, literary content? You see, as one surveys the current art world, one has a clear sense that political art or message-oriented art is in favor. What are your thoughts on these trends? After all, you and I came from a time of different attitudes and beliefs. We were brought up to have a certain faith that the visual, not the temporal message, was primary.

OF: None of my present work contains any of the current issues mentioned in your question. My principal concerns are formal ones. Formal concerns are the length and breadth, the full extent of what I consider the essential qualities in the creative process. Technique concerns me. I am aware that another person looking at my work may indeed see some variety of visual messages. This might be the effect of my titles... . After all, most known musical compositions have titles added long after their creation and are all too often reinterpreted by some listeners with the title in mind. My own titles are mostly fanciful afterthoughts.

KS: Because you are best known for paintings and two-dimensional works, do you regard color any differently here since you are dealing with three dimensions, and with material other than canvas?

OF: I have retained my love of color with my choice of the various metals I use. Also, my love of texture is an important part of my technique. I enhance flat and often shiny metals with a variety of acids brushed on, just like my work on canvas or paper. The shadow and light qualities are another color consideration.

KS: How would you like people to experience your new work? What would you hope they would come away with?

OF: Of course, while working I never think of what the reaction of another will be. There are so many involvements which take over all my concerns during this process. I remember that when I was a small child and I discovered something exciting to look at, I needed to share it immediately. Now I like to wait until a work is definitely finished before showing it to someone else. I do realize that my latest work takes on an added life through the eyes of other people, and that this extension is a necessity. My hope is that others will be able to participate in my work and thereby increase their own visual pleasure.

This Interview was originally published in: Exh.-Cat. *Otto Fried: Metal Relief Structures*, Achim Moeller Fine Arts, New York, November 20 - December 20, 1991.
Reprinted with authorization of Moeller Fine Art, New York.

1 Exhibition *Otto Fried: Metal Relief Sculptures*, 20 November 1990 to 20 Dezember 1990, Achim Moeller Fine Arts, New York.

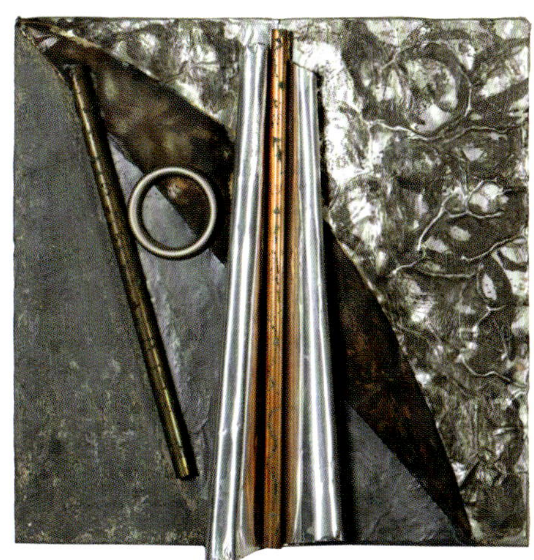

Silence, 1991
Kupfer, Chrom, Aluminium Acide /
Copper, chrom, aluminium acide
39 x 38 x 5 cm
Sammlung des Künstlers /
Collection of the Artist

von jemandem", und natürlich erinnere ich mich gut an die multimedialen Konstruktionen der kubistischen Bewegung, die ich 1947 zum ersten Mal sah. Ich glaube aber, dass mein heutiges Schaffen eine neue Variation ist. Jedes Mal, wenn ich ein neues Stück Metall in die Hand nehme, bin ich unsicher, welche Form es annehmen wird. Metall scheint ein Eigenleben zu führen. Es hat eine widerspenstige Qualität, und ich versuche, diese als eine sich ständig erneuernde Quelle zu nutzen.

KS: Liege ich richtig, wenn ich sie als tiefe Reliefs bezeichne? Oder ziehst du es vor, sie als Skulpturen zu betrachten, die aus einer 180° Perspektive statt aus 360° gesehen werden? Kann man sie auch von der Seite betrachten, oder ist die Frontalansicht die Wesentliche?

OF: Ehrlich gesagt, kann ich mir diese Strukturen nicht als Skulpturen vorstellen. Ich glaube, eine Skulptur beinhaltet eine visuelle Erfahrung, die Form und Licht erlaubt sich vollständig darum zu bewegen. Sie muss aus allen Blickwinkeln betrachtet werden können und, so wie bei deinen Werken, wenn möglich sogar von unten. Ich betrachte meine Werke als Hoch- oder Tiefreliefs, die im Wesentlichen von vorne gesehen werden sollten.

KS: Inwieweit beschäftigst du dich mit vertrauten Themen, Gegenständen, Symboliken, oder literarischen Inhalten? Siehst du, wenn man sich die aktuelle Kunstwelt ansieht, hat man ein klares Gefühl, dass besonders politische oder auf Botschaften ausgerichtete Kunst beliebt ist. Was sind deine Gedanken zu diesen Tendenzen? Schließlich kommen wir aus einer Zeit anderer Einstellungen und Überzeugungen. Wir wurden dazu erzogen, einen gewissen Glauben daran zu haben, dass die visuelle und nicht die zeitliche Botschaft vorrangig ist.

OF: Keines meiner gegenwärtigen Werke enthält eines dieser aktuellen Themen, die du erwähnst. Meine Hauptanliegen sind formaler Natur. Formale Anliegen sind die Länge und Breite, das volle Ausmaß dessen, was ich für die wesentlichen Qualitäten im kreativen Prozess halte. Die Technik interessiert mich. Ich bin mir bewusst, dass eine andere Person, die meine Arbeit betrachtet, in der Tat eine gewisse Vielfalt an visuellen Botschaften sehen kann. Dies könnte der Effekt meiner Werktitel sein... Schließlich werden den meisten bekannten Musikkompositionen erst lange nach ihrer Entstehung Titel hinzugefügt und nur allzu von manchen Zuhörern mit diesem Titel im Hinterkopf neu interpretiert. Meine eigenen Titel sind meist phantasievolle Nachgedanken.

KS: Da du vor allem für Gemälde und zweidimensionale Werke bekannt bist, betrachtest du die Farbe hier anders, da du mit drei Dimensionen und anderem Material als der Leinwand umgehen musst?

OF: Ich habe mir die Liebe zur Farbe bei der Wahl der verschiedenen Metalle, die ich verwende, bewahrt. Auch meine Liebe zur Textur ist ein wichtiger Teil meiner Technik. Ich veredle die flachen und oft glänzenden Metalle mit einer Vielzahl von Säuren, die mit dem Pinsel aufgetragen werden, genau wie bei meinen Arbeiten auf Leinwand oder Papier. Die Schatten- und Lichtqualitäten sind eine weitere Farbüberlegung.

KS: Wie wünschst du dir, dass Menschen deine neuen Arbeiten erleben? Was würdest du dir von Ihnen erhoffen?

OF: Natürlich denke ich während der Arbeit nie daran, wie die Reaktion eines anderen sein wird. Es gibt so viele Aspekte, die alle meine Bedenken während dieses Prozesses angreifen. Ich erinnere mich daran, dass ich, als ich ein kleines Kind war und etwas Spannendes entdeckte, das es zu betrachten galt, ich es sofort mitteilen musste. Jetzt warte ich gerne, bis ein Werk definitiv fertig ist, bevor ich es jemand anderem zeige. Mir ist klar, dass mein neuestes Werk durch die Augen anderer Menschen ein zusätzliches Leben erhält und dass diese Erweiterung eine Notwendigkeit ist. Meine Hoffnung ist, dass andere an meiner Arbeit teilhaben und dadurch ihre eigene visuelle Freude steigern können.

Dieses Interview wurde ursprünglich veröffentlicht in: „Otto Fried: Metal Relief Structures", Ausstellungskatalog, Achim Moeller Fine Arts, New York, 20. November – 20. Dezember 1991.
Nachdruck mit Genehmigung von Moeller Fine Art, New York.

1 Ausstellung „Otto Fried: Metal Relief Sculptures", 20. November 1990 bis 20. Dezember 1990, Achim Moeller Fine Arts, New York.

WERKE WORKS 1980-1987

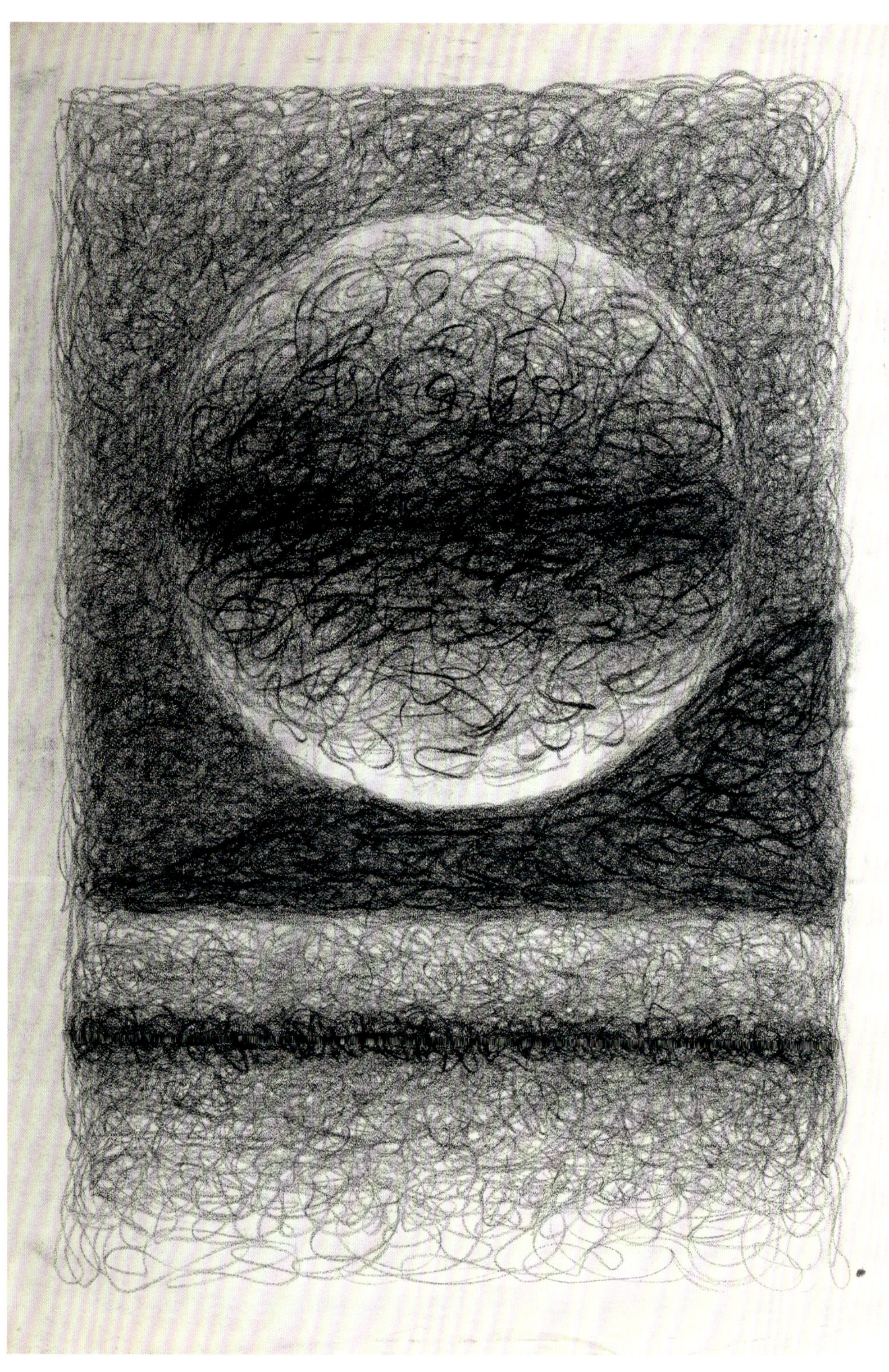

OHNE TITEL / UNTITLED
Circa 1980
Grafit / Kohle auf Papier / Graphite / charcoal on paper

OHNE TITEL / UNTITLED
Circa 1980
Grafit / Kohle auf Papier / Graphite / charcoal on paper

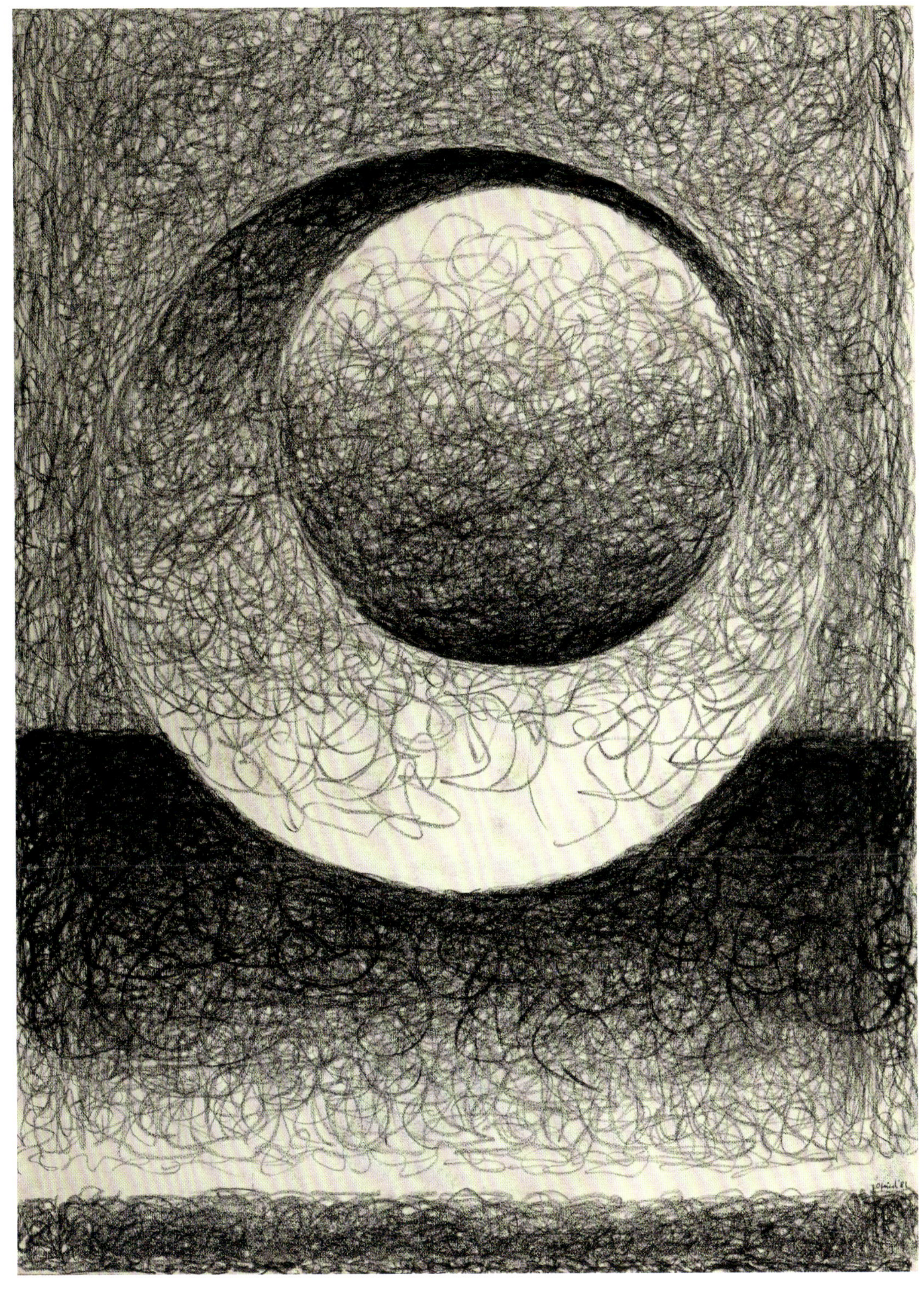

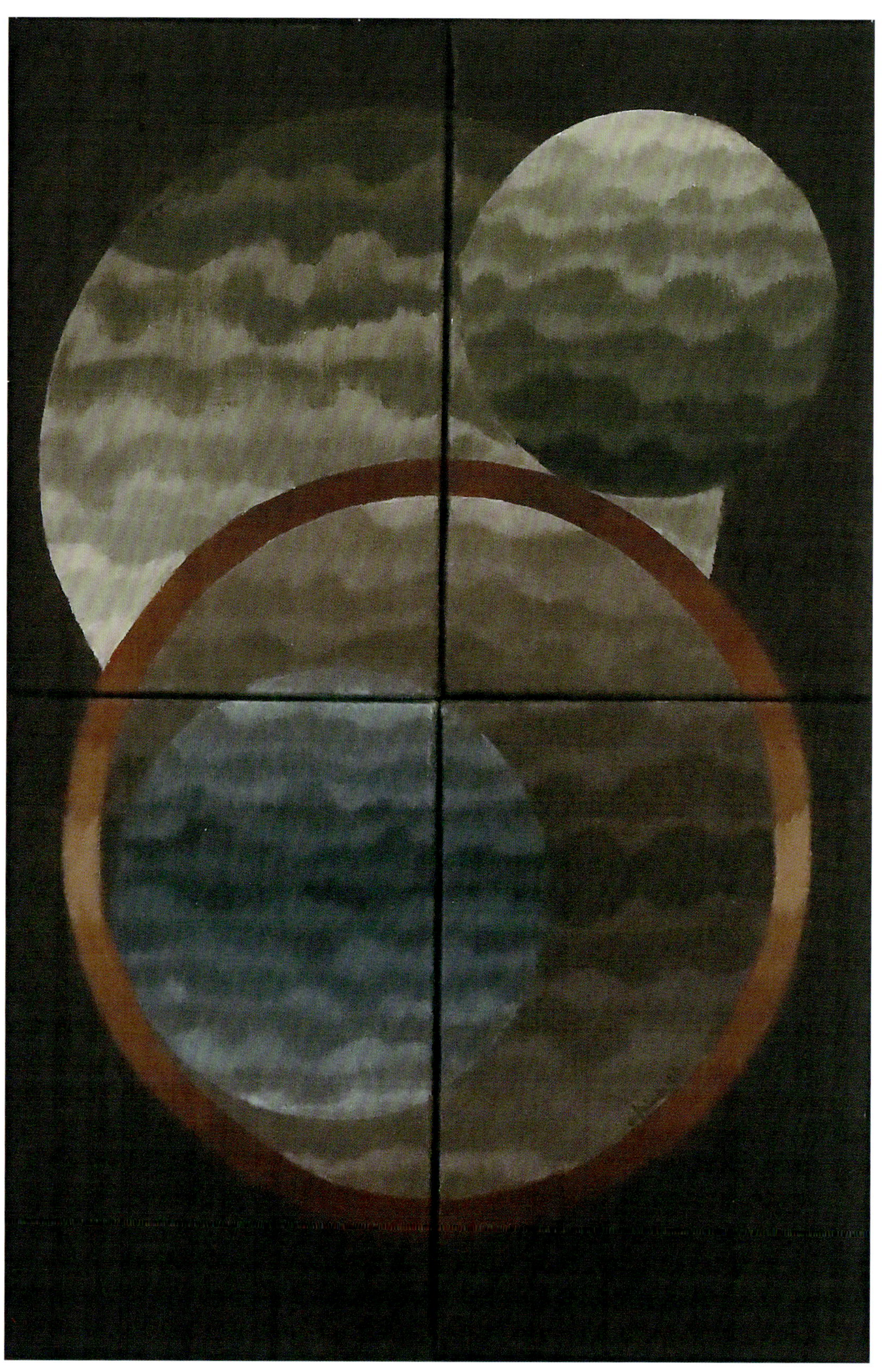

MEASURED INFINITIES
1980
Öl / Acryl auf Leinwand / Oil / acryl on canvas

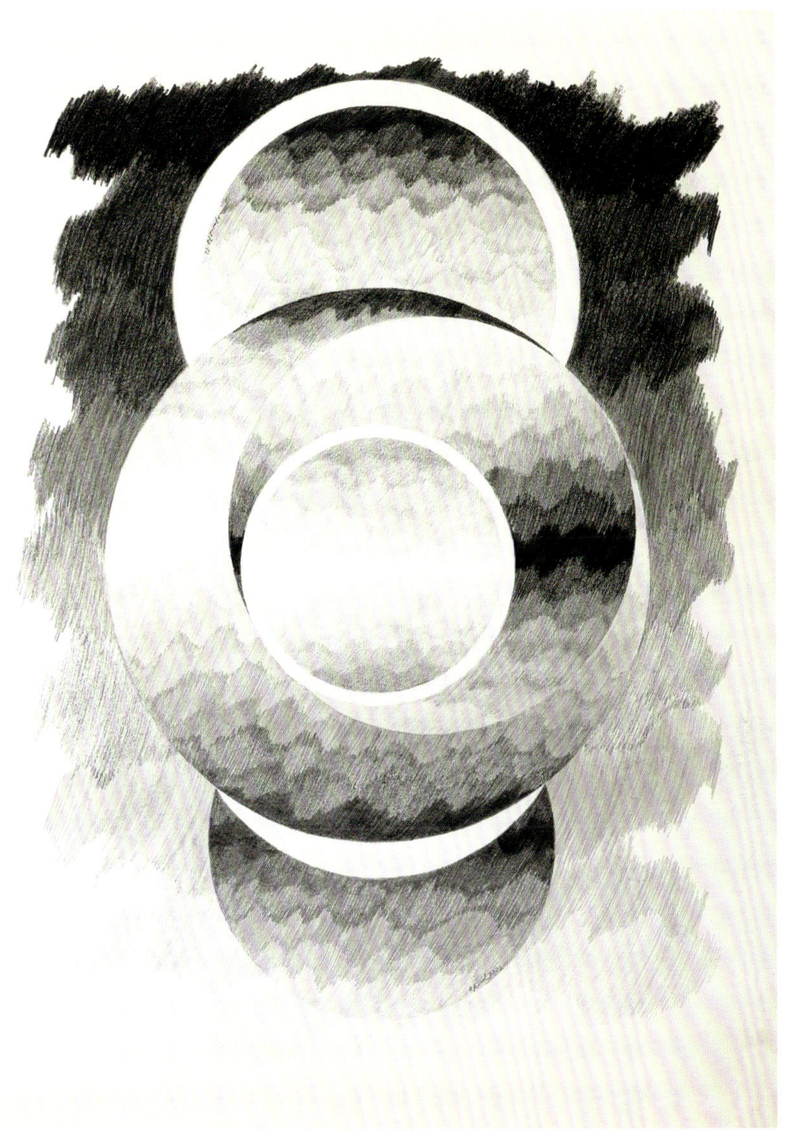

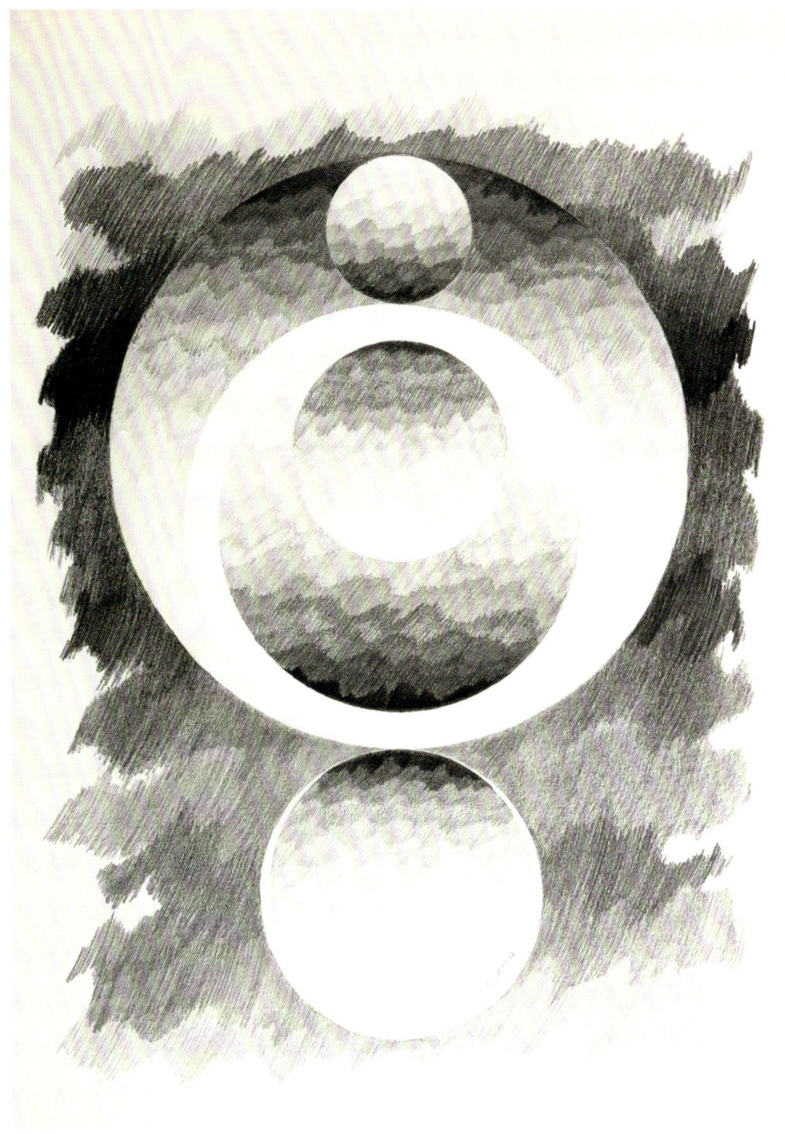

OHNE TITEL / UNTITLED
Circa 1982
Grafit auf Papier / Graphite on paper

OHNE TITEL / UNTITLED
Circa 1983
Grafit auf Papier / Graphite on paper

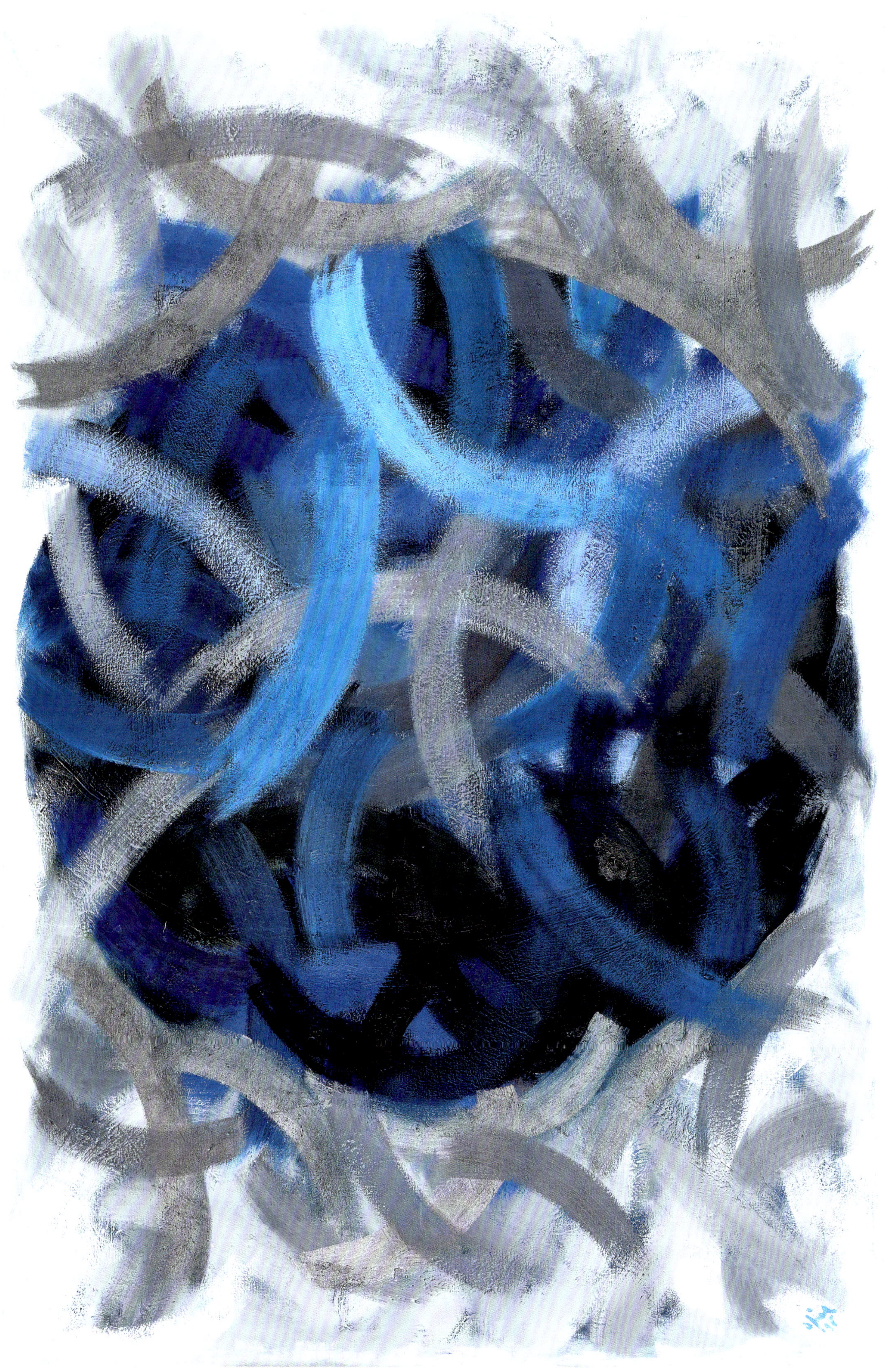

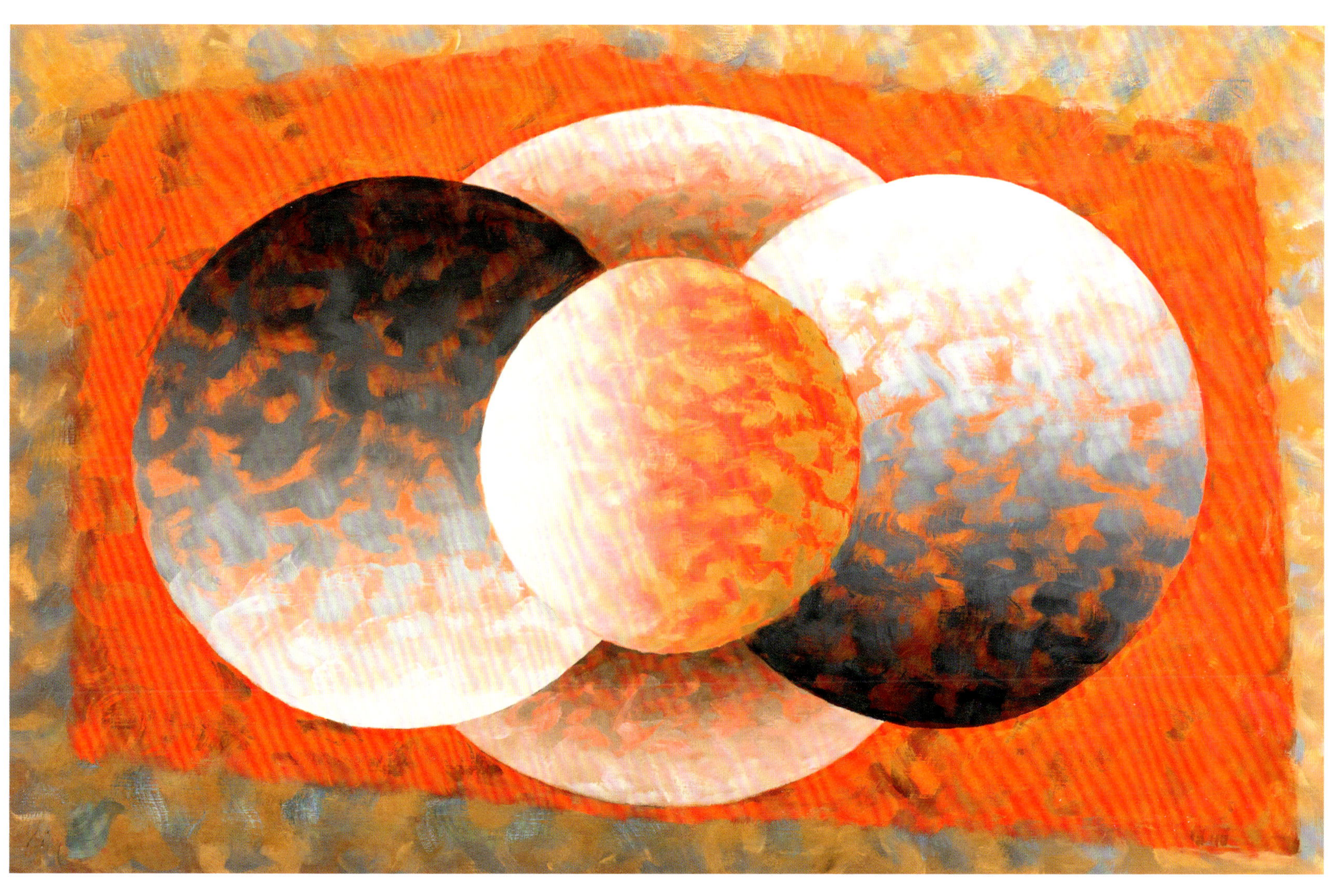

GREVED TAO
1982 / 1983
Öl auf Leinwand / Oil on canvas

SUMMER RAGA / RAGA D'ÉTÉ
1985
Öl auf Leinwand / Oil on canvas

Folgende Seiten / Following pages

TOMORROW'S FIELDS
1985
Öl auf Leinwand / Oil on canvas

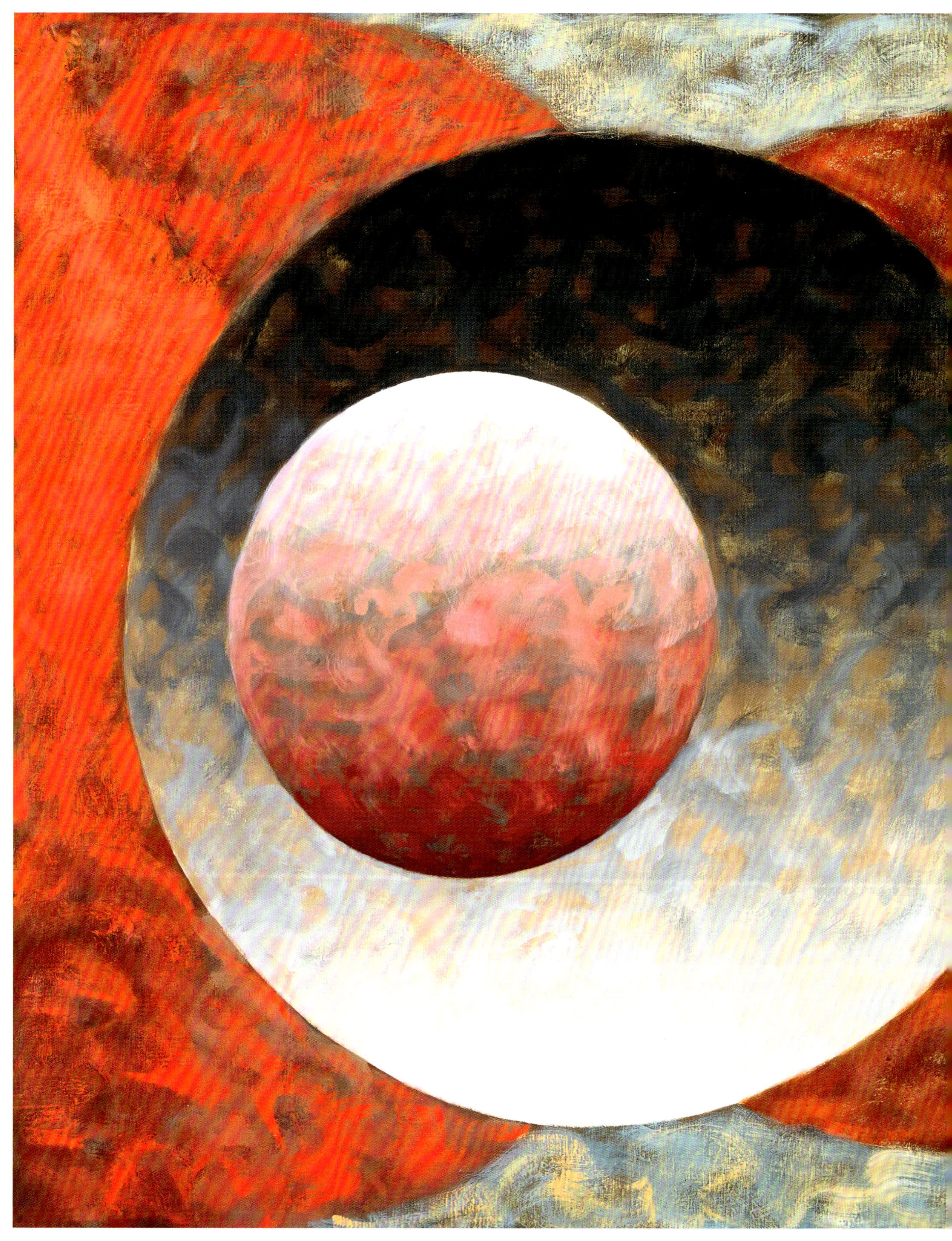

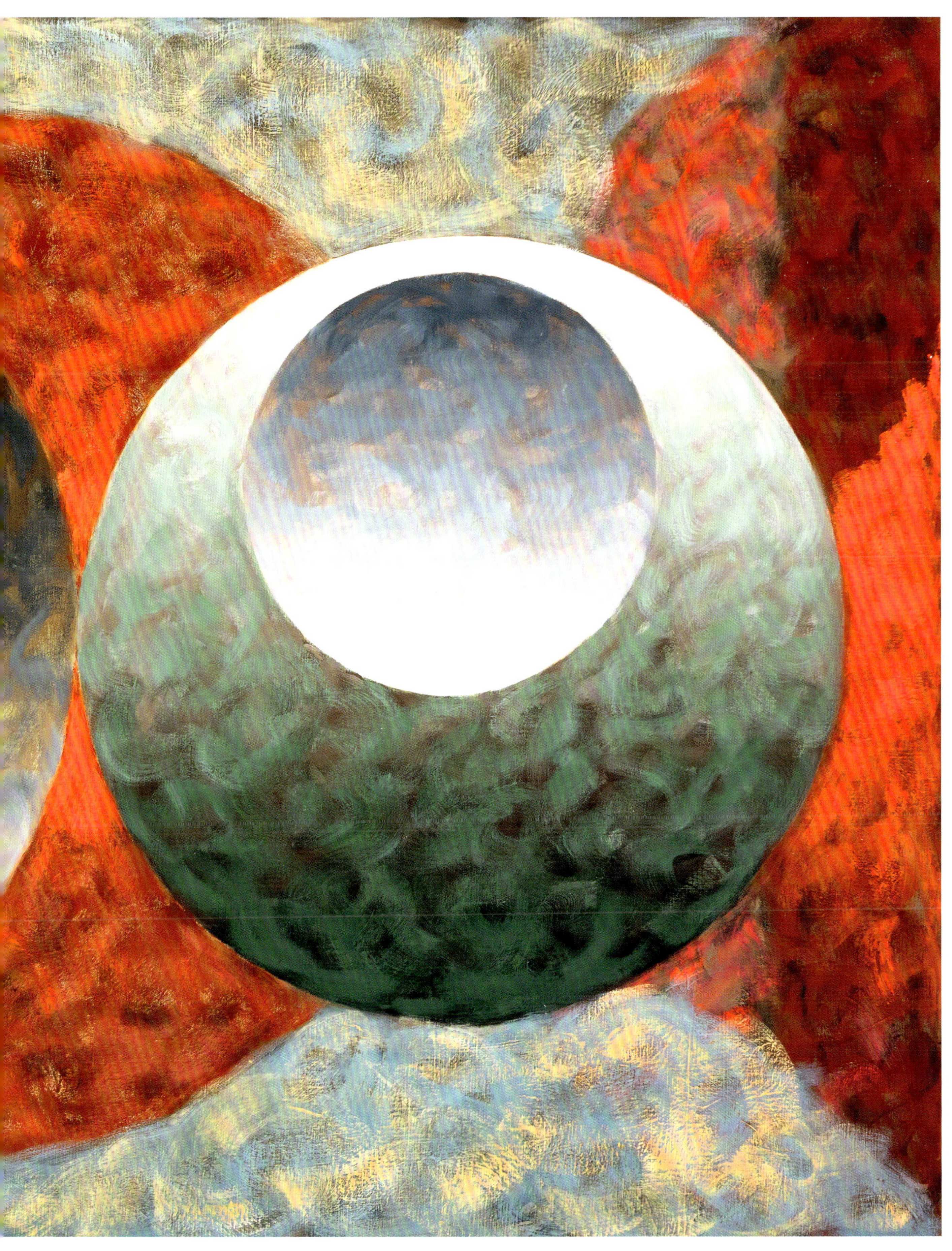

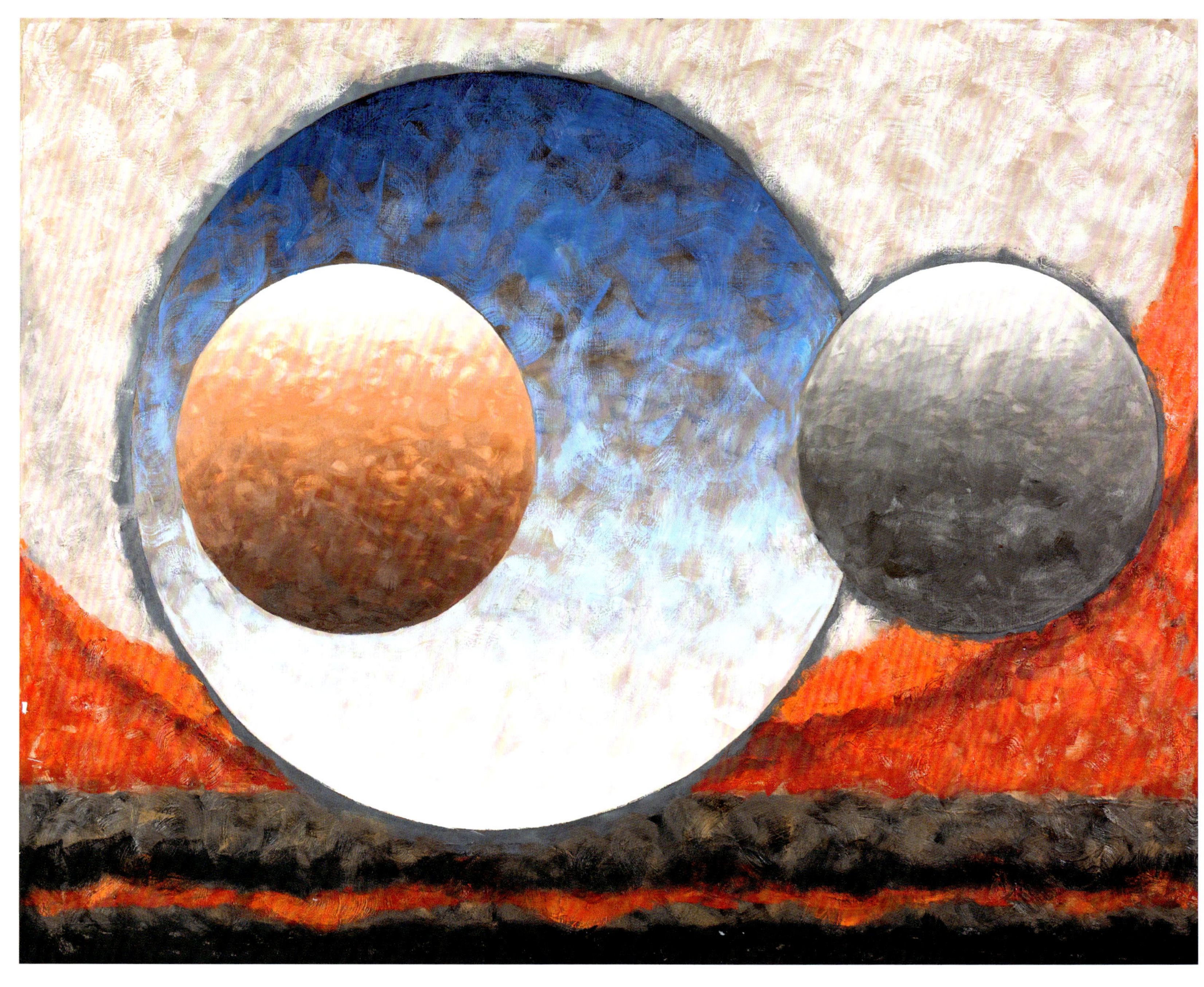

WORLDS APART
1986
Öl auf Leinwand / Oil on canvas

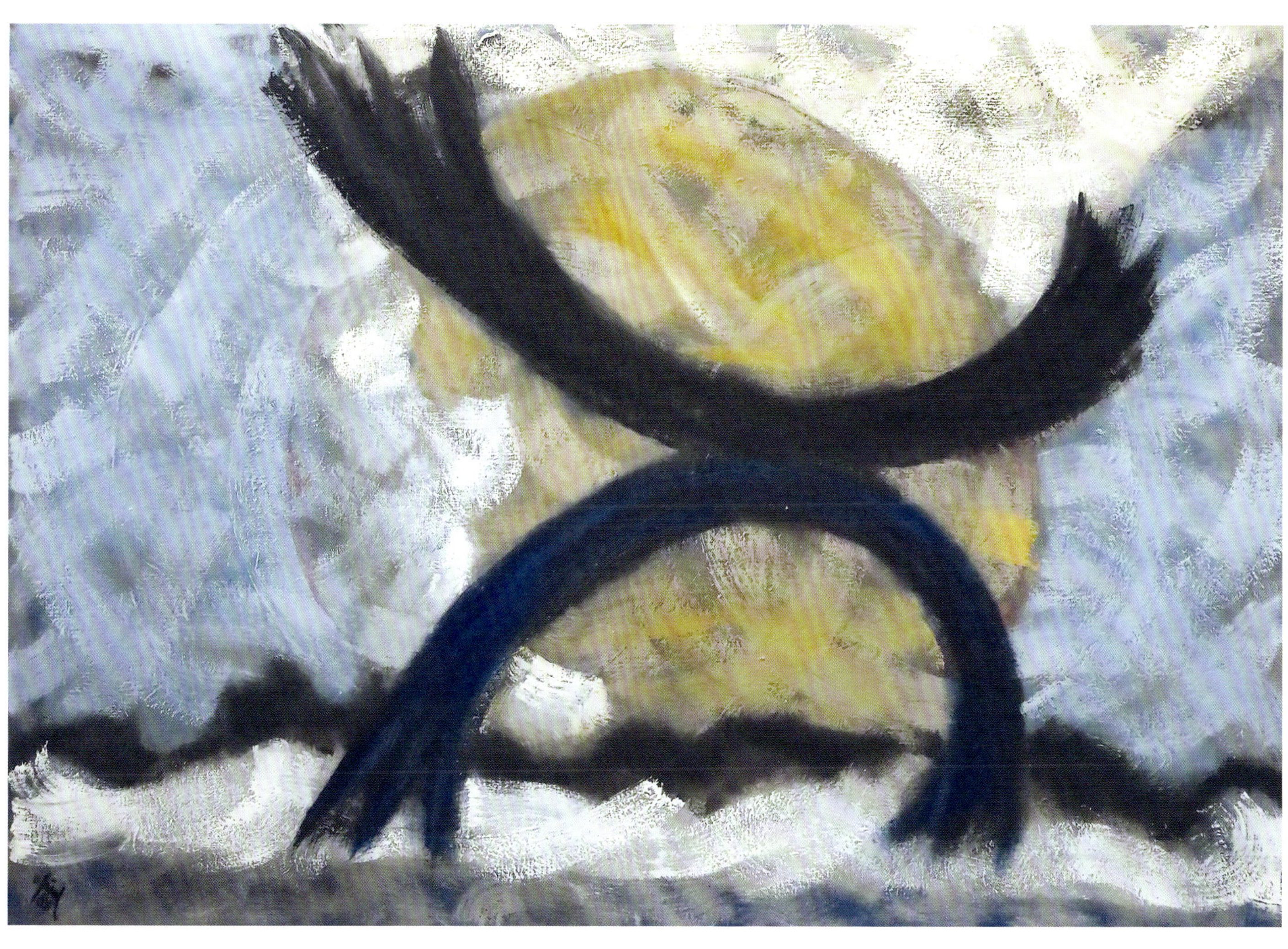

MAGIC ADVICE (ADVICE IN BLUE)
1986
Öl auf Leinwand / Oil on canvas

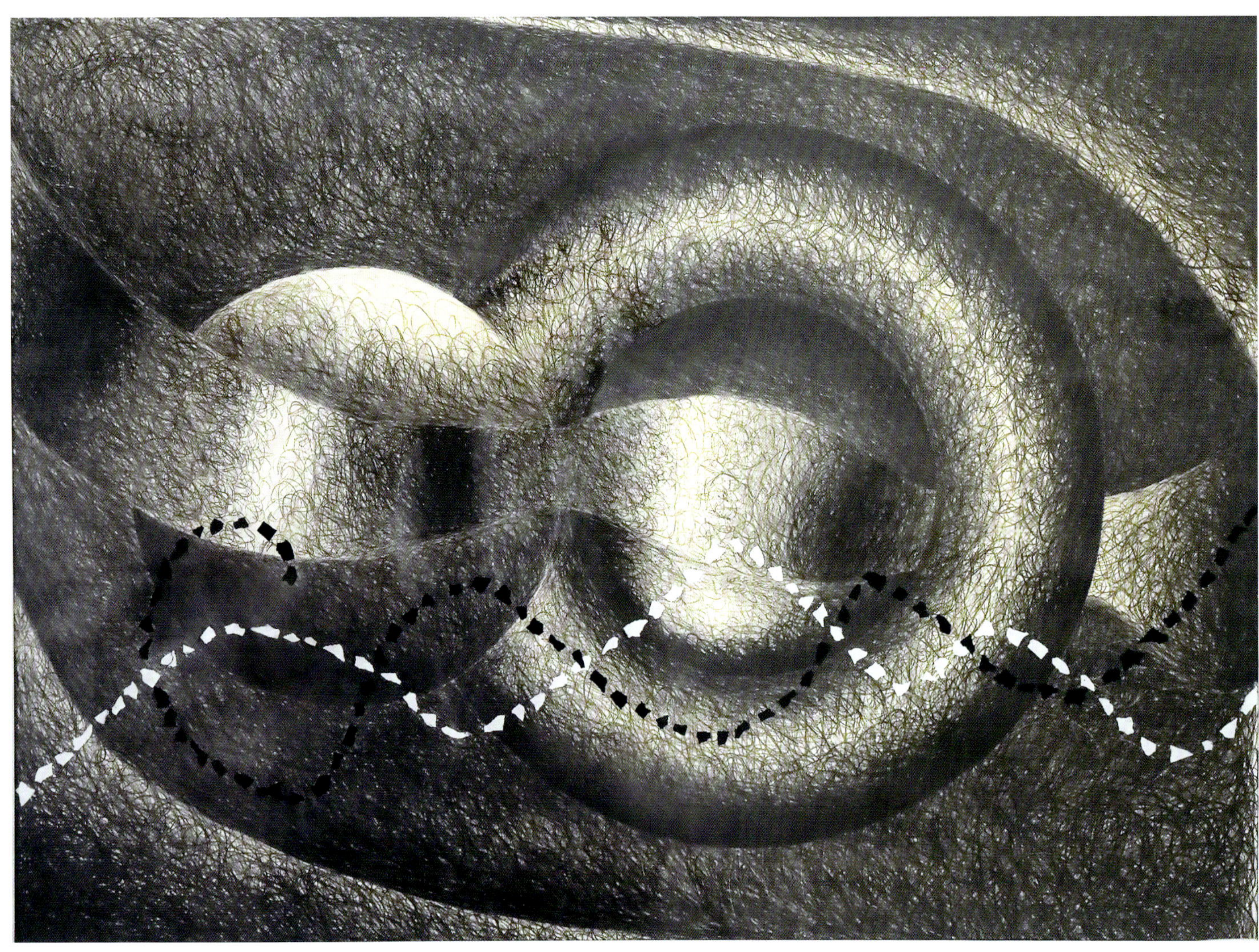

OHNE TITEL / UNTITLED
1987
Collage, Bleistift, Papiercollage auf Papier / Collage, pencil, paper collage on paper

OHNE TITEL / UNTITLED
2008
Grafit auf Papier / Graphite on paper

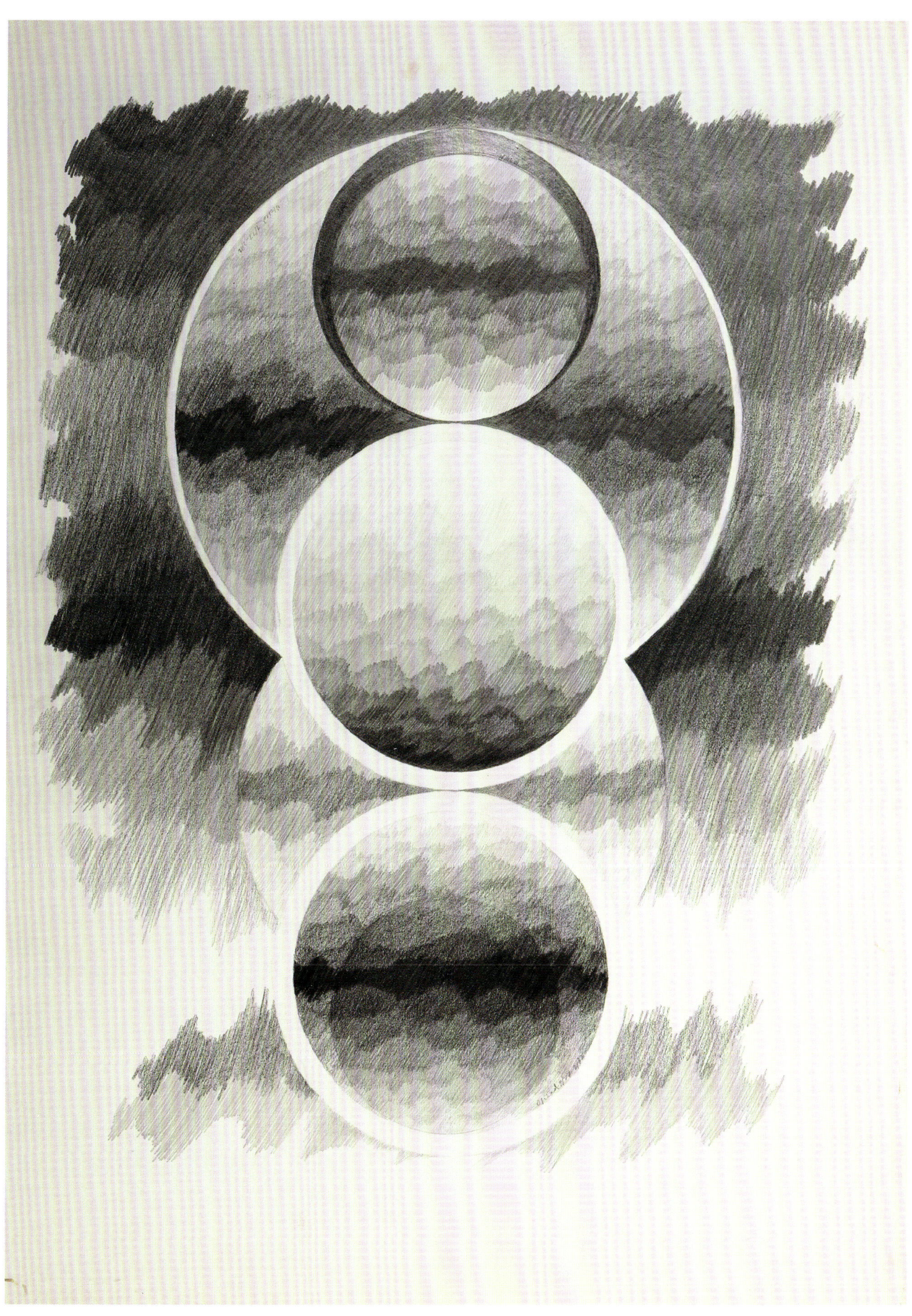

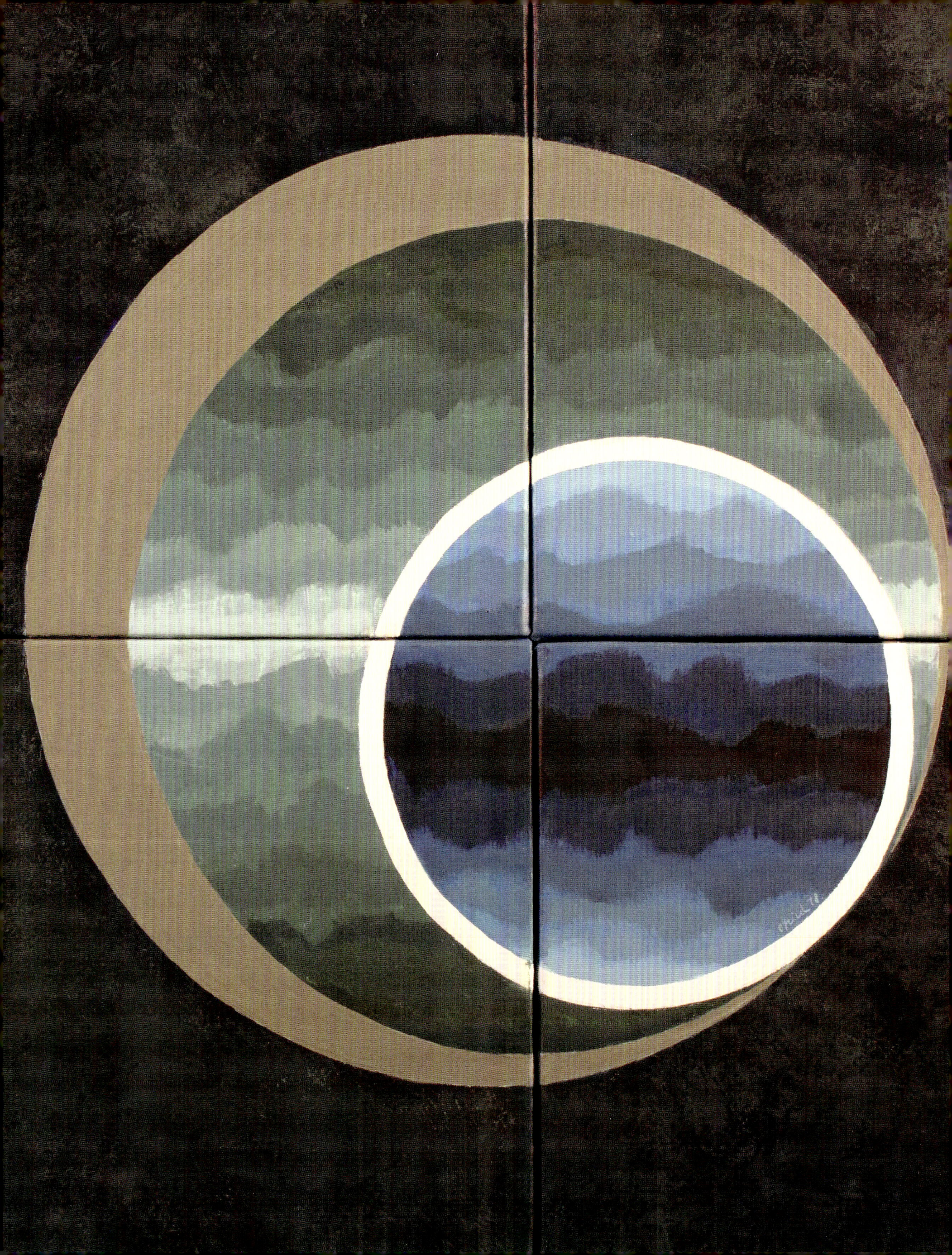

BARBARA WOLBERT

HIMMEL UND FLÜSSE*

Geschichten und Bilder

Auch mit Worten hat Otto Bilder entworfen, die sich mir – seiner Großcousine, *petite cousine* oder *cousin once removed* – eingeprägt haben.
Da kommen mir zuerst die Geschichten aus Diez an der Lahn in den Sinn, die wir – meine Schwestern, meine Cousine und ich – von deren Mutter und unserem Vater kannten. Ihre Cousine Liese und ihr Cousin Otto spielen darin eine große Rolle. Ottos Geschichten aus seiner Kindheit rufen mir diese nur aus Erzählungen bekannten Diez-Bilder wieder ins Gedächtnis und führen mich in Gedanken nach Horchheim und auf die gegenüberliegende Rheinseite, nach Koblenz. Was wir als Kinder „Geschichten" nannten, sind eigentlich Alltagsbeschreibungen. Es sind ambivalente Bilder, weil sie mir das Unheilvolle, das sie auslassen, ins Bewusstsein bringen. Dennoch bleiben es immer auch Bilder vom Glück.

BARBARA WOLBERT

HEAVEN, SKY, AND RIVERS*

Stories and Images

Otto created images, not only as a painter but with words, that I – his cousin once-removed, his *petite cousine*, or *Grosscousine* – have completely committed to memory. These picture-memories are, in a manner of speaking, "stills" of old stories of Diez an der Lahn. I grew up with these stories connecting me to my father's side of the family. Otto played a leading role in these narratives. Growing up in Cologne, I knew Otto from his rare and short visits from America and as a writer of innumerable letters adorned with extraordinary stamps, which my father would read out loud or quote. Otto was my "uncle" in New York.
I first heard Otto's childhood stories, when I was able to visit him on my own. He then lived in Paris, where he'd conjure up images of Diez along with pictures of Horchheim and of Koblenz on the opposite side of the Rhine. What I

Feines Attestat
Detail
1978
Öl auf Leinwand / Oil on canvas
70 x 55 cm
Mittelrhein-Museum Koblenz

as a child called "stories" were, in fact, commonplace descriptions of family life – impossible to be continued. They made no reference to the then creeping, dangerous and sinister reality. They now have an uncomfortable quality as I am painfully aware of that which was unspoken. But nonetheless they remain – just as I understood them as a child – images of happiness.

We need to go back a generation to understand what "Diez" meant for Otto. Otto's father Robert, and his three sisters, who lost their mother at an extremely young age, were raised by their father Leopold and his twin brother Adolph. The twins were butchers, so Robert learned his craft directly from them. When Robert and Ricka, the daughter of the Horchheim butcher Abraham Solomon and his wife Katharina, married, Robert carried on as a butcher. Like Robert, two of his sisters married and left Diez, but the third remained and became known as "Aunt Dora".

In Heaven

Aunt Dora loved her nieces and nephews enormously, especially the four youngest – Otto, Liese, Lore and Heinz Georg – who came respectively from Horchheim, Frankfurt and Cologne during the summer, spending their holidays with *Tante Dora*. Photos still exist: Otto and the others with neighbors' kids, wearing wide-brimmed hats and feather headdresses; all smoking peace pipes in Aunt Dora's garden. Otto and Heinz Georg in knee highs and Liese and Lore in socks line up in various group photographs. Before going to sleep, whispered conversations in the girls and boys' designated rooms. In the mornings, snail races on the garden table and other outdoor games. Lunch at Aunt Dora's kitchen table. Afternoon swimming in the Lahn. Then the children would return to her table hungry for their evening meal. Aunt Dora was Diez; Diez was Aunt Dora. Otto describes being together with his cousins at *Tante Dora's* as being "in heaven."

In the river

Swimming with the others in the Lahn, the river where Otto's father had learned to swim, was Otto's greatest summer pleasure. While our father and his sister only knew what it was like to swim in the Rhine when teenagers in Cologne, Otto, "the Horchheimer kid," became a swimmer in the Rhine very early on. Otto's father would take him and his brother Ernst to the banks of the Rhine often, as it wasn't far. They'd put on red or blue "*Buxen*" – trunks that their parents had chosen "depending on which colors they liked best on their sons". One of the two brothers would always wait along the riverbank while their father, a good swimmer – as Otto emphasizes, every time he tells this story - took the other brother to swim on his back. In this way, Otto was able to swim in the current by the time he got to Diez and bathed in the Lahn with his cousins.

By the river

Otto attended the Horchheim primary school in 1929 where he was taught by nuns. They would bring the children to St. Maximin, the very church to which Otto would donate, seventy-three years later in 2002, his painting *Leeward Illusion*, now hanging over the south portal. In 1933 Otto went on to the St. Kastor school on the other side of the Rhine, where he found an art tutor

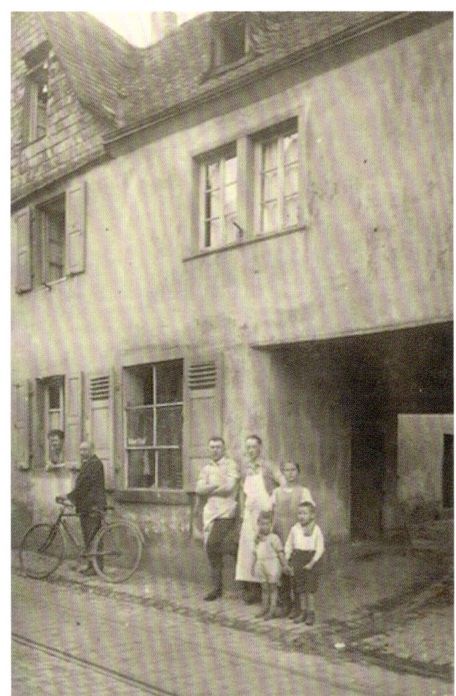

Otto Fried mit seinem Bruder Ernst, seinem Vater Robert (mit Fahrrad), seiner Mutter Ricka (am Fenster) und Mitarbeitern vor ihrer Familienmetzgerei in Horchheim (Koblenz), 1926 / Otto Fried with his brother Ernst, his father Robert (with bicycle), his mother Ricka (at the window) and some workers in front of the family's butcher's shop in Horchheim (Koblenz), 1926

Um zu verstehen, was für Otto und die anderen mit „Diez" gemeint war, müssen wir in Gedanken eine Generation zurückgehen: Ottos Vater Robert und seine drei Schwestern, die früh ihre Mutter verloren, wurden von ihrem Vater Leopold und dessen Zwillingsbruder Adolph großgezogen. Die beiden waren Metzger; bei ihnen lernte Robert sein Handwerk. Als er und Ottos Mutter Ricka, die jüngste Tochter von Katharina und Abraham Salomon, heirateten, konnte Robert daher auch deren Horchheimer Metzgerei weiterführen. Wie Robert hatten auch zwei seiner Schwestern geheiratet und Diez verlassen, die dritte, Dora, war dort geblieben und wurde nun „die Tante Dora."

Im Himmel

Sie hatte ein großes Herz für ihre Nichten und Neffen und vor allem für die vier Jüngsten – Otto, Liese, Lore und Heinz Georg - die im Sommer aus Horchheim, Frankfurt, und Köln anreisten und die Ferien bei ihr verbrachten. Davon gibt es noch Fotos: Otto und die anderen mit Nachbarskindern, unter breitkrempigen Hüten und im Federschmuck Friedenspfeifen rauchend in Tante Doras Garten; Otto und Heinz Georg in Kniestrümpfen und Liese und Lore in Söckchen im Gruppenbild, mal so und mal anders aufgereiht.
Vor dem Einschlafen geflüsterte Unterhaltungen in den Zimmern, die Tante Dora den beiden Mädchen und den beiden Jungen zugeteilt hatte. Morgens Schneckenrennen auf dem Gartentisch und andere Spiele im Freien. Dann das Mittagessen an Tante Doras Küchentisch. Ihren Abendbrothunger holten sich die Kinder beim Schwimmen in der Lahn. Diez - das war Tante Dora. Bei ihr waren Otto und die anderen drei, wie Otto es ausdrückt, „im Himmelreich".

Im Fluss

Mit den anderen in der Lahn zu schwimmen, in dem Fluss, in dem schon sein Vater schwimmen gelernt hatte, war Ottos größtes Sommervergnügen. Während unser Vater und die Mutter unserer Cousine erst als Jugendliche in Köln erlebten, wie es ist, im Rhein zu schwimmen, war Otto, der ‚Horchheimer Jung', schon ganz früh zum Rheinschwimmer geworden: Sein Vater nahm Otto und dessen älterem Bruder Ernst oft mit zum Rhein hinunter. Das war nicht gar weit. Sie zogen kleine rote oder blaue ‚Buxen' an, Badehosen, die ihnen die Eltern ausgesucht hatten - „je nachdem, in welchen Farben sie ihre Söhne am liebsten sahen". Während der eine der beiden Jungen am Ufer wartete, nahm der Vater, der – was Otto immer betont - ein guter Schwimmer war, den anderen auf seinen Rücken und schwamm mit ihm im Rhein. So kannte Otto das Schwimmen in der Strömung schon, als er zum ersten Mal seine Ferien in Diez verbrachte und mit dem Cousin und den Cousinen in der Lahn badete.

Am Fluss

Otto kam 1929 in die Horchheimer Volksschule, wo er von Nonnen unterrichtet wurde. Sie gingen mit den Kindern auch in die St. Maximin Kirche, der er 2002, also dreiundsiebzig Jahre später, das Gemälde „Leewärtige Illusion" schenkte, das jetzt über dem Südportal der Kirche hängt. 1933 wechselte Otto in die St. Castor Schule auf der anderen Rheinseite. Die Schule hatte einen Zeichenlehrer, der ihn sehr förderte. Aber auch seine Eltern, die wussten, wie gern er malte und zeichnete, haben ihn darin immer bestärkt – das sagt er mit Nachdruck. Im Gegensatz zu seinem Bruder, der den Beruf seines Vater ergreifen

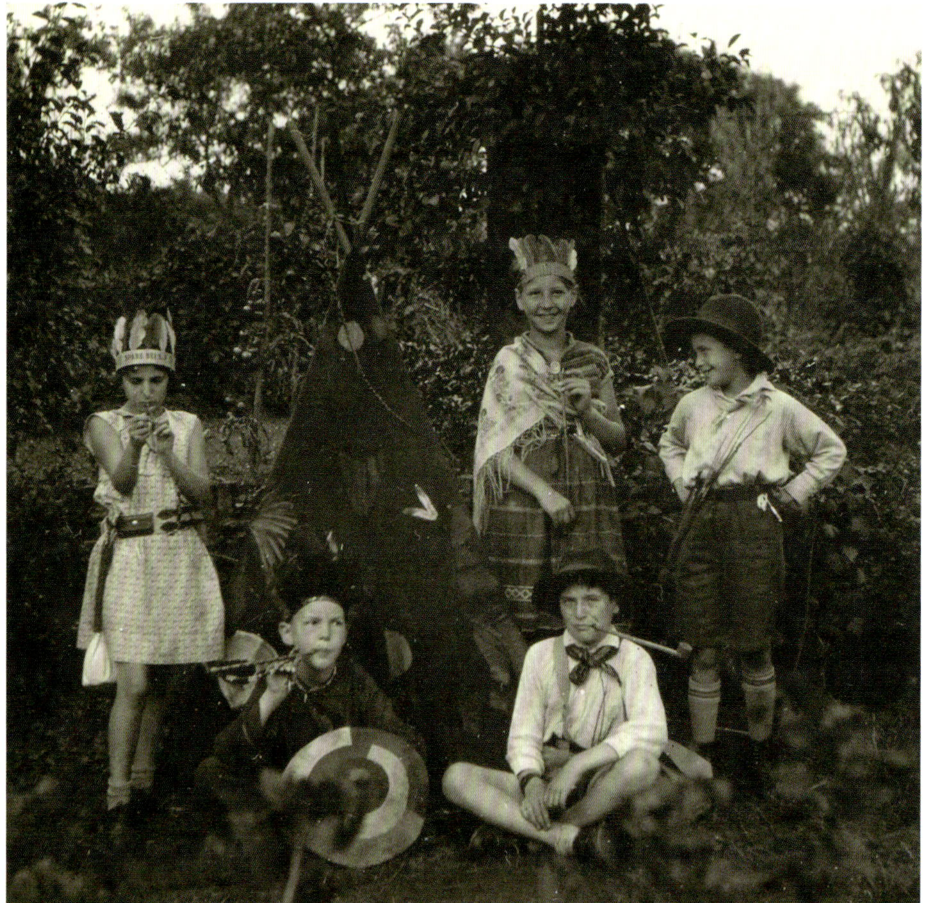

Otto Fried (rechts oben) mit seiner Cousine Lore, seinem Cousin Heinz Georg und Nachbarskindern im Garten ihrer Tante Dora in Diez an der Lahn / Otto Fried (standing on the right) with his cousins Lore und Heinz Georg and kids from the neighborhood in his Aunt Dora's garden in Diez an der Lahn

who encouraged him greatly. Otto says, with huge appreciation, that his parents, knowing how much he liked to draw and paint, encouraged him as well. Unlike his brother Ernst who wanted nothing more than to follow his father's profession, Otto was not interested in the slaughterhouse but rather in his mother's world, whether working in the hillside orchard – the *Bangert* – or the back garden. Otto had his own vegetable and flower bed which he enjoyed sowing and watering in spring and harvesting in summer and autumn. He liked to draw what he saw and discovered when working and playing in the orchards or during walks in the forest. As carefully as his father might have butchered the skin, the bones and the flesh of his raw animals into pieces, so too did Otto cut up plants and dead insects to inspect their forms and structures and then to draw his observations.
As a child of a Jewish family, Otto was given a free period while his classmates were given Catholic lessons. He would then leave the school, whose post-war building can be seen today by looking out from the Western windows of the upper rooms of the *Deutschherrenhaus* that houses the permanent collection of the Ludwig Museum. To the south of the museum is the Sankt Kastor Basilica. Looking east, one can see the Rhine and from the northern side, the buttocks of the oversized horse of *Kaiser Wilhelm I*. Horse and rider stare into the so-called *Deutsches Eck*, the fortified headland between the Moselle and the Rhine. In this exact place Otto would spend his free time. From high up on the base of the German emperor's monument, where he was unable to see the equestrian statue itself, he had the best view of the flowing water from

wollte, interessierte sich Otto weniger für die Arbeit im Schlachthaus als vielmehr für das, was in der Domäne der Mutter geschah und zu tun war, ob auf der Streuobstwiese am Hang, dem Bangert, oder im Garten hinter dem Haus. Er hatte ein eigenes Beet; er genoss es, im Frühjahr zu sähen und zu gießen und im Sommer und Herbst zu ernten. Gern zeichnete er, was er dabei oder bei Ausflügen im Wald entdeckt hatte. Vermutlich ähnlich beherzt und sorgsam wie der Vater Haut, Knochen und Fleisch der Tiere, die er geschlachtet hatte, voneinander löste und in einzelne Stücke zerteilte, schnitt Otto Pflanzen und tote Insekten auf, um die Strukturen, die sich da auftaten, genau anzuschauen und sie zu zeichnen.

Als Kind einer jüdischen Familie hatte Otto frei, wenn den Mitschülern katholischer Religionsunterricht erteilt wurde. Er verließ dann die Schule, deren Neubau man heute sieht, wenn man aus den westlichen Fenstern der oberen Räume des Deutschherrenhaus blickt, in denen die ständige Sammlung des Ludwig Museums ausgestellt ist. Auf der Südseite des Museums steht die Sankt Kastor Basilika. Wenn man nach Osten schaut, sieht man den Rhein und aus den Nordfenstern guckt man auf das Hinterteil des überdimensionalen Gauls von Kaiser Wilhelm. Starren Blicks sind Ross und Reiter auf das Deutsche Eck ausgerichtet, auf die befestigte Landspitze zwischen Mosel und Rhein. Genau diesen öffentlichen Platz hatte Otto sich für seine Freistunden ausgesucht. Da saß er dann auf dem Sockel des Kaiser-Wilhelm-Denkmals. Von da oben, wo das Reiterstandbild selbst nicht in seinem Blickfeld lag, hatte er die beste Sicht auf das Wasser der Mosel, das sich vor ihm mit dem des Rheins vermischte. Wenn er an diesem Platz sein Butterbrot aß, belegt mit Wurst oder Schinken aus der Produktion des Vaters – für ihn auch ein „Mutterbrot", weil die Mutter es für ihn geschmiert hatte – fühlte er sich „im Himmel". Wenn er damals hätte ahnen können, dass in dem Deutschherrenhaus, dem er dabei den Rücken zukehrte, einmal seine Bilder ausgestellt werden würden ... kann er sich das vorstellen? Aus seiner Antwort spricht Gewissheit anstelle der unterstellten Verwunderung: „Der Maler steckte damals schon in mir!"

Am Himmel

Die Koblenzer Schulzeit endete für Otto abrupt, als er 13 Jahre alt war und die Stadt am Rhein verließ. Für ihn und für seine und andere jüdische Familien war sie nicht mehr sicher, nachdem „ein Mann namens Adolf Hitler an die Regierung gekommen war" – so seine heutige euphemistische Kurzformel für die Katastrophe. Zuerst konnte nur Otto fliehen, ganz allein. Von Hamburg aus, wohin der Vater ihn noch hatte begleiten können, reiste er auf einem Frachtschiff über den Atlantik, durch den Panamakanal, auf dem Pazifischen Ozean nach San Francisco und von da aus schnell mit dem Zug weiter nach Portland, Oregon, wo das Schuljahr gerade begann. Seine Eltern hatten dort in ihrer Not entfernte Verwandte ausfindig gemacht. Diese unbekannten Verwandten, deren Väter bereits in Amerika geboren waren, hatten die Einreisepapiere beschafft. In der neuen Schule wurde er sofort in das Swim-Team aufgenommen. Er schwamm auch in der Mannschaft des YMCA, des Christlichen Vereins Junger Männer, „wo es kein Problem war, dass ich Jude war." Er lebte nun wieder in einer Stadt an zwei Flüssen, dem Columbia River und dem Willamette River. Er liebte den Staat Oregon, die Wälder, die Berge, das Meer und die Küste, die Seen und Flüsse. Das ging seinen Eltern ebenso, die ihm erst drei Jahre später

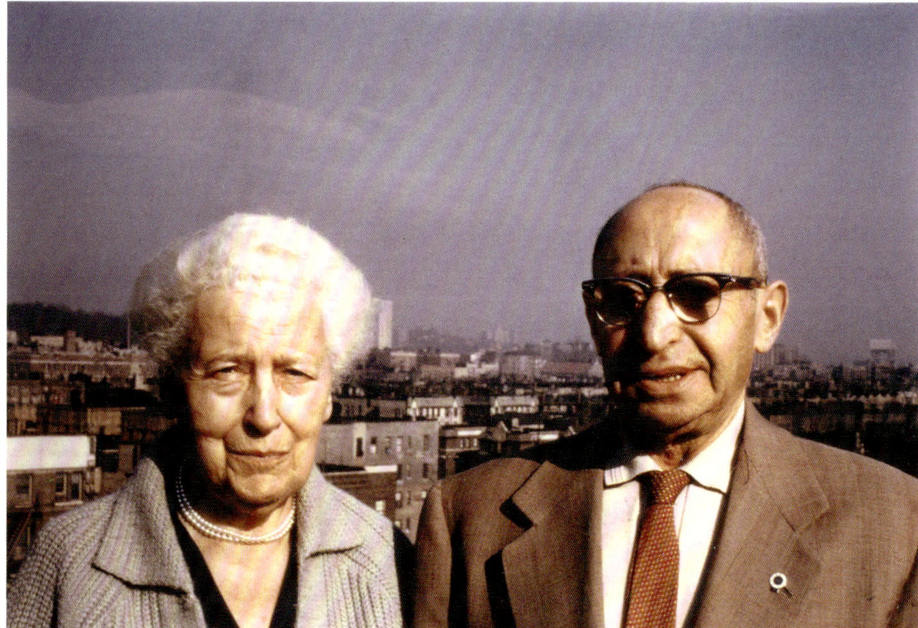

Frieds Eltern Ricka und Robert in Washington Heights, New York, 1966 / Fried's parents Ricka and Robert in Washington Heights, New York, 1966

the Moselle mixing with that of the Rhine. There he would unpack his sandwich made with his father's sausages or ham and prepared by his mother. Concentrating on the rivers while eating this *Butterbrot* that he called "*Mutterbrot*" – mother's bread – Otto thought he was "in heaven".

If he could ever imagine that his paintings would be exhibited in the very *Deutschherrenhaus* against which he turned his back all those years ago, what would he say? His answer is self-assured rather than amazed: "The painter in me was already there."

In the Sky

The Koblenz schooldays ended abruptly when he was forced to leave the city on the Rhine at the age of thirteen. It was no longer safe for him, his family, or other Jewish families after "a man named Adolf Hitler came to power" – Otto's euphemistically short reference to the Holocaust. At first only Otto was able to escape. His father accompanied him to Hamburg, where he got passage on a cargo ship bound across the Atlantic. Otto was all alone. The ship took the Panama Canal route into the Pacific and on to San Francisco. From there he boarded a train to Portland, Oregon where the school year had just started.

His parents had managed to discover distant relatives. Hitherto unknown, these relatives, both of whose fathers were born in America, managed to obtain entry documents for Otto. He was put immediately into his new American school and accepted into the swimming teams at his school and at the YMCA, "where it was no problem that I was a Jew."

He found himself living in another city on other two rivers: the Columbia and Willamette Rivers. Otto loved the State of Oregon, its forests, mountains, lakes and its coast. Three years later his parents managed to follow him to Oregon. However, there were only the two of them. The third, his brother Ernst, lost his life because of anti-Semitic violence in Germany.

After graduating from high school in 1943, Otto was conscripted into the US

nach Oregon folgen konnten. Allerdings kamen sie nur zu zweit, ohne Ihren ältesten Sohn. Ottos Bruder Ernst hatte die antisemitische Gewalt in Deutschland das Leben gekostet.
Nach der High School 1943 zum Militär eingezogen, kam Otto in das US Army Air Corps. Erst wurde er im Kriegsgebiet von Indien, Burma und China eingesetzt und dann brachte er - wahrscheinlich mit derselben Sicherheit, die ihm sein Vater beim Schwimmen im Rhein vermittelt hatte - jüngeren Piloten das Fliegen am Himmel über der Wüste Arizonas bei. 1946 nahm er als guter Schwimmer und Taucher an einem militärischen Forschungsprojekt zur Rettung von Piloten in der Karibik teil. Begeistert für die Farben, Formen und Bewegungen der Lebewesen des Meeres entdeckte er für sich dabei die amerikanischen Virgin Islands als einen Ort unter blauem Himmel, den er immer wieder aufsuchen sollte.
Otto sammelte Meteoriten, Himmelskörper also, die anders als die übrigen Steine auf der Erde gar nicht von diesem Planeten stammen sondern von außerhalb der Erde. Als ich ihn im November 1984 in New York besuchte, bestand Otto, der sich sonst nicht für das Fernsehprogramm interessierte, darauf, die Außenbordeinsätze der Astronauten Joseph P. Allen und Dale Gardner an der Space Shuttle Discovery anzuschauen, die das Fernsehen übertrug, um wenigstens auf dem Bildschirm zu sehen, wie die Erde aus dem All erscheint. Ich dachte an Ottos Bilder, und seine Faszination für die Mission im All wunderte mich keineswegs.

Man steigt nicht zweimal in denselben Fluss

Zu seinem großen Glück ermöglichte ihm die ‚GI-Bill', ein 1944 verabschiedetes Gesetz zur Wiedereingliederung von Veteranen, ein Studium. Zuerst hatte sich Otto, der sich weiterhin für Pflanzen und Tiere interessierte, am Oregon State College in Portland für Biologie eingeschrieben. Als ihm klar wurde, dass er sich vor allem künstlerisch mit der Natur auseinandersetzen und sich ganz dem Zeichnen und Malen widmen wollte, wechselte er an das Art and Architecture Department der University of Oregon in Eugene. Dort studierte auch Kenneth Snelson, der ein guter Freund werden und ebenfalls nach Paris und New York gehen sollte. Ihr Professor war Jack Wilkinson, der den Kontakt zu Fernand Léger vermittelte. Nach Abschluss seines Studiums in Eugene arbeitete und studierte Otto Fried in dessen Pariser Atelier an der Académie de Montmarte weiter.
Von Paris aus reiste Otto nach Horchheim, wo er Walter Bode, seinen Freund aus der Kindheit, besuchte. Ottos Elternhaus und das Haus der Bodes lagen einander gegenüber. Sie hatten korrespondiert, als Otto noch ganz allein in Portland war. Otto hatte sich gefragt, weshalb die Briefe von zuhause mit einem Mal nicht mehr die Handschrift beider Eltern trugen sondern nur noch die der Mutter. Walter war wohl derjenige, der ihm geschrieben hatte, dass sein Vater, der bald - vermutlich als einer der sogenannten 'Aktionsjuden' - aus dem Konzentrationslager freikam, nach Buchenwald deportiert worden war, und möglicherweise auch, dass sein Bruder nicht mehr lebte – Nachrichten, vor denen seine Eltern ihn, solange sie nicht bei ihm waren, hatten verschonen wollen oder die im Brief mitzuteilen für sie zu riskant gewesen wäre. Nach dem Krieg nahmen Walter und er die Korrespondenz wieder auf. Zusammen mit einem dritten Wanderfreund unternahmen die beiden Jahrzehnte später jedes Jahr im September mehrtägige Touren, meist in Deutschland, aber auch in Frankreich.

Army and joined the Air Corps. First he was deployed to the war zones in India, Burma and China and then – probably with the same confidence that his father had proved teaching him to swim – he taught young pilots to fly in the skies of the Arizona desert. After the end of the war, he remained in the military until 1946 – as a good swimmer participating in a research project on methods of rescuing pilots at sea – on the American Virgin Islands. Thrilled by the colors, shapes and movements of the living sea creatures, he fell for these islands under the blue sky to which he would return often.

Otto collected meteorites, celestial bodies that, unlike other stones, do not come from planet Earth but from a place beyond. When I visited him in New York in 1984, Otto, who was not normally interested in television programs, was glued to the TV screen, showing the space missions of the astronauts Joseph P. Allen and Dale Gardner of the Space Shuttle Discovery. I thought of his paintings of the 1970s and his fascination with the outer space came as no surprise.

You cannot step into the same river twice

Luckily for Otto, the GI Bill, passed in 1944 for the re-integration of veterans into society, enabled him to study as he had wanted. At first Otto, who was still fascinated in plants and insects, enrolled in biology at the Oregon State College in Portland. As soon as he realized that he was more interested in engaging with nature artistically, he switched to the Art and Architecture Department of the University of Oregon in Eugene. There Otto met Kenneth Snelson, who became a life-long friend and accompanied Otto to Paris and later New York. His professor, Jack Wilkinson, put Otto in touch with Fernand Léger so that following his studies in Oregon, Otto was able to work and study in Léger's famous studio at the Académie de Montmartre in Paris. It was only then that he travelled again to Horchheim, visiting his childhood friend Walter Bode. Otto's parents' home and that of the Bodes faced each other. Walter had written to him during Otto's time alone in Portland. Otto had wondered why the letters from home no longer bore the usual handwriting of both parents but only that of his mother. Walter was probably the neighbor who told him about the deportation of his father. Robert Fried was – probably as one of the so-called *Aktions-Juden* – released from Buchenwald early in 1939 as part of the campaign to speed up the expropriation of Jewish property in order to gain the political support of the "*Aryan*" beneficiaries. Through Walter he may also have learned that his brother was no longer alive. It seems that Otto's parents wanted to spare him these facts, as he was alone and they found it probably too risky to reveal them in a letter. After the war, Walter and he resumed correspondence. Decades later every year in September, together with a friend, Otto and Walter went on hiking tours mostly in Germany but also in France.

Returning to Portland from Paris in 1951, Otto decided to go to New York as a freelance artist instead of teaching in Oregon. By the time the United States Information Service, the USIS, started to establish American cultural institutes in Germany, the *Amerika-Häuser*, Otto had already participated in numerous group exhibitions in France and the USA and indeed had had some solo exhibitions. Warren Robbins, later a well-known collector of African art, then the director of USIS, Germany, and cultural attaché at the US Embassy in Bonn, offered Otto exhibition opportunities in three West German cities. Before Ot-

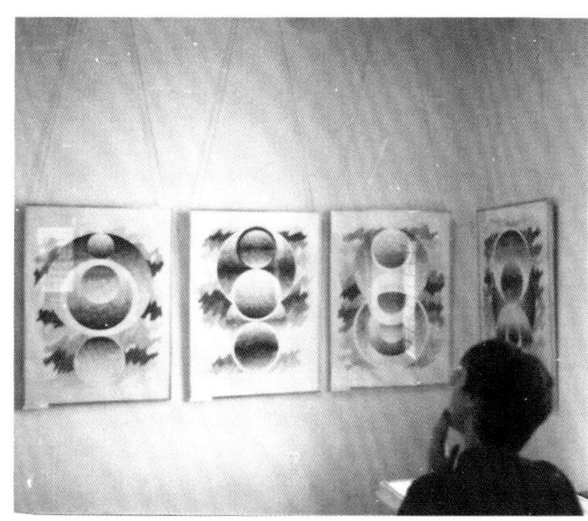

Otto Frieds Ausstellung im Mittelrhein-Museum Koblenz, 1978 / Otto Fried's Exhibition at the Mittelrhein-Museum Koblenz, 1978

Im Herbst 1951 aus Paris nach Portland zurückgekehrt, hatte Otto sich entschieden, statt in Oregon Kunst zu unterrichten, als freier Künstler nach New York zu gehen. Als der United States Information Service, der USIS, der 1950 begonnen hatte, in Deutschland amerikanische Kulturinstitute, die sogenannten Amerika-Häuser, aufzubauen, war Otto Fried sowohl in Frankreich als auch in den Vereinigten Staaten schon an etlichen Gruppenausstellungen beteiligt gewesen und hatte auch schon eine Reihe Einzelausstellungen gehabt. Es war der später als Sammler afrikanischer Kunst bekannt gewordene Warren Robbins, der damals Direktor des Informationsdienstes der Vereinigten Staaten für Deutschland und Kulturattaché der amerikanischen Botschaft in Bonn war, der ihm seine ersten Ausstellungsmöglichkeiten in drei westdeutschen Städten anbot. Bevor Arbeiten von Otto Fried, darunter vor allem auch die Monotypien, für die er in den USA bekannt war, in Darmstadt und Tübingen zu sehen waren, wurden sie 1958 in Koblenz ausgestellt. Diese Ausstellung war für ihn ganz besonders wichtig, sagt Otto. Eine Kooperation des Amerikahauses mit der Stadt Koblenz machte die Ausstellung möglich, die ausgerechnet im Deutschherrenhaus stattfand – am Zusammenfluss von Rhein und Mosel, auf den er als Schuljunge, sein Pausenbrot essend, so gern geschaut hatte.
In den 1960er Jahren, nachdem er Micheline Haardt, damals in New York als Modejournalistin tätig, geheiratet hatte, verlegte er seinen Lebensmittelpunkt in deren Stadt, nach Paris. Neben seinem Pariser Atelier behielt er aber sein *Studio* in der Nähe des East River, wo er vor allem im Frühjahr und Herbst arbeitete, wenn die beiden jeweils zwei Monate in New York verbrachten.
1978 gab es erneut eine Otto Fried Ausstellung in Koblenz. Ihr Titel „Ströme" reflektierte Ottos Verhältnis zum Rhein, zu Flüssen, zum Wasser und zur Bewegung. Erstmals kam die Einladung zu einer Ausstellung federführend von einer deutschen Institution, dem Mittelrhein-Museum Koblenz, namentlich von dessen Direktor Kurt Eitelbach – 42 Jahre nachdem Otto Deutschland hatte verlassen müssen und 33 Jahre nach dem Ende des nationalsozialistischen Regimes, das ihn dazu getrieben hatte!
Seit 2010 lebt Otto Fried ausschließlich in Frankreich, nicht weit von der Seine entfernt, im Zentrum von Paris. Wieder nach Deutschland zu ziehen, kam nie mehr in Frage. Heute nun, wiederum mehr als vierzig Jahre danach sind Arbeiten von Otto Fried im Koblenzer Museum für internationale Kunst zu sehen – in dem 1992 im Deutschherrenhaus eröffneten Ludwig Museum. In diesem Museum, dessen Sammlungskern aus deutscher, französischer und amerikanischer Kunst nach 1945 besteht, ermöglichen die Werke des gebürtigen Koblenzer und in Paris lebenden, amerikanischen Künstlers nicht nur einen weit gespannten Dialog mit diesen, sondern erscheinen selbst wie ‚im Fluss'.

*Diesen Text verstehe ich nicht als Otto-Fried-Biografie; weder beansprucht er Vollständigkeit, noch gewichtet er einzelne Begebenheiten entsprechend. Er hebt Berührungen des amerikanischen Künstlers aus Paris mit Koblenz hervor. Mit ‚Himmel' und ‚Flüssen' greift er zwei der Motive auf, die sein Leben und Werk durchziehen. Sie finden sich im Ausstellungsort und im Titel der Ausstellung, der auf einen Werktitel von Otto Fried zurückgeht, wieder. Neben dem, was Otto Fried berichtet und beschreibt, liegen diesem Text auch die Quellen der Vita zugrunde: die 1995 erschienene Monographie über Otto Frieds Leben und Werk, Essays, Kataloge, Zeitungsartikel, Briefe und Dokumente aus Archiven. Nicht zuletzt stützt sich dieser Text auf Gespräche mit Verwandten und mit den Kindern enger New Yorker, Pariser und Horchheimer Freunde von Otto Fried. Die Autorenschaft

to's monotypes, for which he'd become known in the States, would be seen in Darmstadt and Tübingen, they were – to Otto most importantly – exhibited in Koblenz. Cooperation between the *Amerika-Haus* and the city of Koblenz made this possible. This exhibition of 1958 took place in the *Deutschherrenhaus* at *Deutsches Eck* – the very place where Otto had enjoyed his "Mother's Bread" looking out at the confluence of the two rivers.

After marrying Micheline Haardt, then a French fashion journalist in New York, he moved to Paris to live in her city. In addition to his *atelier* in Paris, he kept his East River studio where he worked during his four month *per annum* visits to New York. In 1978 there was another Otto Fried exhibition in Koblenz. Its title, "Ströme – Streams", reflected Otto's relationship with the Rhine, with rivers, water, and movement. For the first time, the invitation to exhibit in Germany came through a German institution, the Middle Rhine Museum Koblenz, through its director, Kurt Eitelbach – 42 years after Otto had to leave this country and 33 years after the end of the Nazi regime which had forced him to do so in the first place!

Since 2010 Otto has lived exclusively in France, not far from the river Seine, in the center of Paris. Moving back to Germany was never an option.

Today, more than forty years after his last exhibition there, works by Otto Fried can once again be seen in Koblenz. They will be on display in Koblenz' Museum of International Art – in the Ludwig Museum that opened in 1992 in the *Deutschherrenhaus*, the place where he had his first exhibition in Germany, more than sixty years ago. The core of the Museum's collection consists of post-War German, French and American art. The works of Otto Fried, the Paris-based American artist, born in Koblenz, will find themselves in comfortable dialogue with the works of his international colleagues, which keeps his as well as their works 'in the flow.'

* I do not consider this text to be a biography of Otto Fried. It neither claims completeness nor gives weight to individual events appropriately. It emphasizes the links of the American artist from Paris with Koblenz. With the "sky" and "rivers" it evokes two of the motifs that run through his work and – with regard to the scope of the German notion of *Himmel* a third one as well: "heaven". The title of this text references the location of the exhibition and its title, which goes back to one of Otto Fried's works. Together with his comments and descriptions, this text relies on the same sources as the biography, the 1995 monograph on his life and work; catalogues, essays, newspaper clippings, letters and documents from archives. Last but not least, this text is based on conversations with relatives and the children of close friends of Otto's from New York, Paris and Horchheim. I gratefully share the authorship with them, while of course taking responsibility for mistakes that I may have made inadvertently. I am thankful to the editor, Beate Reifenscheid, for her invitation to contribute to this catalogue. I thank her and curatorial assistant Larissa Wesp as well as my cousin Anne Oebele, her husband Werner and my daughter Leonie Wolbert for their comments. My special thanks go to Lisa Forrell, Otto's godchild, for her invaluable help with this translation and for her particularly critical reading of my text. With respect to the circumstances of Otto's brother's death, what Lisa knows and what I know does not correspond. The contradictory and incomplete "facts" serve to clarify just how much anti-Semitic violence continues to torment, as such violence attempts to efface traces of these crimes. Equally, such discrepancies demonstrate the 'legitimacy' of forgetting. Even within the family, the unbearable truth had to be 'forgotten' again and again in order to carry on living, in spite of everything, as Otto has done in such a tremendous and generous way. I extend my heartfelt thanks to him, to my favorite cousin and "*Onkel*", to Otto Fried.

Otto Fried in seinem Atelier in Paris, 1989 / Otto Fried in his studio in Paris, 1989

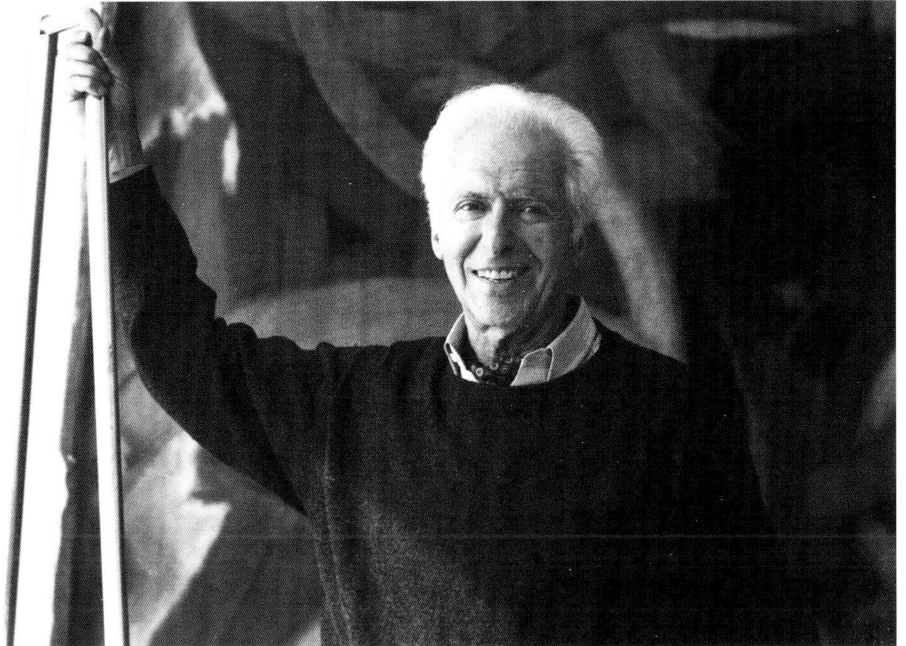

teile ich dankbar mit ihnen, während ich selbstverständlich die Verantwortung für Fehler, die mir unterlaufen sein können, übernehme. In diesem Sinne danke ich auch den Kuratorinnen und Editorinnen dieses Katalogs, Beate Reifenscheid und Larissa Wesp, meiner Cousine Anne Oebels und ihrem Mann Werner für ihre Kommentare. Lisa Forrell, Ottos Patenkind, danke ich für ihr in besonderer Weise kritisches Lesen meines Texts: Was die Umstände des Todes von Ottos Bruder betrifft, stimmt, was sie und was ich darüber weiß nicht überein. Auf der einen Seite machen die widersprüchlichen und lückenhaften lokalen Quellen deutlich, wie sich die antisemitische Gewalt im Verwischen der Tat- und Täterspuren fortsetzt. Auf der anderen Seite weisen solche Diskrepanzen auf die Legitimität des Vergessens. Selbst innerhalb der Familie musste die unerträgliche Wahrheit immer wieder aktiv vergessen werden, um sich – wie es Otto auf so großzügige und großartige Weise vermocht hat und vermag – trotz allem dem Leben zuwenden zu können. Von Herzen danke ich vor allem ihm, Otto Fried, als dem eigentlichen Autor dieses Textes.

WERKE WORKS 1987–2005

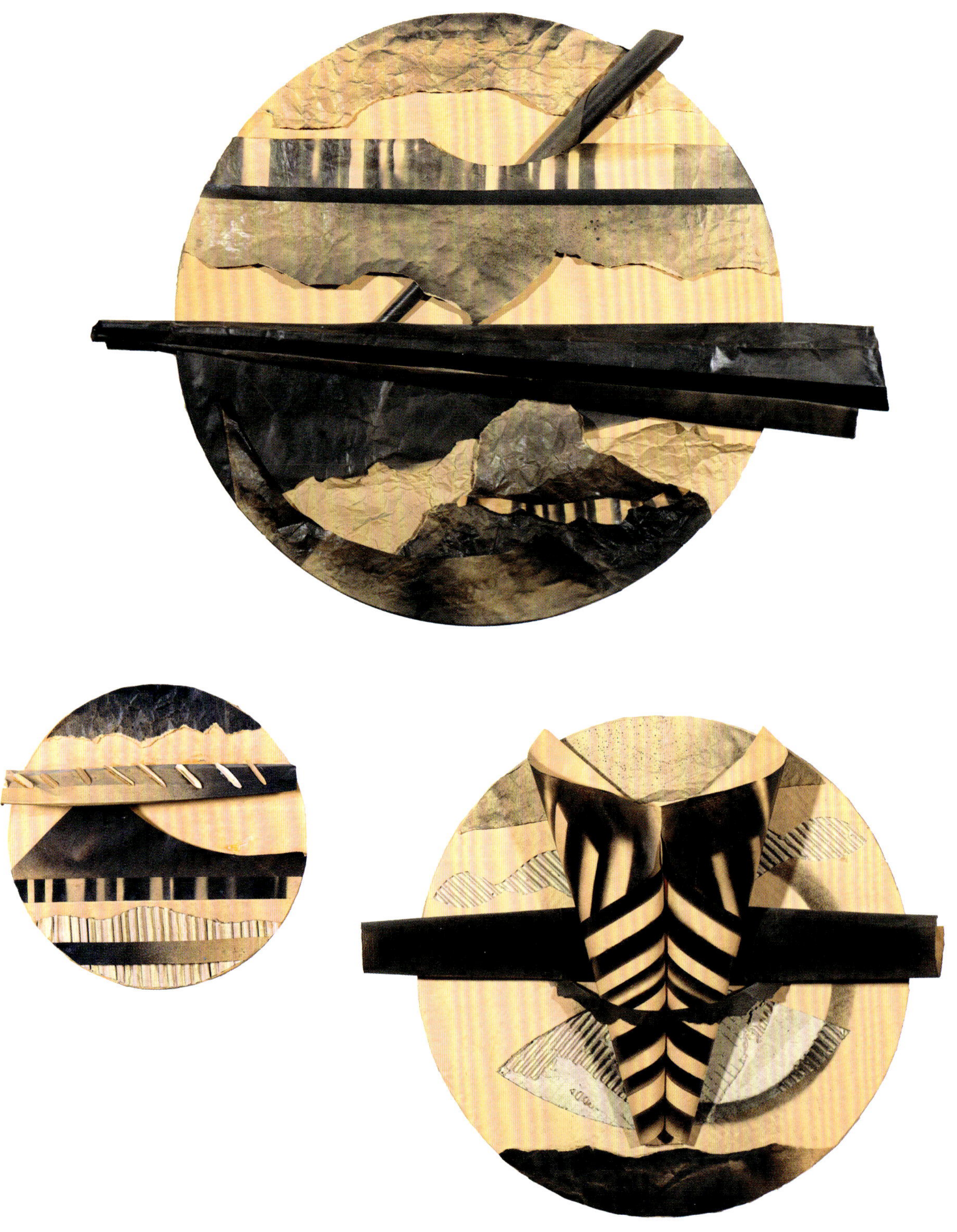

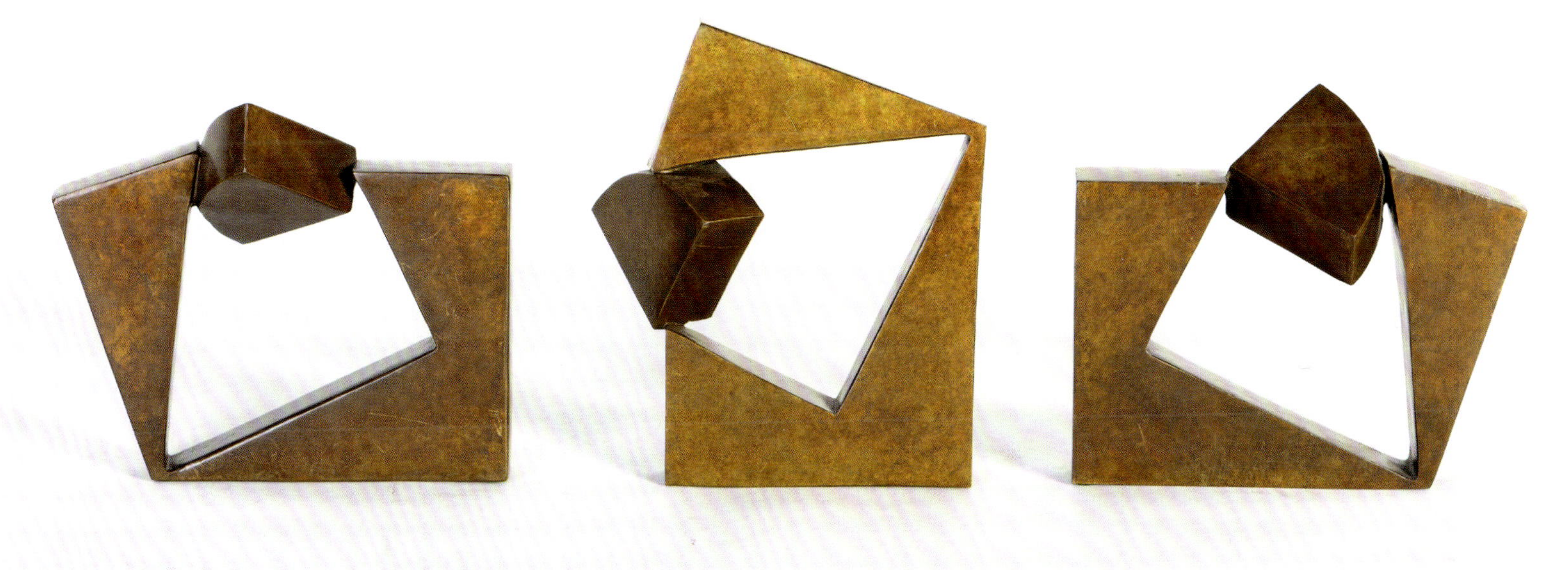

OHNE TITEL / UNTITLED
Circa 1987
Kraftpapier, (Well-)pappe, Tinte oder Gouache / Craft paper, (corrugated) cardboard, ink or gouache

OHNE TITEL / UNTITLED
Circa 1990
Geschmiedetes Eisen / Forged iron

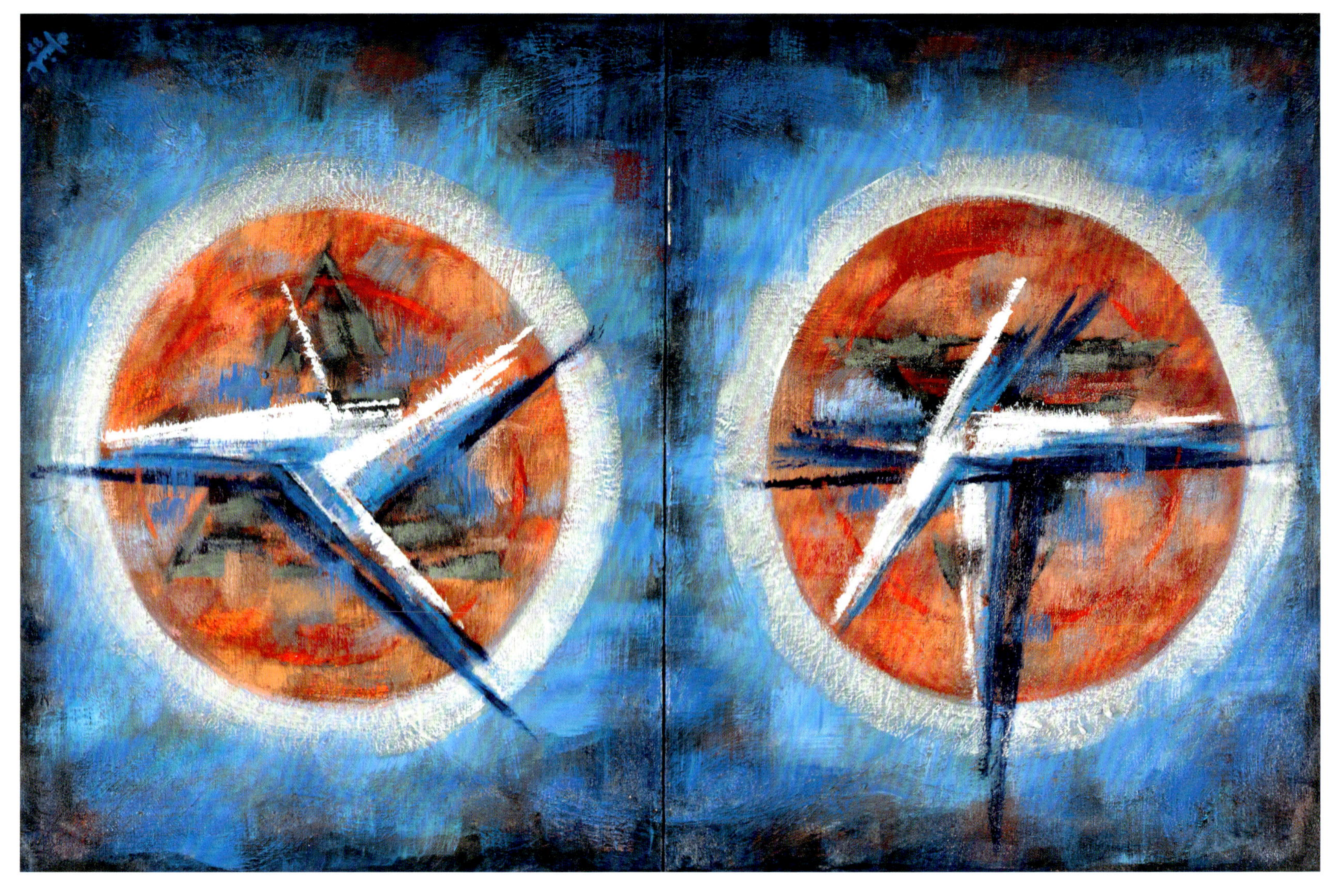

FOURTH ZONE
1988
Öl auf Leinwand / Oil on canvas

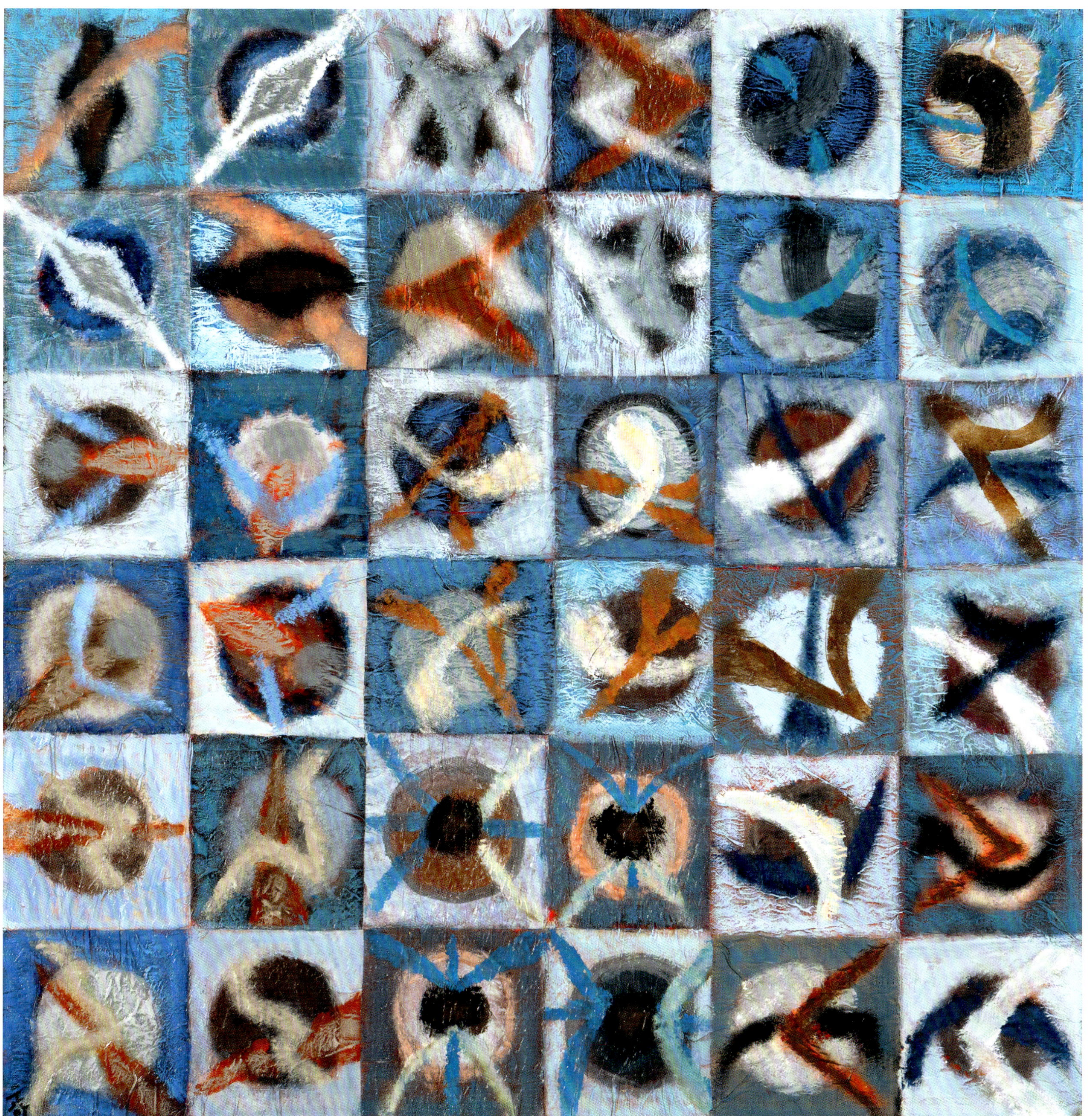

ECRITURE D'UN MONDE Á PART
1990
Collage: Öl auf Papier-Servietten appliziert auf Leinwand / Collage: Oil on paper napkins laid down on canvas

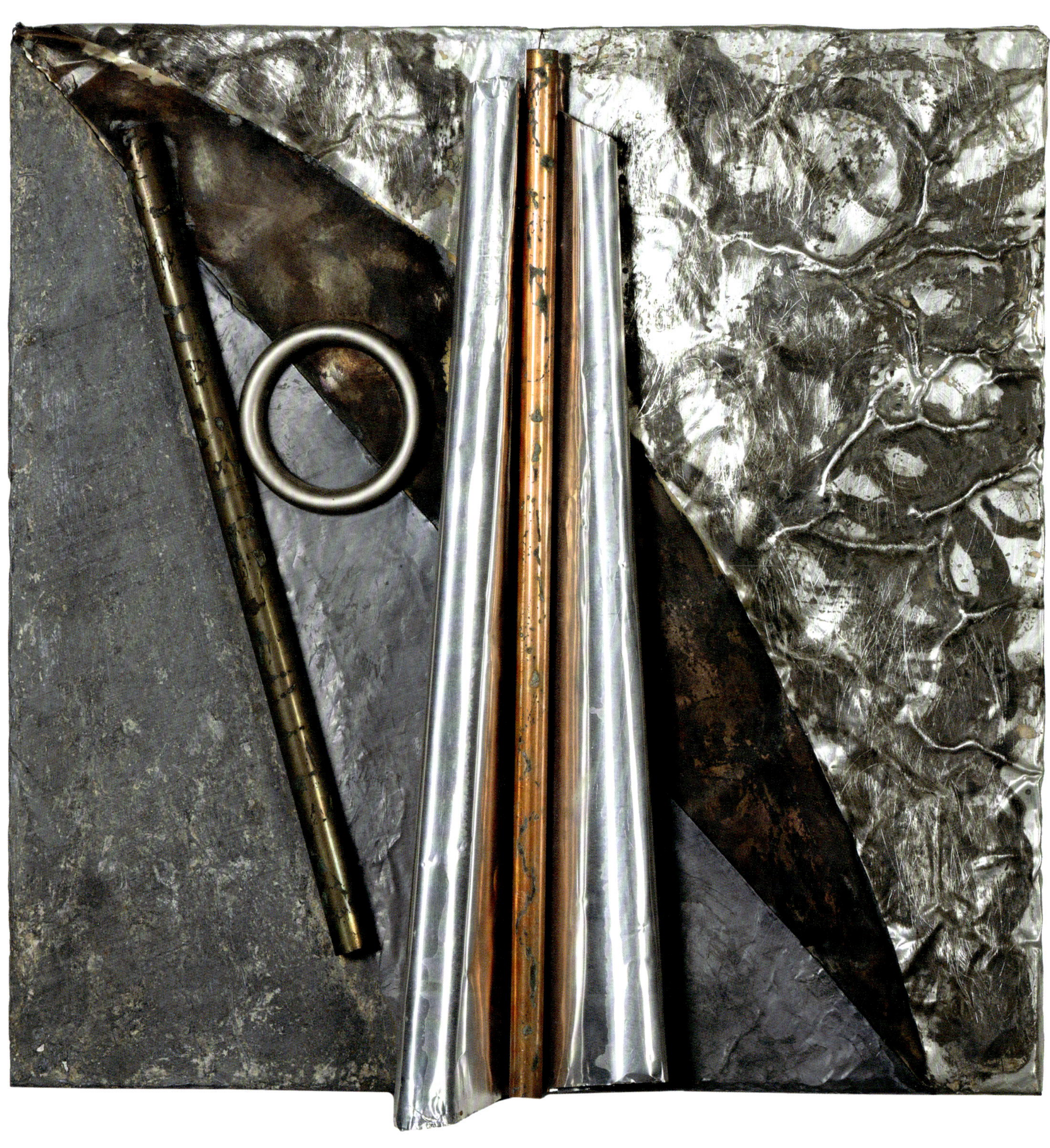

SILENCE
1991
Kupfer, Chrom, Aluminium Acide / Copper, chrom, aluminium acide

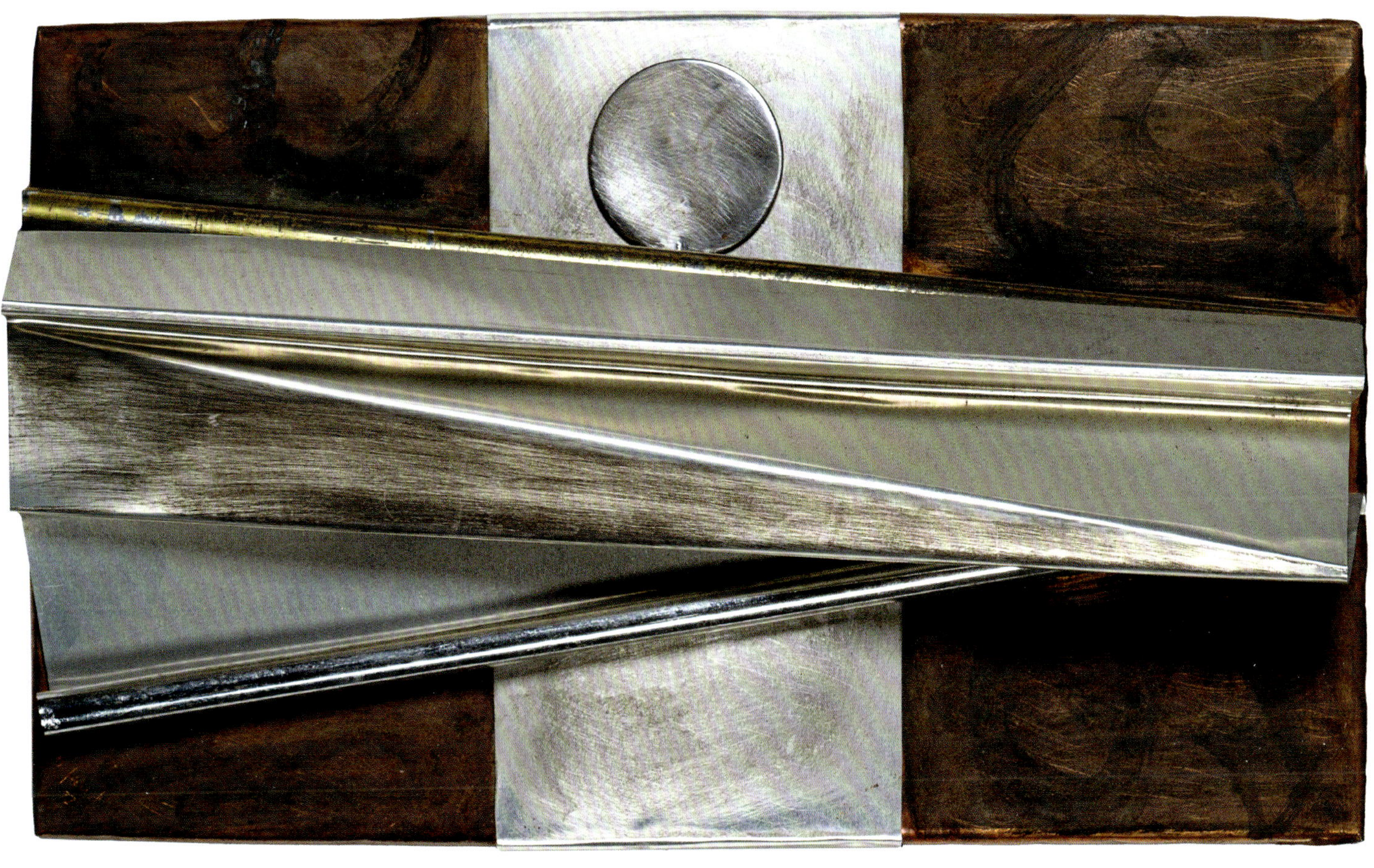

ROCKET WITH PLANET
1992
Kupfer, Chrom, Aluminium Acide / Copper, chrom, aluminium acide

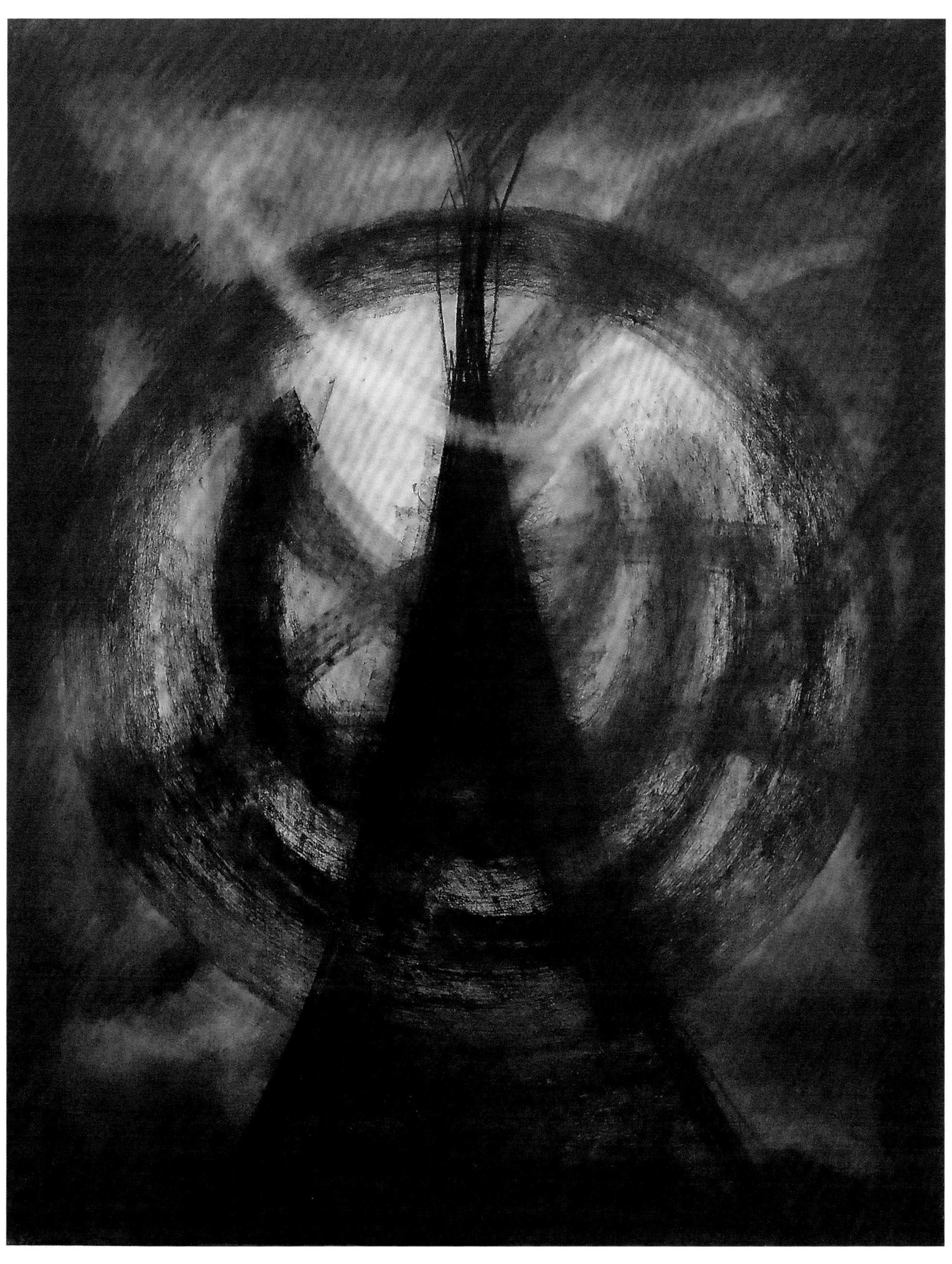

TIPI
1995
Bleistift und Kohle auf Papier / Pencil and charcoal on paper

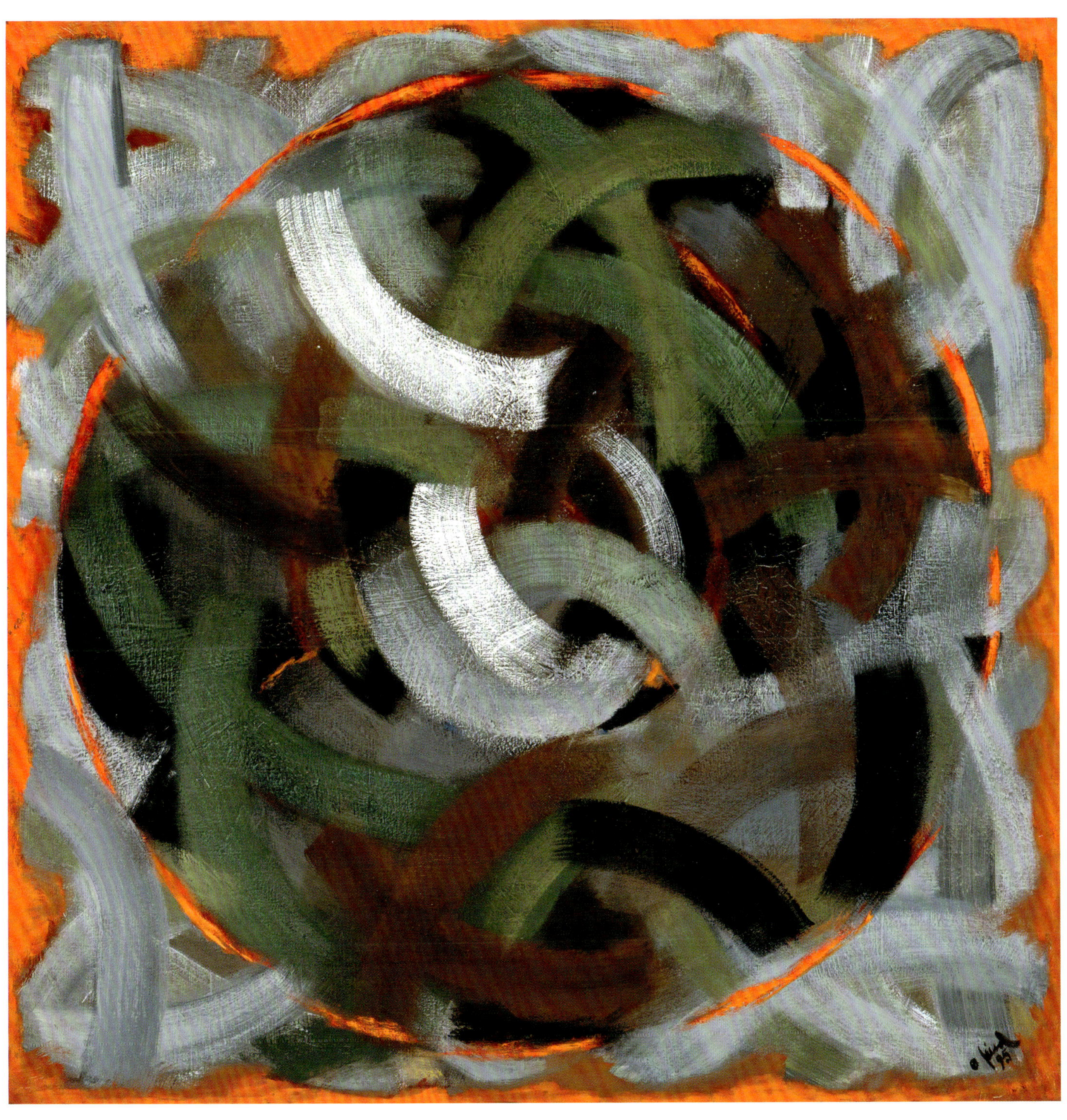

COREOPTIC
1995
Öl auf Leinwand / Oil on canvas

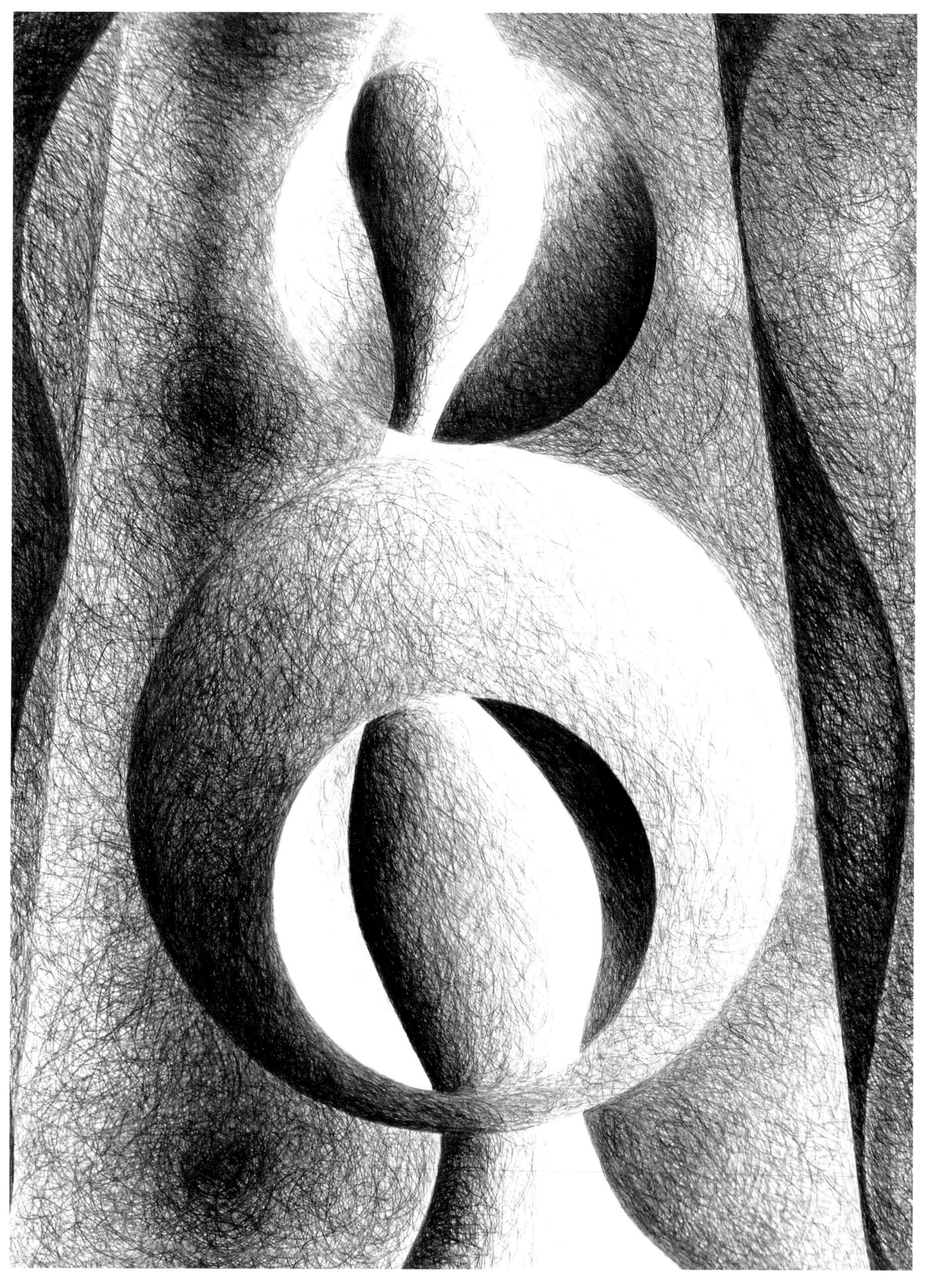

A FRESH TEAM
1996
Grafit auf Papier / Graphite on paper

VOLTIGEURS
1996
Geschmiedetes Eisen / Forged iron

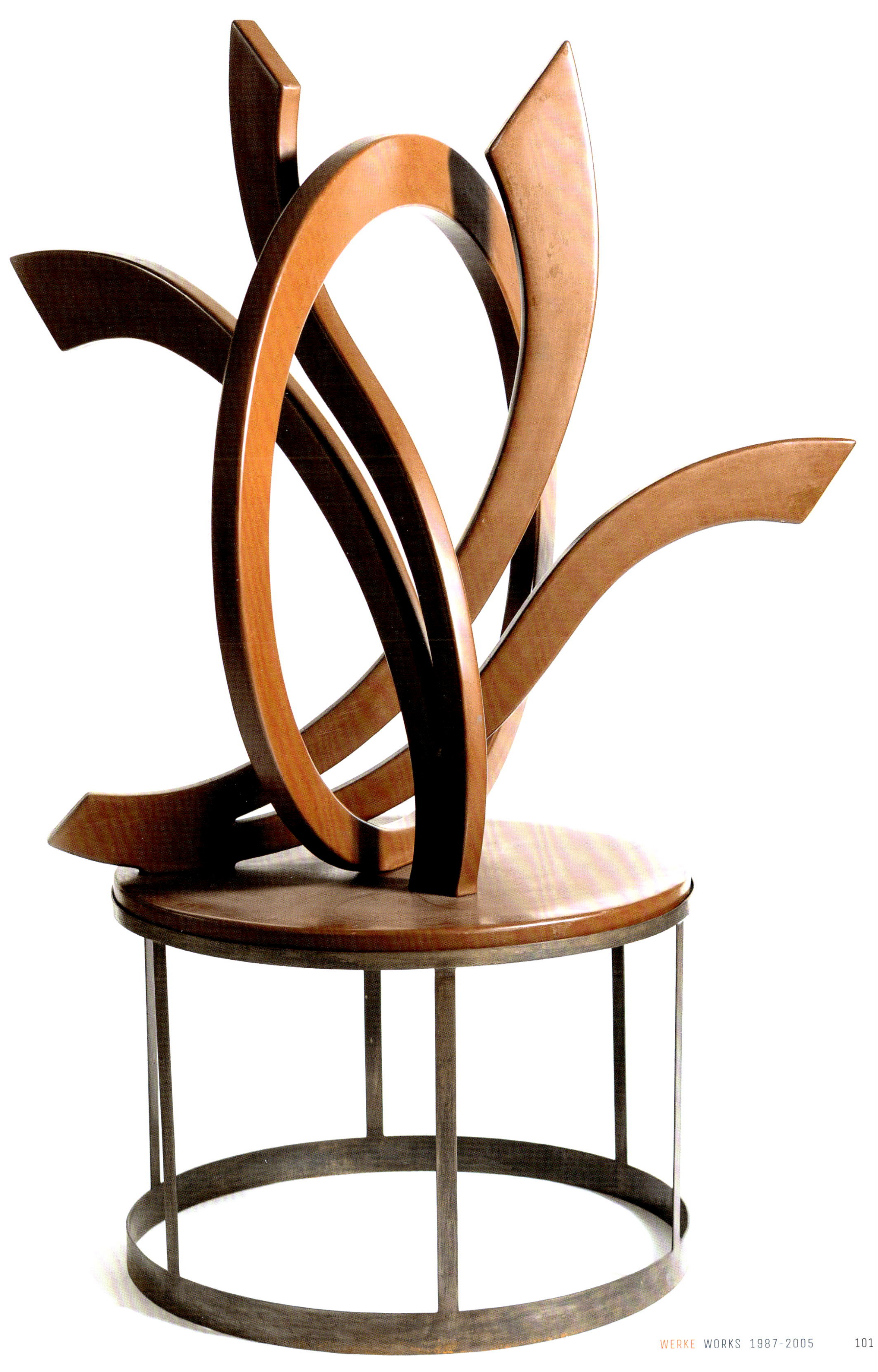

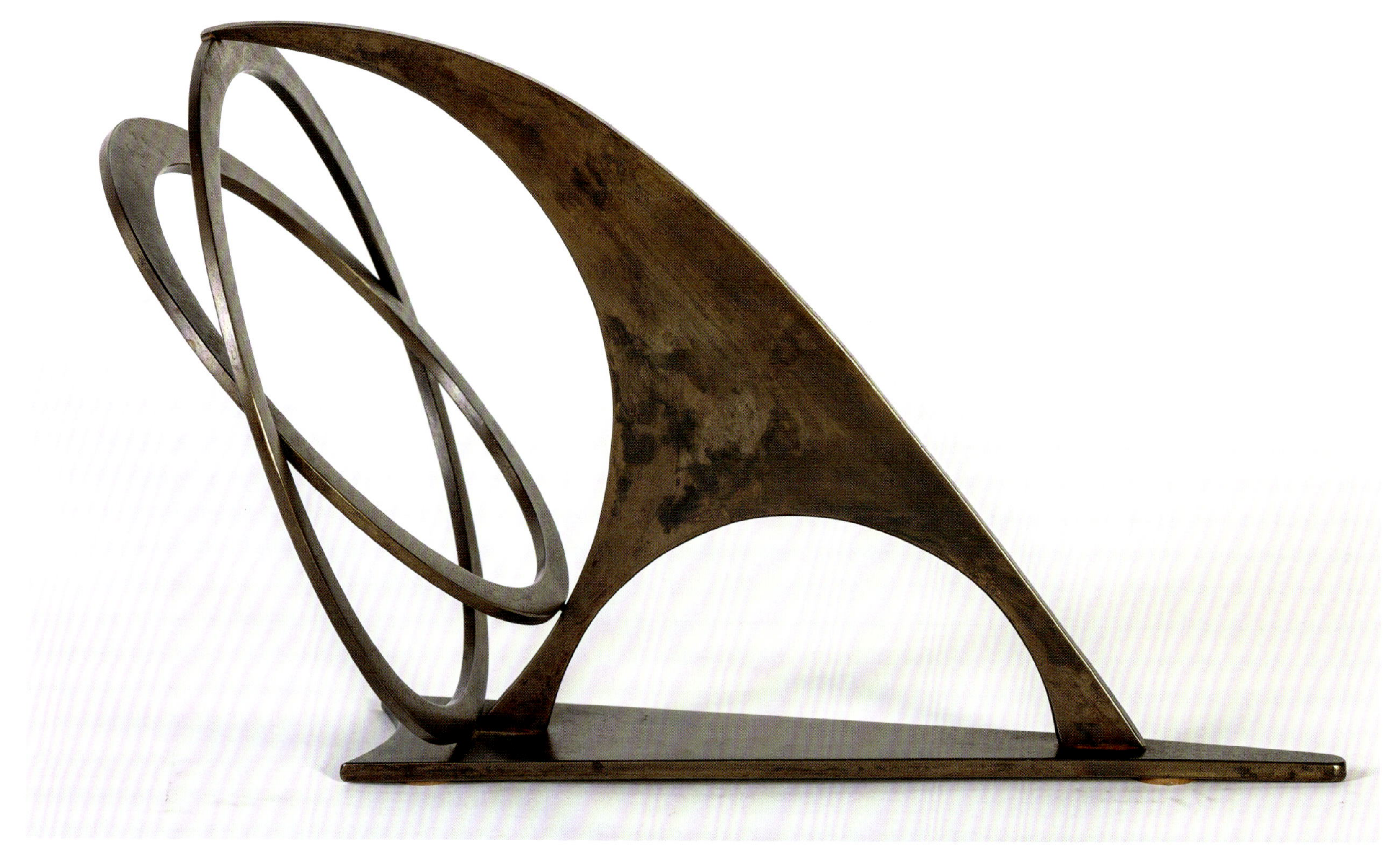

AMITIÉS
1996
Bronze mit Patina / Patinated bronze

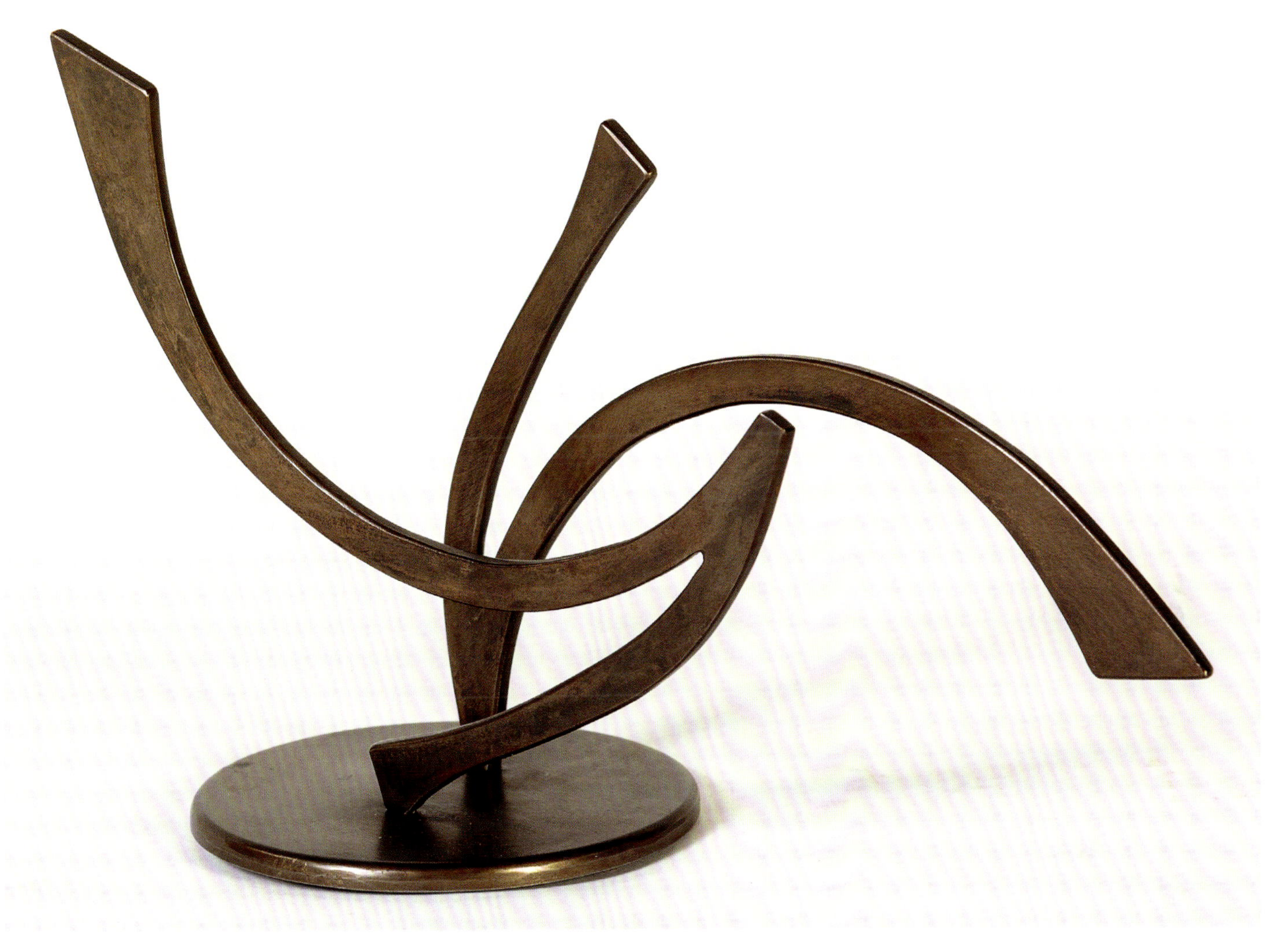

C'EST L'AMOUR
1996
Bronze mit Patina / Patinated bronze

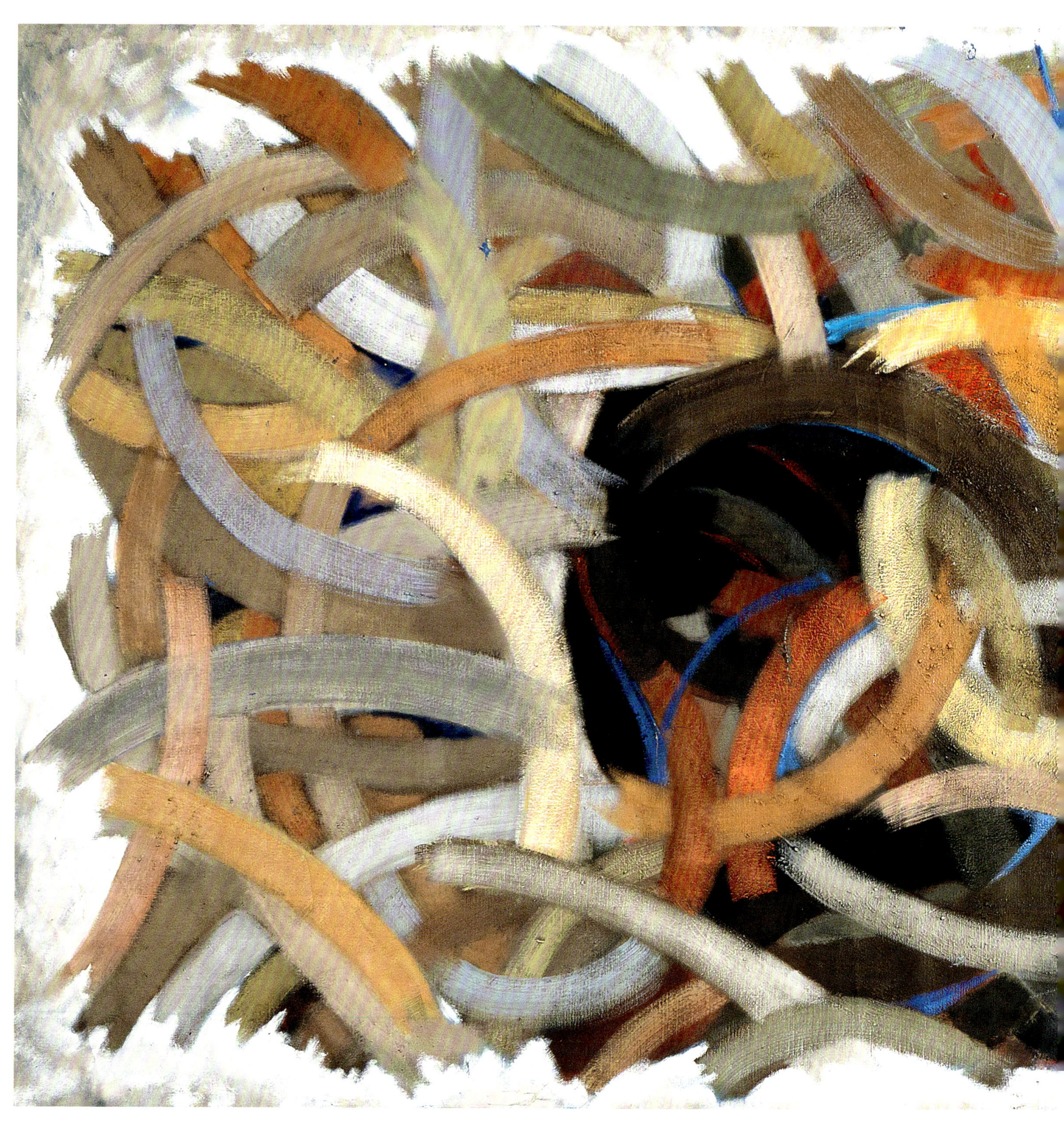

OHNE TITEL / UNTITLED
1998
Öl auf Leinwand / Oil on canvas

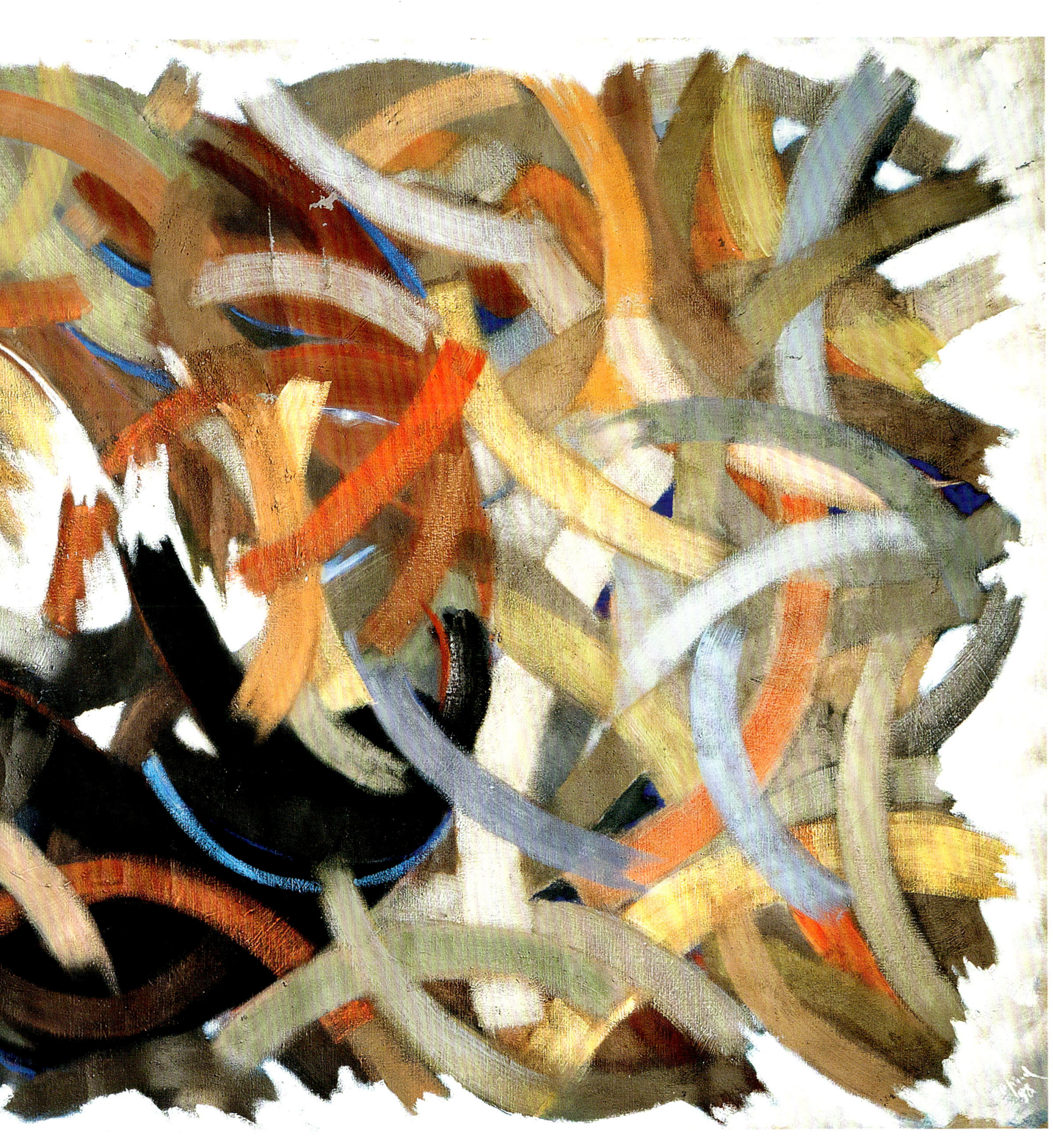

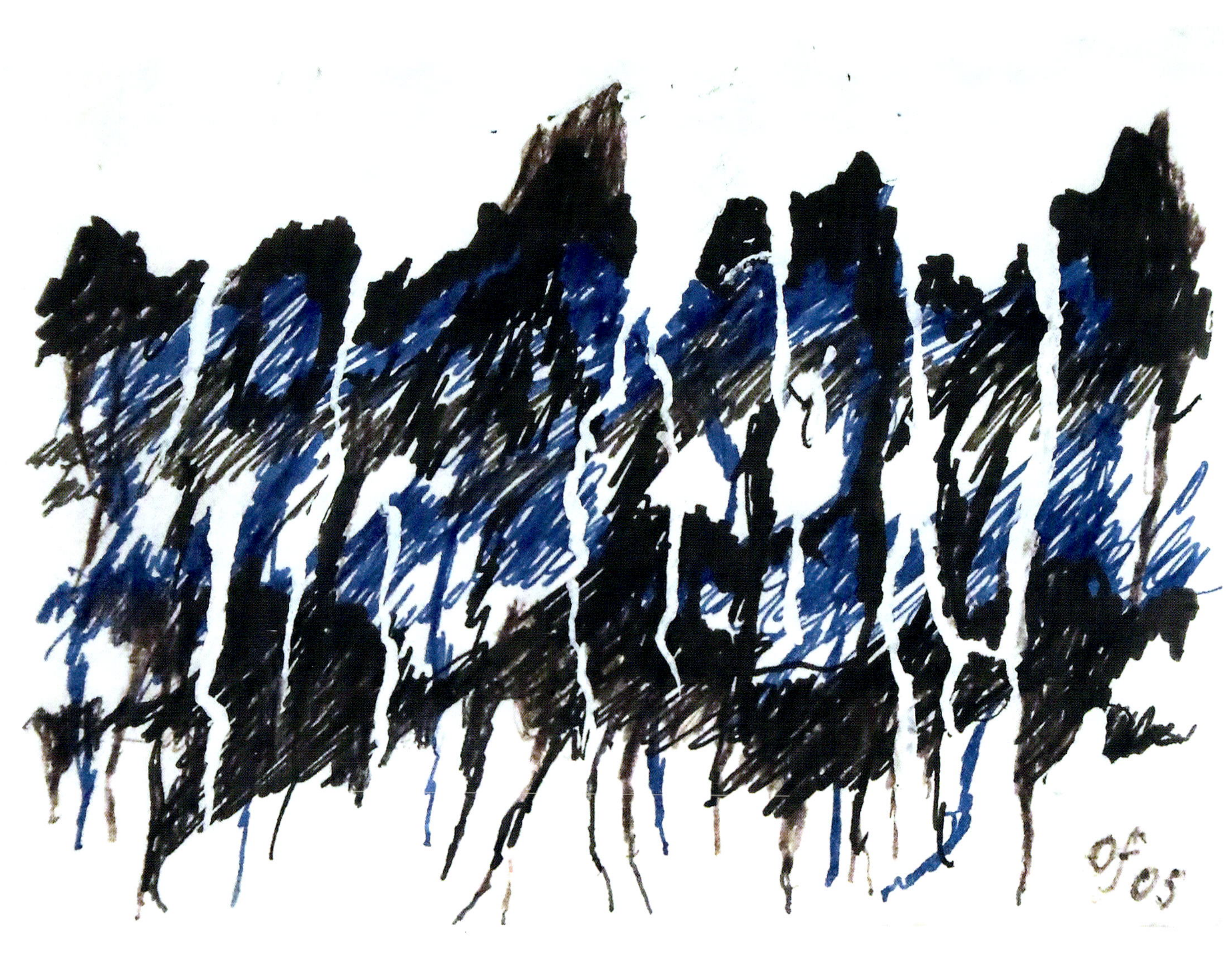

OHNE TITEL
2005
Zeichnung / Drawing

WERKVERZEICHNIS LIST OF WORKS

OHNE TITEL / UNTITLED
Circa 1948–1950
Grafit auf Papier / Graphite on paper
56 x 36,5 cm
Sammlung des Künstlers / Collection of the Artist
Seite / page 38

OHNE TITEL / UNTITLED
Circa 1948–1950
Grafit auf Papier / Graphite on paper
55 x 37 cm
Sammlung des Künstlers / Collection of the Artist
Seite / page 39

LANDSCAPE WITH BRIDGE
1951
Öl auf Leinwand / Oil on canvas
50 x 100 cm
Sammlung des Künstlers / Collection of the Artist
Seite / page 40

PARISIAN WINDOW
1952
Öl auf Leinwand / Oil on canvas
60 x 40 cm
Sammlung des Künstlers / Collection of the Artist
Seite / page 41

JONES BEACH
1956
Öl auf Leinwand / Oil on canvas
89 x 127 cm
Sammlung des Künstlers / Collection of the Artist
Seite / page 42

BLOSSOMING APPLE TREES
1958
Monotypie / Monotype
68,70 x 46,70 cm
Mittelrhein-Museum Koblenz
Seite / page 43

OHNE TITEL / UNTITLED
1973
Öl auf Leinwand / Oil on canvas
50 x 75 cm
Privatsammlung / Private collection
Seite / page 44

OVERLAPPING TEMPERATURES
1975
Öl auf Leinwand / Oil on canvas
97 x 146 cm
Sammlung des Künstlers / Collection of the Artist
Seite / page 45

FLOWERING ATMOSPHERE
1976
Öl auf Leinwand / Oil on canvas
97 x 130 cm
Sammlung des Künstlers / Collection of the Artist
Seite / page 45

OHNE TITEL / UNTITLED
Circa 1975–1978
Öl / Acryl auf Leinwand /
Oil / acryl on canvas
48,5 x 55 cm
Privatsammlung / Private collection
Seite / page 46

SPHÄREN
1976
Bleistift auf Papier / Pencil on paper
50 x 32 cm
Privatsammlung Familie Oebels / Private Collection, Oebels Family
Seite / page 47

JACKHAMMER BLUES
1978
Öl auf Leinwand / Oil on canvas
146 x 89 cm
Sammlung des Künstlers / Collection of the Artist
Seite / page 48

FEINES ATTESTAT
1978
Öl auf Leinwand / Oil on canvas
70 x 55 cm
Mittelrhein-Museum Koblenz
Seite / page 49

RUHE BITTE
1976
Zeichnung / Drawing
Bleistift auf Papier / Pencil on paper
65 x 50 cm
Privatsammlung / Private collection
Seite / page 50

EXPANSION
1979
Öl auf Leinwand / Oil on canvas
100 x 73 cm
Sammlung des Künstlers /
Collection of the Artist
Seite / page 51

OHNE TITEL / UNTITLED
Circa 1980
Grafit / Kohle auf Papier / Graphite / charcoal on paper
110 x 75 cm
Sammlung des Künstlers / Collection of the Artist
Seite / page 68

OHNE TITEL / UNTITLED
Circa 1980
Grafit / Kohle auf Papier / Graphite / charcoal on paper
99 x 72,5 cm
Sammlung des Künstlers / Collection of the Artist
Seite / page 69

MEASURED INFINITIES
1980
Öl / Acryl auf Leinwand /
Oil / acryl on canvas
49 x 33 cm
Privatsammlung / Private collection
Seite / page 70

OHNE TITEL / UNTITLED
Circa 1982
Grafit auf Papier / Graphite on paper
99,5 x 72,5 cm
Sammlung des Künstlers / Collection of the Artist
Seite / page 71

OHNE TITEL / UNTITLED
Circa 1983
Grafit auf Papier / Graphite on paper
99,5 x 72,5cm
Sammlung des Künstlers / Collection of the Artist
Seite / page 71

GREVED TAO
1982–1983
Öl auf Leinwand / Oil on canvas
130 x 195 cm
Sammlung des Künstlers / Collection of the Artist
Seite / page 72

SUMMER RAGA / RAGA D'ÉTÉ
1985
Öl auf Leinwand / Oil on canvas
73 x 116 cm
Sammlung des Künstlers / Collection of the Artist
Seite / page 73

TOMORROW'S FIELDS
1985
Öl auf Leinwand / Oil on canvas
2 Teile / 2 parts:
je / each 100 x 163 cm
Sammlung des Künstlers / Collection of the Artist
Seiten / pages 74–75

WORLDS APART
1986
Öl auf Leinwand / Oil on canvas
127 x 162 cm
Sammlung des Künstlers / Collection of the Artist
Seite / page 76

MAGIC ADVICE (ADVICE IN BLUE)
1986
Öl auf Leinwand / Oil on canvas
81,2 x 115,5 cm
Privatsammlung / Private collection
Seite / page 77

OHNE TITEL / UNTITLED
1987
Collage, Bleistift, Papiercollage auf Papier /
Collage, pencil, paper collage on paper
71 x 99 cm
Privatsammlung Familie Oebels / Private Collection, Oebels Family
Seite / page 78

OHNE TITEL / UNTITLED
2008
Grafit auf Papier / Graphite on paper
100 x 73 cm
Sammlung des Künstlers / Collection of the Artist
Seite / page 79

OHNE TITEL / UNTITLED
Circa 1987
Kraftpapier, (Well-)pappe, Tinte oder Gouache / Craft paper, (corrugated) cardboard, ink or gouache
3 Stücke / 3 pieces: 78 x 102 cm, 28 x 28 cm, 48 x 58 cm
Sammlung des Künstlers / Collection of the Artist
Seite / page 92

OHNE TITEL / UNTITLED
Circa 1990
Geschmiedetes Eisen / Forged iron
3 Stücke / 3 pieces:
je / each 20 x 15 cm
Sammlung des Künstlers / Collection of the Artist
Seite / page 93

FOURTH ZONE
1988
Öl auf Leinwand / Oil on canvas
2 Teile / 2 parts:
je / each 66 x 102,5 cm
Sammlung des Künstlers / Collection of the Artist
Seite / page 94

ECRITURE D'UN MONDE Á PART
1990
Collage: Öl auf Papier-Servietten applizierte auf Leinwand / Collage: Oil on paper napkins laid down on canvas
128 x 128 cm
Sammlung des Künstlers / Collection of the Artist
Seite / page 95

SILENCE
1991
Kupfer, Chrom, Aluminium Acide /Copper, Chrom, Aluminium acide
39 x 38 x 5 cm
Sammlung des Künstlers / Collection of the Artist
Seite / page 96

ROCKET WITH PLANET
1992
Kupfer, Chrom, Aluminium Acide /Copper, Chrom, Aluminium acide
38 x 23 x 1 0 cm
Sammlung des Künstlers / Collection of the Artist
Seite / page 97

TIPI
1995
Bleistift, Kohle / Pencil, charcoal
60 x 47,5 cm
Privatsammlung Familie Oebels / Private Collection, Oebels Family
Seite / page 98

COREOPTIC
1995
Öl auf Leinwand / Oil on canvas
122 x 122 cm
Sammlung des Künstlers / Collection of the Artist
Seite / page 99

A FRESH TEAM
1996
Grafit auf Papier / Graphite on paper
98 x 123 cm
Sammlung des Künstlers / Collection of the Artist
Seite / page 100

VOLTIGEURS
1996
Geschmiedetes Eisen / Forged iron
170 x 100 x 100 cm
(mit Fuß / incl. Base)
Sammlung des Künstlers / Collection of the Artist
Seite / page 101

AMITIÉS
1996
Bronze mit Patina / Patinated bronze
31 x 48 x 29 cm
Privatsammlung / Private collection
Seite / page 102

C'EST L'AMOUR
1996
Bronze mit Patina / Patinated bronze
21 x 35 x 14 cm
Privatsammlung / Private collection
Seite / page 103

OHNE TITEL / UNTITLED
1998
Öl auf Leinwand / Oil on canvas
208 x 408 cm
Sammlung des Künstlers / Collection of the Artist
Seiten / pages 104–105

BLADED CAVERNS
2000
Öl / Acryl auf Leinwand / Oil / acryl on canvas
27 x 46 cm
Privatsammlung / Private collection
Seite / page 35

OHNE TITEL / UNTITLED
2005
Tusche auf Papier / Ink on paper
Privatsammlung / Private collection
Seite / page 106

BIOGRAPHY

1922
Born in Koblenz district Horchheim on December 13, 1922.

1936
He succeeds in escaping from the growing threat of the National Socialists to Portland, Oregon at 13 thanks to the help of distant relatives living there. The trip through the Caribbean and Panama Canal via San Francisco impressed him deeply. In Portland, he initially lives with a host family.

1939
Fried's parents follow him to Oregon. Anti-semitism costs his brother's life.

1942
Graduation from Grant High School, Portland, Oregon.

1943
Conscription to the United States Army.

1944
Military draft at Air Corps, including the war area "India-China-Burma", till 1946.

1946
Got back to Portland.
Starts a biology course at Oregon State College, Portland, Oregon.

1947
After a summer course at the Art and Architecture Department of the University of Oregon, Eugene, he joins the painting class by Jack Wilkinson.

1949
Completes his studies in art at the University of Oregon, Eugene.
Northwest Artists Exhibition, Kharouba Gallery, Portland
Travels to France, to work at the Atelier of Fernand Legér at the Académie de Montmartre.

1950
On the recommendation of Fernand Léger, Fried's works are exhibited several times in Paris.
Salon d'Autonmne, Paris
Galerie Jeanne Bucher, Paris
Grand Cycle de Peintures, Deauville, France
Salon de l'Art libre, Paris

1951
American Library of Paris (first solo show)
Prima Biennale Internazionale d'Arte Marinara, Genoa, Italy
Gets back to Portland in October.

1952
Reed College Gallery, Portland, Oregon (solo show)
Instead of taking an opportunity to teach art in Oregon, he prefers living as a freelance artist in New York.
Meeting in New York with Richard Buckminster Fuller, philosopher and architect well known for his dome constructions.

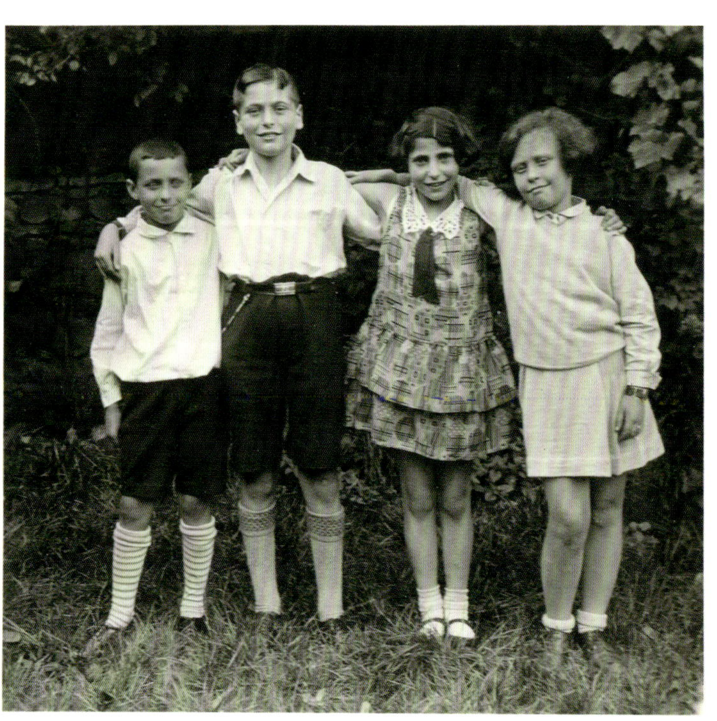

Otto Fried (links) mit seinem Cousin Heinz Georg und seinen Cousinen Lore und Liese in Diez an der Lahn / Otto Fried (left) with his cousins Heinz Georg, Lore and Liese in Diez an der Lahn

Biografie

1922
Geboren im Koblenzer Stadtteil Horchheim am 13. Dezember 1922.

1936
Kann als 13-Jähriger mit Hilfe dort lebender entfernter Verwandter nach Portland, Oregon, der zunehmenden Bedrohung durch die Nationalsozialisten in Deutschland entkommen. Die Reise durch die Karibik, den Panama Kanal über San Francisco beeindruckt ihn nachhaltig. In Portland lebt er zunächst bei einer Gastfamilie.

1939
Frieds Eltern können ihm nach Oregon folgen; seinen Bruder kostet der Antisemitismus das Leben.

1942
Schulabschluss an der Grant High School, Portland, Oregon.

1943
Einberufung in die United States Army.

1944
Militärdienst im Air Corps, u.a. im Kriegsgebiet „Indien-China-Burma", bis 1946.

1946
Rückkehr nach Portland.
Beginnt zunächst ein Biologie-Studium am Oregon State College, Portland, Oregon.

1947
Nach einem Sommerkurs am Art and Architecture Department der University of Oregon, Eugene, nimmt er das Malereistudium bei Jack Wilkinson auf.

1949
Schließt im Juni sein Kunststudium an der University of Oregon, Eugene, ab.
Northwest Artists Exhibition, Kharouba Gallery, Portland
Reist nach Frankreich, um dort im Atelier Fernand Légers an der Académie de Montmartre zu arbeiten.

1950
Auf Empfehlung von Fernand Léger werden Frieds Werke mehrfach in Paris ausgestellt.
Salon d'Automne, Paris
Galerie Jeanne Bucher, Paris
Grand Cycle de Peintures, Deauville, Frankreich
Salon de l'Art libre, Paris

1951
American Library of Paris (Erste Einzelausstellung)
Primera Biennale Internazionale d'Arte Marinara, Genua, Italien
Rückkehr nach Portland im Oktober.

1952
Reed College Gallery, Portland, Oregon (Einzelausstellung)
Zieht ein Leben als freier Künstler in New York der Option, in Oregon Kunst zu lehren, vor. Treffen mit Richard Buckminster Fuller, dem Philosophen und durch seine Kuppelkonstruktionen bekannten Architekten, in New York, vermittelt über seinen Freund Kenneth Snelson, der mit ihm bei Jack Wilkinson und Fernand Léger studiert hatte. Fried arbeitet zunächst figurativ, trifft bald die führenden Vertreter des Abstrakten Expressionismus und lernt Musiker, Filmemacher und weitere Intellektuelle kennen. Erste Ehe, die nur wenige Jahre Bestand hat.
The Oregon Journal (Lobby), Portland, Oregon (Einzelausstellung)
Ausstellung von Zeichnungen, Portland Art Museum, Portland, Oregon

1953
University of Oregon, Eugene, Oregon

1955
New York City Center Gallery, New York City

1956
Wellons Gallery, New York City (Einzelausstellung)
Les Arts Décoratifs (Heute: Union centrale des Arts décoratifs), Paris

1957
Hastings-on-Hudson, New York
Warren Robbins, Leiter des United States Information Service in Deutschland und Kulturattaché an der amerikanischen Botschaft in Bonn, bittet Fried um die Zusendung von Kunstwerken für eine Ausstellungsreihe.

1958
Zweijährig tourende Einzelausstellung des United States Information Service (U.S.I.S.): Deutschherrenhaus, Koblenz (1958) / Kunstgewerbeschule, Tübingen (1959) / German American Cultural Institute, Darmstadt (1960)
Fried entwirft einen Paravent aus Metall und Glas für die New York Glas Factory.

1960
Das Metropolitan Museum of Art, New York, kauft eine Monotypie Frieds für die Sammlung des Museums. Die Kunst der Monotypie war zu diesem Zeitpunkt weitgehend unbekannt in den USA.
Welser Gallery, Salzburg, Österreich (Einzelausstellung)
Nester Gallery, New York
Columbia Museum, Columbia, South Carolina
Irving Gallery, Milwaukee, Wisconsin
Greenville Museum, Greenville, South Carolina
Drawing Exhibition, Cober Gallery, New York

Ein „Amerika-Schängel“ stellt aus

50 Originalwerke des in Koblenz geborenen Malers Otto Fried

Die Stadt Koblenz veranstaltet in Zusammenarbeit mit dem Amerika-Haus eine Ausstellung von etwa 50 Originalwerken des in Koblenz geborenen amerikanischen Malers Otto Fried. Diese Ausstellung wird vom 1. bis 7. Juli, täglich von 11 bis 19 Uhr, im Kapitelsaal des Koblenzer Deutsch-Herren-Hauses gezeigt. Der Eröffnung werden Vertreter der Stadt Koblenz und der amerikanischen Botschaft beiwohnen.

Der Maler und Graphiker Otto Fried wurde am 13. Dezember 1922 in Koblenz-Horchheim als Sohn der Metzgerfamilie Fried-Salomon geboren. Schon in früher Jugend zeigte sich seine Vorliebe für das Zeichnen und Malen. Nach seiner Emigration über Spanien nach den Vereinigten Staaten im Jahre 1937 wurde er durch Anregung und Förderung seiner Universitätslehrer ermutigt, sich in vollem Maße einer künstlerischen Ausbildung zuzuwenden.

Als „Bachelor of the Fine Arts“ der Universität Oregon arbeitete Otto Fried anschließend in Paris unter Fernand Léger und André Lhôte. In dieser Zeit wurden durch die besondere Empfehlung Légers die Ölbilder und Monotypien des Malers in mehreren Städten Frankreichs ausgestellt. Nach seiner Rückkehr in die Vereinigten Staaten folgten weitere Ausstellungen im Staat Oregon. Von Portland, Oregon, zog Fried nach New York, wo er auch heute wohnt.

Otto Frieds Bilder entstehen zunächst scheinbar aus einem unmittelbaren Erlebnis der realen Dingwelt, deren Zeichen er dann aber durch eine Verflechtung mit abstrakten Formelementen verhüllt. Die Pinsel- und Flächenstrukturen verändern sich nur selten. Trotzdem entsteht jedes Werk immer wieder als das Ergebnis einer neuen malerischen Erfahrung oder Entdeckung. [illegible] er auch jedes Blatt [illegible] schlossenes Werk und [illegible] Bilderfolge betrachtet w[illegible]

Seine Monotypien weisen mehr in die experimentelle Richtung seiner künstlerischen Arbeit. Diese Technik bot ihm vor allem einfache Mittel, mit denen er in vielfacher Abwandlung zu einer neuen stofflichen Bereicherung und Oberflächenstruktur im Bild gelangen konnte. Dieses Können erwarb sich Fried im Laufe von sechs Jahren steter Experimente. Heute ist er einer der bekanntesten Vertreter der Monotypie in den Vereinigten Staaten und bewirkt geradezu eine Wiedergeburt dieser Bildgattung unter den Künstlern seines Landes. Werke von Otto Fried befinden sich in Privatbesitz und in Kollektionen in England, Frankreich, den Vereinigten Staaten, in Australien, Chile und in vielen anderen Ländern.

Herausgeber und Verlag: Mittelrhein-Verlag GmbH, Koblenz, Schloßstr. 13, Fernsprech-Sammel-Nr. [illegible]
[illegible]
Druck: Mittelrhein-Verlag GmbH, Koblenz.
[illegible]
Verantwortlich für den Anzeigenteil: [illegible] Antwerpen.
[illegible]
Geschäftsstelle Koblenz, [illegible] Fernsprech-Sammel-Nr. [illegible]

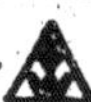

Ein Meister der Monotypie

Die Ausstellung Otto Frieds im Deutschherren-Haus eröffnet

Am Montagvormittag wurde die von der Stadt Koblenz in Gemeinschaft mit dem Amerika-Haus veranstaltete Ausstellung von nahezu 50 Werken des 1922 in Koblenz-Horchheim geborenen, 1936 nach den USA ausgewanderten und dort ausgebildeten Malers und Graphikers Otto Fried im Kapitelsaal des Koblenzer Deutschherren-Hauses eröffnet. Vor dem Kreis der Geladenen – ex officio-Anwesenden und Kunstinteressenten – machte Museumsdirektor Dr. Metzger in seiner Begrüßungsansprache einige recht anregende Ausführungen, die uns die Bekanntschaft mit dem Künstler und seiner Technik erleichtern und in das Verständnis für das Gesamtwerk einführen sollten.

Der Hauptakzent von Frieds Schaffen liegt auf seinen graphischen Werken, auf seinen Monotypien. Davon sieht man an den Wänden 36 Beispiele, während von seiner Malweise nur zehn Bilder Auskunft geben. Erfreulich ist an dem Ganzen, daß es ikonographisch keine Rätsel aufgibt, daß der Betrachter immer noch erkennt, mühelos erkennt, was dargestellt werden soll. Ein wirklicher Stimmungsgehalt ist da, der in Farbe, Linie und Schattierung beim Betrachter Resonanz finden kann, weil dies er im Sehen begreift und ihn weder bloße Farbflecke noch Linienchaos düpieren. Dabei ist Otto Fried natürlich schon ein Moderner, aber in den Grenzen des Sinnvollen. In dem Vorausartikel (Rhein-Zeitung vom 26. Juni) über ihn und seine Malweise heißt es, daß das Gegenständliche „durch eine Verflechtung mit abstrakten Formelementen verhüllt“ werde. Gewiß: diese Symbiose von Realität und Abstraktion ist an seinen Bildern wahrnehmbar, freilich auch erkennbar. Das Verhülltwerden entartet nicht in Auflösung des Objektes. Und dies ist eben der Gewinn.

Die graphischen Werke der Ausstellung, die Monotypien, zeigen, daß es der Künstler hier verstanden hat, in vielfacher Abwandlung der Technik zu neuen Wirkungen der Körperlichkeit, der Farbe und der Linie zu gelangen. Sechs Jahre hat Otto Fried seinen Versuchen obgelegen, so daß er in dieser Technik zu einer Meisterschaft gediehen ist, der vor allem er seinen Ruf in den Vereinigten Staaten zu danken hat. Menschliche Figuren, Tiere – dies vor allem –, Landschaft und Wasser sind hauptsächlich die Motive, für die gedeckte Valeurs bevorzugt werden. GM.

"Ein 'Amerika-Schängel' stellt aus", Ausstellungsankündigung Koblenz 1958 / Exhibition Announcement Koblenz 1958, *Rhein-Zeitung* 26.06.1958

"Ein Meister der Monotypie", Ausstellungsbericht Koblenz 1958 / Exhibition-Review Koblenz 1958, *Rhein-Zeitung* 02.07.1958

arranged by his friend Kenneth Snelson, who had studied with him under Jack Wilkinson and Fernand Léger. Fried initially chooses figurative art, but soon meets the leading representatives of Abstract Expressionism and gets to know musicians, filmmakers and other intellectuals. First marriage that lasts only a few years.
The Oregon Journal (Lobby), Portland, Oregon (solo show)
Exhibition of drawing, Portland Art Museum, Portland, Oregon

1953
University of Oregon, Eugene, Oregon

1955
New York City Center Gallery, New York City

1956
Wellons Gallery, New York City (solo show)
Les Arts Décoratifs (now: Union centrale des Arts décoratifs), Paris

1957
Hastings-on-Hudson, New York
Warren Robbins, head of the United States Information Service in Germany and cultural attaché at the American embassy in Bonn, asks Fried to send some of his works of art for an exhibition series.

1958
Biennial travelling solo show of the United States Information Service (U.S.I.S.): Deutschherrenhaus, Koblenz (1958) / Kunstgewerbeschule, Tübingen (1959) / German American Cultural Institute, Darmstadt (1960)
Fried designs a metal and glass screen for the New York Glass Factory.

1960
The Metropolitan Museum of Art, New York, buys a monotype by Fried for the museum's collection. At the time, the art of monotype was largely unknown in the United States.
Welser Gallery, Salzburg, Österreich (solo show)
Nester Gallery, New York

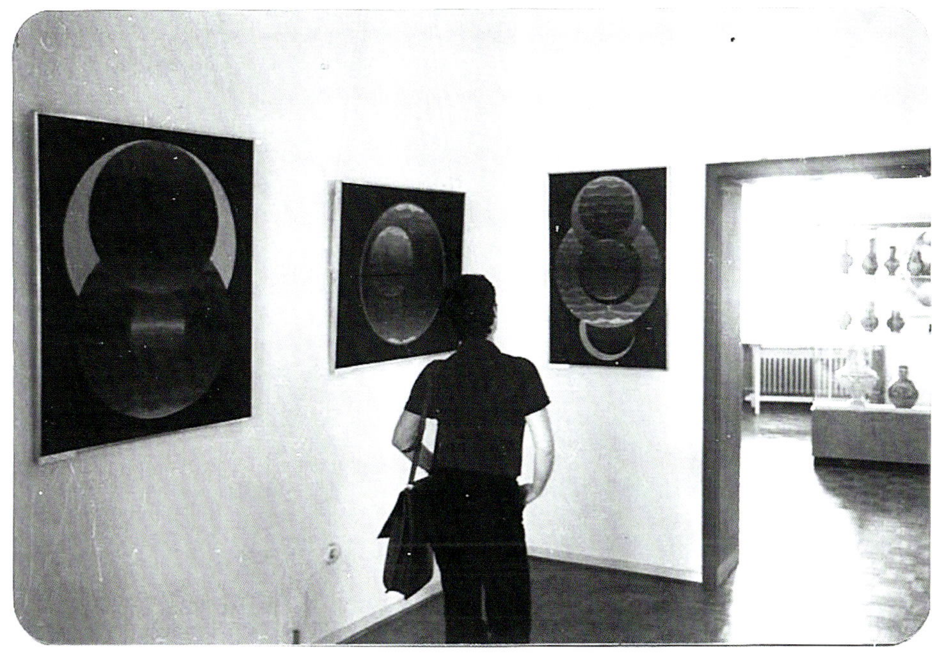

Otto Frieds Ausstellung im Mittelrhein-Museum Koblenz, 1978 / Otto Fried's exhibition at the Mittelrhein-Museum Koblenz, 1978

Critic's Choice Exhibition, City and Country School, New York
Gallery 10, New Hope, Pennsylvania

1961
Das Metropolitan Museum of Art und das Rose Art Museum der Brandeis University, Waltham, Massachusetts, kaufen je eine Monotypie für ihre Sammlungen.
Leger-Gallery, White Plains, New York (Einzelausstellung)
„Otto Fried", Arlan Gallery, Pittsburgh, Pennsylvania (Einzelausstellung)

1962
Heiratet die französische Modejournalistin Micheline Haardt und zieht nach Paris. Zusätzlich zu seinem Atelier in Paris behält Fried sein Studio in New York, wo das Paar jährlich einige Monate verbringt
Oshkosh Museum, Oshkosh, Wisconsin (Einzelausstellung)
Robbins Collection, Howard University Gallery, Washington D.C.

1963
Revel Gallery, New York (Einzelausstellung)
Das Museum der Syracuse University, New York (heute „SUArt Galleries") kauft ein Ölgemälde für seine Sammlung.

1964
Gallery Vendome, Pittsburgh, Pennsylvania (Einzelausstellung)
Galerie Hector Brame, Paris (Einzelausstellung)
Ankauf eines Ölgemäldes für die Sammlung des Museum of Art, University of Oregon, (heute Jordan Schnitzer Museum) in Eugene, Oregon.

1966
Byron Gallery, New York City (Einzelausstellung)
Galerie Hector Brame, Paris (Einzelausstellung)

1968
„Otto Fried: Recent Painings", The Fountain Gallery, Portland, Oregon (Einzelausstellung)
Museum of Art, University of Oregon, Portland (Einzelausstellung)

1969
Irving Gallery, Milwaukee, Wisconsin (Einzelausstellung)
Galerie Hector Brame, Paris (Einzelausstellung)

1972
Auftrag zur Gestaltung eines Wandgemäldes in Grimaud, Frankreich.
Für American Express Co. entwirft er ein Set aus Trinkgläsern, Schalen und einem Teller, die in einer Werkstatt in Murano produziert werden.
Kreise, die bereits in den 1950er und 60er Jahren in Fried's Strand- oder Stadtlandschaften auftauchten, beginnen Anfang der 1970er Jahre seine Arbeiten zu prägen.

1973
The Fountain Gallery, Portland, Oregon (Einzelausstellung)
„Otto Fried: Paintings", Coe Kerr Gallery, New York City (Einzelausstellung)

1975
„Important New Oils by Otto Fried", Coe Kerr Gallery, New York City (Einzelausstellung)

1977
„Otto Fried: Le monde des sphères", Galerie des Grands Augustins, Paris (Einzelausstellung)
Ankauf von vier Monotypien für die Sammlung des Musée d'art moderne, Centre Pompidou, Paris

1978
„Otto Fried: Ströme" Mittelrhein-Museum, Koblenz (Einzelausstellung)

1979
The Fountain Gallery, Portland, Oregon (Einzelausstellung)
Schenkung seines Werkes „Feines Attestat" (1978) an das Mittelrhein-Museum, Koblenz.
„Otto Fried", Fuji TV Gallery, Tokyo, Japan (Einzelausstellung)
Reise nach Tokio, wo Fried ein Fernsehinterview gibt, durch das Zen-Buddhisten auf seine Gemälde aufmerksam werden.

1980
Ausstellung von Zeichnungen, Galerie Valmay, Paris

1982
The Fountain Gallery, Portland Oregon (Einzelausstellung)

1983
The Washington D.C. Design Center (Einzelausstellung)

1985
Fuji TV Gallery, Tokyo, Japan (Einzelausstellung)
Zweiwöchige Reise nach Japan; Treffen mit japanischen Künstlern.
Arbeitet erstmals an runden Reliefs aus Packpapier und Pappe.

1986
Galerie Gianna Sistu, Paris

Columbia Museum, Columbia, South Carolina
Irving Gallery, Milwaukee, Wisconsin
Greenville Museum, Greenville, South Carolina
Drawing Exhibition, Cober Galley, New York
Critic's Choice Exhibition, City and Country School, New York
Gallery 10, New Hope, Pennsylvania

1961
The Metropolitan Museum of Art and the Rose Art Museum of the Brandeis University, Waltham, Massachusetts, buy a monotype each for their collections.
Leger-Gallery, White Plains, New York (solo show)
"Otto Fried", Arlan Gallery, Pittsburgh, Pennsylvania (solo show)

1962
Marries the French fashion journalist Micheline Haardt and moves to Paris. However, the couple spends several months each year in the United States. Beside his studio in Paris, Fried keeps one also in New York, where the couple spends several months each year.
Oshkosh Museum, Oshkosh, Wisconsin (solo show)
Robbins Collection, Howard University Gallery, Washington D.C.

1963
Revel Gallery, New York (solo show)
The Museum of Syracuse University, New York (now "SUArt Galleries") buys an oil painting for its collection.

1964
Gallery Vendome, Pittsburgh, Pennsylvania (solo show)
Galerie Hector Brame, Paris (solo show)
Purchase of an oil painting for the collection of the Museum of Art, University of Oregon, (now Jordan Schnitzer Museum) in Eugene, Oregon.

1966
Byron Gallery, New York City (solo show)
Galerie Hector Brame, Paris (solo show)

1968
"Otto Fried: Recent Paintings", The Fountain Gallery, Portland, Oregon (solo show)
Museum of Art, University of Oregon, Portland (solo show)

1969
Irving Gallery, Milwaukee, Wisconsin (solo show)
Galerie Hector Brame, Paris (solo show)

1972
Commission to design a wall painting in Grimaud, France.
For American Express, he designs a set of drinking glasses, bowls and a plate, which are produced in a glasswork.
The circles, that had already appeared in Fried's beach- or cityscapes as early as the 1950s and 60s, begin to shape his work in the early 1970s.

1973
The Fountain Gallery, Portland, Oregon (solo show)
"Otto Fried: Paintings", Coe Kerr Gallery, New York City (solo show)

1975
"Important New Oils by Otto Fried", Coe Kerr Gallery, New York City (solo show)

1977
"Otto Fried: Le monde des spheres", Galerie des Grands Augustins, Paris (solo show)
Purchase of four monotypes for the Collection of Musée d'art moderne, Centre Pompidou, Paris

1978
"Otto Fried: Ströme" Mittelrhein-Museum, Koblenz (solo show)

1979
The Fountain Gallery, Portland, Oregon (solo show)
Donation of his work *Feines Attestat* (1978) to the Mittelrhein-Museum, Koblenz.
"Otto Fried", Fuji TV Gallery, Tokyo, Japan (solo show)
Travels to Tokyo, where Fried gives a television interview that draws Zen Buddhists' attention towards his paintings.

1980
Exhibition of drawings, Galerie Valmay, Paris

1982
The Fountain Gallery, Portland, Oregon (solo show)

1983
The Washington D.C. Design Center (solo show)

1985
Fuji TV Gallery, Tokyo, Japan (solo show)
Two-week travel to Japan; He meets Japanese artists.
Works for the first time on round reliefs which are made of wrapping paper and cardboard.

1986
Galerie Gianna Sistu, Paris
The Fountain Gallery, Portland, Oregon (solo show)
Purchase of an oil painting for the Collection of Portland Art Museum, Portland.

1987
Invited to produce reliefs for outdoor spaces, Fried begins to work with metal
Paris-New York-Kent Gallery, Kent, Connecticut (solo show)
Galerie Gianna Sistu, Paris (solo show)

1988
Commission by the Friends of Musée d'art moderne, Centre Georges Pompidou, Paris, to design fireplace instruments made of brass and iron as well as a set of plates of Limoges porcelain and a series of large serving plates.
Bachelier Cardonsky Gallery, Kent, Connecticut

1989
"Otto Fried: Recent Paintings", Foster/White Gallery, Seattle, Washington (solo show)

1990
"Otto Fried: œuvres récentes", Galerie Gianna Sistu, Paris (solo show)
Commission by the Friends of Musée d'art moderne, Centre Georges Pompidou, Paris, to design door knobs made of brass and iron.
In addition to painting and drawing, Fried increasingly works as a sculptor and designer in the 1990s. He designs furniture like consoles, tables, shelves and smaller items such as bookends, door handles and candle holders as well as carpets. In addition to small everyday objects and sculptures, he creates also large metal sculptures in collaboration with the blacksmith Jean Prévost.

1991
"Otto Fried: Metal Relief Structures", Achim Moeller Fine Art, New York (solo show)

1992
Commission by the Friends of Musée d'art moderne, Centre Georges Pompidou, Paris, to design vases made of wrought iron and ceramics.
Commission for an outdoor sculpture for the city of Grimaud, Var, France.

1993
"Otto Fried", Laura Russo Gallery, Portland, Oregon
Lecture at the University of Oregon, Eugene

The Fountain Gallery, Portland, Oregon (Einzelausstellung)
Ankauf eines Ölgemäldes für die Sammlung des Portland Art Museum, Portland.

1987
Eingeladen, Reliefs für den Außenraum zu produzieren, beginnt Fried mit Metall zu arbeiten.
Paris-New York-Kent Gallery, Kent, Connecticut (Einzelausstellung)
Galerie Gianna Sistu, Paris (Einzelausstellung)

1988
Auftrag der Freunde des Musée d'art moderne, Centre Georges Pompidou, Paris, zur Gestaltung von Kamininstrumenten aus Messing und Eisen sowie von einem Tellerset aus Limoges-Porzellan und einer Serie von großen Serviertellern.
Bachelier Cardonsky Gallery, Kent, Connecticut

1989
„Otto Fried: Recent Paintings", Foster/White Gallery, Seattle, Washington (Einzelausstellung)

1990
„Otto Fried: œuvres récentes", Galerie Gianna Sistu, Paris (Einzelausstellung)
Auftrag der Freunde des Musée national d'art moderne, Centre Georges Pompidou, Paris, Türknäufe aus Messing und Eisen zu gestalten.
Neben dem Malen und Zeichnen, arbeitet Fried in den 1990er Jahren zunehmend als Bildhauer und Designer. Er entwirft Möbel wie Konsolen, Tische, Regale und kleinere Gegenstände wie Buchstützen, Türklinken und Kerzenhalter sowie Teppiche. Neben kleinen Gebrauchsgegenständen und Skulpturen entstehen in Zusammenarbeit mit dem Schmied Jean Prévost auch große Skulpturen aus Metall.

1991
„Otto Fried: Metal Relief Structures", Achim Moeller Fine Art, New York (Einzelausstellung)

1992
Auftrag der Freunde des Musée national d'Art moderne, Centre Georges Pompidou, Paris, Vasen aus geschlagenem Eisen und Keramik zu gestalten.
Auftrag für eine Außenskulptur für die Stadt Grimaud, Var, Frankreich.

1993
„Otto Fried", Laura Russo Gallery, Portland, Oregon
Vortrag an der University of Oregon, Eugene

1994
Das Museum of Modern Art in New York kauft eine Zeichnung für seine Sammlung.
Zwei Aufträge für Skulpturen.
Auftrag zur Gestaltung eines drei Meter hohen Brunnens für den Skulpturengarten der Sammler Paul und Jeanette Haim, nahe Biarritz, Frankreich.

1995
Arbeit an Metallreliefs
Ausstellung von Skulpturen im Salon des Beaux-Arts
Achim Moeller Fine Arts, Paris

1996
Auftrag zur Gestaltung einer Außenskulptur für eine Skulpturenpark in Newton, Connecticut.

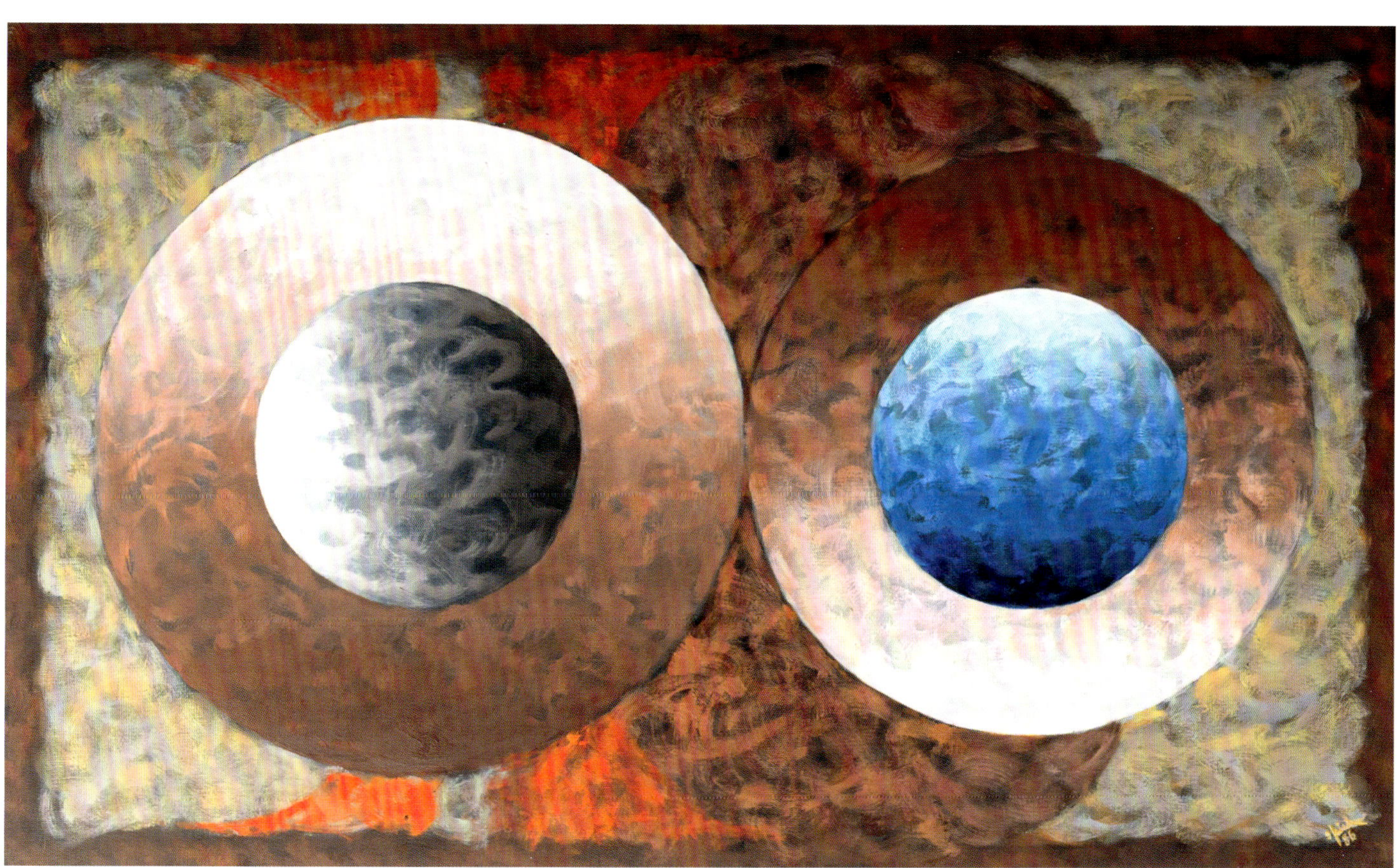

Otto Fried, *Leewärtige Illusion*, 1986
Öl auf Leinwand / Oil on canvas
Pfarrkirche St. Maximin, Horchheim, Koblenz

1994
The Museum of Modern Art in New York buys a drawing for its collection.
Two commissions of sculptures.
Commission to design a 3-meter-high fountain for the sculpture garden of collectors Paul and Jeanette Haim, near Biarritz, France.

1995
Works on metal reliefs.
Exhibition of sculptures at Salon des Beaux-Arts
Achim Moeller Fine Arts, Paris

1996
Commission to design an outdoor sculpture for the sculpture garden in Newton, Connecticut.

1997
"Otto Fried: Sculptures et dessins", Galerie Brame & Lorenceau, Paris (solo show)
"Artistes Américains en France", Mona Bismark Foundation, Paris

1999
Otto Fried - Retrospektive, Portland Art Museum, Oregon (solo show)
On the occasion of his retrospective, the Portland Art Museum installs a monumental sculpture by Otto Fried.
"Otto Fried, Recent Works", Portland Museum of Art, Portland, Oregon (solo show)
"Otto Fried", Laura Russo Gallery, Portland, Oregon (solo show)
"Otto Fried: High Relief Paper Series, 1987-1989", Denis Cadé Gallery, New York City (solo show)

2001
Commission to design a dinnerware set for the Union centrale des arts décoratifs (UCAD).
Exhibition, Centrale des Arts décoratif, (now: Musée des Arts Décoratifs), Paris
With the beginning of the 21st century, Fried concentrates once again on drawing and painting. Completely new, remembered and invented landscapes or "skyscapes" are created.

2002
Donation of the painting *Leewärtige Illusion* to the Sankt Maximin Church in Koblenz-Horchheim.
"Otto Fried: Meubles et Objects", Galerie Brame & Lorenceau, Paris (solo show)

2006
"Otto Fried", Galerie Brame & Lorenceau, Paris (solo show)

2010
Fried renounces his studio and house in the United States; from then on, Otto und Micheline Fried have lived only in France.

2017
Micheline Fried, born Haardt, dies in May.

2020
"Otto Fried – Heaven Can Wait / Heaven Can't Wait", Ludwig Museum Koblenz (solo show)

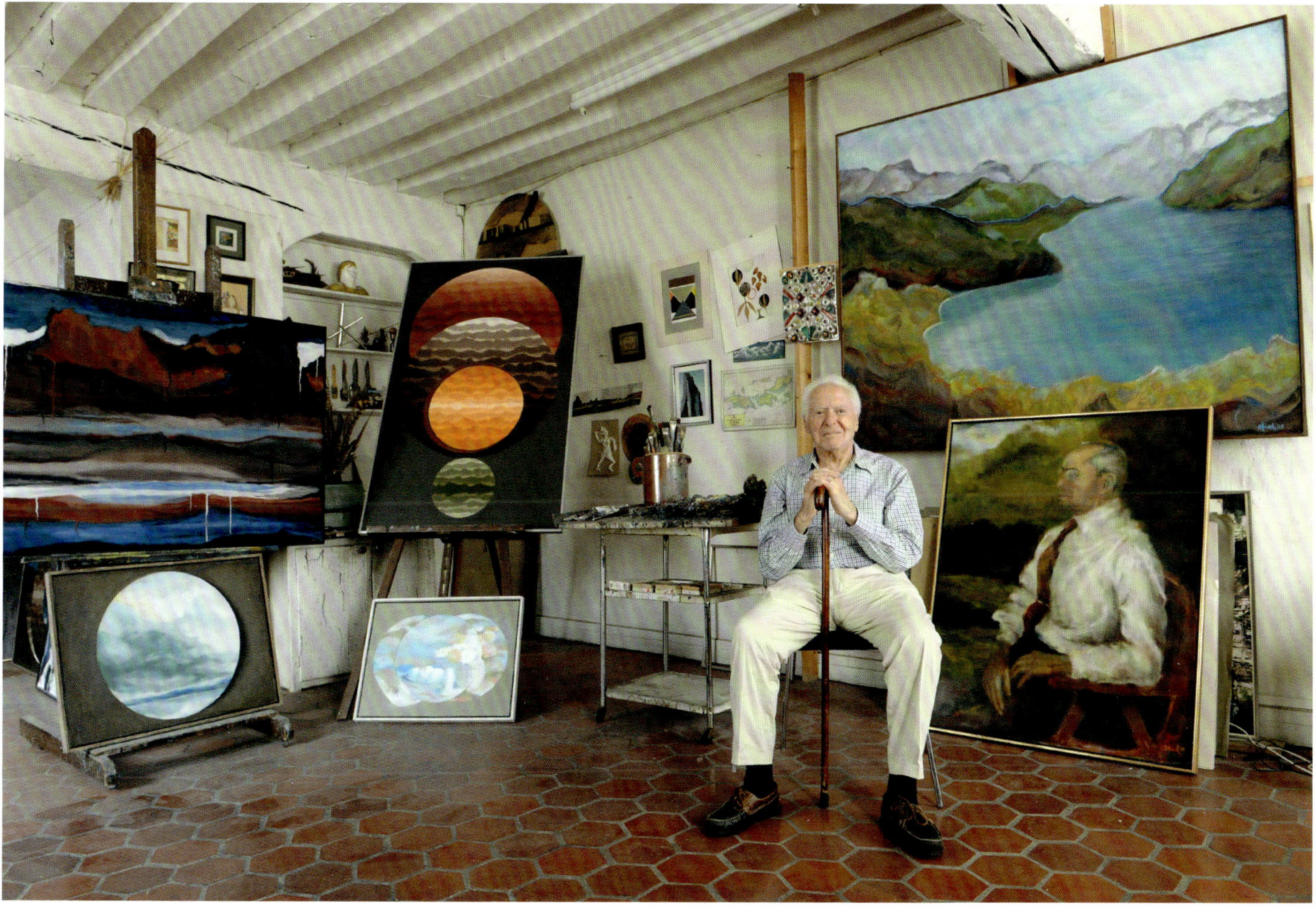

Otto Fried in seinem Atelier in Paris, 2018 / Otto Fried in his Paris studio, 2018

1997

„Otto Fried: Sculptures et dessins", Galerie Brame & Lorenceau, Paris (Einzelausstellung)
„Artistes Américains en France", Mona Bismark Foundation, Paris

1999

Otto Fried - Retrospektive, Portland Art Museum, Oregon (Einzelausstellung)
Anlässlich seiner Retrospektive installiert das Portland Art Museum eine monumentale Skulptur von Otto Fried.
„Otto Fried, Recent Works", Portland Museum of Art, Portland, Oregon (Einzelausstellung)
„Otto Fried" Laura Russo Gallery, Portland, Oregon (Einzelausstellung)
„Otto Fried: High Relief Paper Series, 1987-1989", Denis Cadé Gallery, New York City (Einzelausstellung)

2001

Auftrag zur Gestaltung eines Geschirrsets für die Union centrale des arts décoratifs (UCAD).
Ausstellung, Centrale des Arts décoratif, (heute: Musée des Arts Décoratifs), Paris
Seit dem Beginn des 21. Jahrhunderts konzentriert sich Fried wieder mehr aufs Zeichnen und Malen. Dabei entstehen ganz neue, erinnerte und erfundene Landschaften oder ‚Himmelschaften'.

2002

Schenkung des Gemäldes „Leewärtige Illusion" an die Sankt Maximin Kirche in Koblenz-Horchheim.
„Otto Fried: Meubles et Objects", Galerie Brame & Lorenceau, Paris (Einzelausstellung)

2006

„Otto Fried", Galerie Brame & Lorenceau, Paris (Einzelausstellung)

2010

Fried gibt sein Atelier und die Wohnung in den Vereinigten Staaten auf; Otto und Micheline Fried leben nun ausschließlich in Frankreich.

2017

Micheline Fried, geb. Haardt, stirbt im Mai.

2020

„Otto Fried – Heaven Can Wait / Heaven Can't Wait", Ludwig Museum Koblenz (Einzelausstellung)

Museen und Sammlungen
Museums and Collections

Museen / Museums

Metropolitan Museum of Art, New York

Mittelrhein-Museum Koblenz

Musée national d'art moderne, Centre Georges Pompidou, Paris

Museum of Modern Art, New York

The Museum of the University of Syracruse (heute / now: SUArt Galleries), Syracruse, New York

The Museum of Art of the University of Oregon (heute / now: Jordan Schnitzer Museum of Art), University of Oregon, Eugene, Oregon

Portland Art Museum, Portland, Oregon

Rose Art Museum, Brandeis University, Waltham, Massachusetts

Weitere Sammlungen / Further Collections

Bank of California, Portland, Oregon

Georgia Pacific Company (heute / now: Georgia Pacific), Portland, Oregon

Continental Grain Cooperation, (heute / now: ContiGroup Companies), New York City

Collection of Paul and Jeannette Haim, Paris (heute / now: „Collection La Petite Escalère", geleitet von / directed by Dominique Haim, Strasbourg)

Collection of Terry and Jean de Gunzburg, Paris/London

Coopers & Lybrand, San Francisco (heute / now: Pricewaterhouse Coopers International, London)

Far West Federal Bank, Portland, Oregon

First National Bank of Oregon (heute / now: First Interstate Bank of Oregon), Portland, Oregon

Frana, Co. Geneva (heute / now: Socotab Frana SA), Geneva

Fuji Mic Computer, Inc., (heute / now: Fujitsu Ltd.), Tokyo

Georgia Pacific Corparation (heute / now: Georgia Pacific, Atlanta, Georgia

Guerlain Collection, (heute / now: Fondation d'art contemporain Daniel et Florence Guerlain), Paris

Goldman Sachs & Co, New York City

Hans & Elsbeth Juda Collection, London

Haseltine Collection, Portland, Oregon

Hoffman Construction Co., Portland, Oregon

Merrill Lynch, Portland, Oregon

N.E.C., (heute / now: NEC Corporation of America), San Francisco, California

Nippon Broadcasting System, Inc., Tokyo

Pacific Power and Light, San Francisco, California (heute / now: Porland, Oregon)

Rainier Corporation (heute / now: Rainier Industries), Seattle, Washington

Seattle Telephone Co., Seattle, Washington

Sparkasse Koblenz

United States Bank of Oregon

Willamette Industries, Portland, Oregon

Darüber hinaus waren Werke von Otto Fried Bestanteil einiger inzwischen aufgelöster Sammlungen, die hier nicht aufgeführt sind. Zu diesen Sammlungen zählen beispielsweise die IBM Collection oder die Privatsammlungen von Laurence Rockefeller, Arthur G. Altschul, R. Buckminster Fuller und Warren M. Robbins. Der Verbleib der Otto Fried Werke aus diesen Sammlungen ist nicht nachvollziehbar. Bis heute befindet sich eine Vielzahl von Werken Frieds in privatem Besitz. /
Furthermore, works by Otto Fried belonged to some collections that have since been dismantled and are not listed here. These collections include, for example, the IBM Collection or the private collections of Laurence Rockefeller, Arthur G. Altschul, R. Buckminster Fuller and Warren M. Robbins. The new locations of Otto Fried's works from these collections are unknown. So far, a large number of Fried's works are privately owned.

BIBLIOGRAPHIE
BIBLIOGRAPHY

Antiques & Art Weekly, April 1987.

Arts & Antiques, Mai / May 1988.

Arts Magazine, März / March 1956.

Arts Magazine, April 1963.

Art News, Mai / May 1963.

Art News, März / March 1966.

Ausstellungskatalog / Exhibition catalogue *Fuji Television Gallery*, Tokyo, April 5 - April 24, 1979, Tokyo 1979.

Ausstellungskatalog / Exhibition catalogue *Otto Fried, Metal Relief Structures*, New York, Achim Moeller Fine Arts, November 20 – Dezember / December 20, 1991, New York 1991.

Ausstellungskatalog / Exhibition catalogue *Otto Fried, Sculptures et Dessins*, Paris, Brame & Lorenceau, Februar / February 6 - März / March 8, 1997, Paris 1997.

Ausstellungskatalog / Exhibition catalogue *Otto Fried, Recent Work*, Oregon, Portland Art Museum, Mai / May 14 – Juli / July 18, 1999, Hg. von / Ed. by John E. Buchanan and Kathryn Kanjo, Portland 1999.

Bouret, Jean: Artikel / Article in: *La Pensée française*, Dezember / December 1, 1966.

Bouyeure, Claude: *Les Iliades du Cercle / The Iliads of the circle*, in: *Cimaise*, Juni / June 1990, Paris 1990.

Brunhammer, Yvonne: *Otto Fried, Meubles et Objets*, Turin 2000.

Cabanne, Pierre: Artikel / Article in: *Arts*, Paris, Mai / May 27, 1964.

Charmet, Raymond: Artikel / Article in: *Arts*, Dezember / December 1, 1966.

Courthion, Pierre: Ausstellungskatalog / Exhibition catalogue *Otto Fried*, Paris, Galerie des Grands Augustins, Februar / February 1977, Paris 1977.

Crespelle, Jean Paul: Artikel / Article in: *France Soir*, November 25, 1966.

Eitelbach, Kurt (Hg. von / Ed.): Ausstellungskatalog / Exhibition catalogue *Ströme*, Koblenz, Mittelrhein-Museum, 1978, Koblenz 1978.

Fried, Otto: *Sélection de dessin et d'œuvres sur papier*, Hg. von / Ed. by Sylvie Brame, Paris 2009.

Gibson, Michael: Artikel / Article in: *International Herald Tribune*, Januar / January 29, 1977.

Gleiny, Christine: Artikel / Article in: *Les Arts*, Februar / February 1, 1977.

Hinshaw, Tim: Artikel / Article in: *Encore Magazine*, Januar / January 1979.

Margolis, Larry (Text); Fried, Otto (Gemälde / Paintings): *WE 3*. Paris 1950.

Nakahara, Yusuke; Haim, Paul: Ausstellungskatalog / Exhibition catalogue *Otto Fried*, Tokyo, Fuji Television Gallery, 1985, Tokyo 1985.

Offin, Charles Z.: Artikel / Article in: *Pictures on Exhibit*, Oktober / October 1975.

Pictures on Exhibit, Mai / May 1963.

Snelson, Kenneth: *Otto Fried – Interviewed by Kenneth Snelson*, Sommer / Summer 1991, in: Ausstellungskatalog / Exhibition catalogue *Otto Fried, Metal Relief Structures*, New York, Achim Moeller Fine Arts, November 20 – Dezember / December 20, 1991, New York 1991.

Thierry, Solange: Artikel / Article in: *L'Oeil*, Juni / June 1990.

Thierry, Solange: Artikel / Article in: *L'Oeil*, Juni / June 1987.

Vezin, Luc: Artikel / Article in: *Beaux Arts*, Juni / June 1987.

Werner, Alfred: Ausstellungskatalog / Exhibition catalogue *Recent Paintings, Oil Sketches, Monotypes by Otto Fried*, Milwaukee, Irving Gallery, 1960–1961, Milwaukee, Wisconsin, 1960–1961.

West, Thomas: *Otto Fried*, Hg. von / Ed. by Foundation Fine Art of the Century, Genf / Geneva, Genf / Geneva 1995.

Bildnachweis / Photo Credits

Umschlagbild / Cover
Vor / Front: Otto Fried: *Coreoptic*, 1995
Sammlung des Künstlers / Collection of the Artist
Photo: Jost Gabriel, newcut werbefilme e.K.
Hinter / Back: Otto Fried in seinem Atelier in Paris / working in his studio in Paris, 2004
Photo: Eric Bardeau, Atelier de Photographe,
312 St Honoré, 75001 Paris.

Otto Fried (vermutlich / presumably): S. / p. 86
Jost Gabriel, newcut werbefilme e.K.: S. / p. 7, 13, 16, 26, 28, 32, 34, 38, 39, 40, 41, 42, 44, 45, 48, 51, 56, 59, 67, 68, 69, 71, 73, 74, 75, 76, 79, 82, 83, 84, 85, 86, 87, 89, 100, 101, 102, 103, 104/105, 106
Mittelrhein-Museum Koblenz: S. / p. 19, 43, 49
Werner Oebels: S. / p. 60/61, 89, 113
Axel Ronnisch: S. / p. 31, 35, 46, 47, 50, 70, 77, 78, 88
Unbekannt / Unknown: S. / p. 17, 61, 83, 84, 86
Lothar Schmidt: S. / p. 54/55
Susanne Schmidt-Dominé, Düsseldorf: S. / p. 52, 117
Marc Waymel, Atelier de Photographe, 312 St Honoré, 75001 Paris: S. / p. 91

Dieser Katalog erscheint anlässlich der Ausstellung /
This catalogue is published on the occasion of the exhibition

OTTO FRIED
Heaven can wait / Heaven can't wait

Ludwig Museum im Deutschherrenhaus, Koblenz
21. Juni 2020 – 16. August 2020 /
June 21, 2020 until August 16, 2020

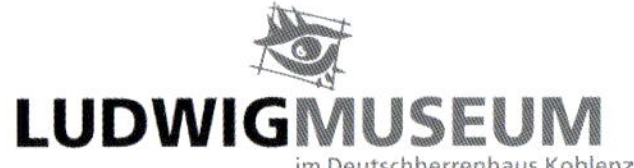

Herausgeber / Editor
Beate Reifenscheid

Kurator / Curator
Beate Reifenscheid

Kuratorische Assistenz / Curatorial Assistance
Larissa Wesp

Redaktion / Editing
Barbara Leers, Ludwig Museum, Koblenz
Suzana Leu, Ludwig Museum, Koblenz
Larissa Wesp, Ludwig Museum, Koblenz

Texte / Texts
Lisa Forrell
Beate Reifenscheid
Larissa Wesp
Barbara Wolbert

Haustechnik und Aufbau / Building services and construction
Holger Schumacher, Haustechnik, Ludwig Museum, Koblenz
Jonathan Borsch
Thomas Topuksöker

Verwaltung / Administration
Thomas Rinck

Pädagogik / Educational Program
Marko Sommer, Museumspädagogik, Ludwig Museum, Koblenz
KunstKontakt-Team, Ludwig Museum, Koblenz

Die Ausstellung wird gefördert von /
The exhibition is supported by

Peter und Irene
Ludwig Stiftung

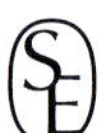

Silvana Editoriale

Verlagsleiter / Direction
Dario Cimorelli

Art Director
Giacomo Merli

Redaktionskoordinator / Editorial Coordinator
Sergio Di Stefano

Redakteurin / Copy Editor
Cristina Pradella

Deutsche Übersetzungen
Cristina Pradella

English translations
Cristina Pradella

Layout und Textsatz / Layout
Annamaria Ardizzi

Produktionskoordination / Production Coordinator
Antonio Micelli

Redaktionsassistentin / Editorial Assistant
Ondina Granato, Giulia Mercanti

Photo Editor
Alessandra Olivari, Silvia Sala

Pressestelle / Press Office
Lidia Masolini, press@silvanaeditoriale.it

Available through ARTBOOK | D.A.P.
155 Sixth Avenue, 2nd Floor, New York, N.Y. 10013
Tel: (212) 627-1999 Fax: (212) 627-9484

Silvana Editoriale S.p.A.
via dei Lavoratori, 78
20092 Cinisello Balsamo, Milano
tel. 02 453 951 01
fax 02 453 951 51
www.silvanaeditoriale.it

Reproduktionen, Druck und Einbindung
wurden in Italien ausgeführt
Reproductions, printing and binding in Italy
Gedruckt von / Printed by Intergrafica Verona S.r.l.
Fertig gedruckt im Juni 2020
Printed in June 2020